Authenticity in Contemporary Theatre and Performance

Methuen Drama Engage offers original reflections about key practitioners, movements and genres in the fields of modern theatre and performance. Each volume in the series seeks to challenge mainstream critical thought through original and interdisciplinary perspectives on the body of work under examination. By questioning existing critical paradigms, it is hoped that each volume will open up fresh approaches and suggest avenues for further exploration.

Series Editors

Mark Taylor-Batty
Senior Lecturer in Theatre Studies, Workshop Theatre,
University of Leeds, UK

Enoch Brater
Kenneth T. Rowe Collegiate Professor of Dramatic Literature &
Professor of English and Theater, University of Michigan, USA

Titles

Adaptation in Contemporary Theatre
by Frances Babbage
ISBN 978-1-4725-3142-1

Social and Political Theatre in Twenty-First Century Britain
by Vicky Angelaki
ISBN 978-1-474-21316-5

Beat Drama: Playwrights and Performances of the 'Howl' Generation
edited by Deborah R. Geis
ISBN 978-1-472-56787-1

Drama and Digital Arts Cultures
by David Cameron, Michael Anderson and Rebecca Wotzko
ISBN 978-1-4725-9220-0

The Contemporary American Monologue: Performance and Politics
by Eddie Paterson
ISBN 978-1-472-58501-1

Watching War on the Twenty-First Century Stage: Spectacles of Conflict
by Clare Finburgh
ISBN 978-1-472-59866-0

Theatre in the Dark: Shadow, Gloom and Blackout in Contemporary Theatre
edited by Adam Alston and Martin Welton
ISBN 978-1-4742-5118-1

Theatre of Real People: Diverse Encounters from Berlin's Hebbel am Ufer and Beyond
by Ulrike Garde and Meg Mumford
ISBN 978-1-4725-8021-4

Authenticity in Contemporary Theatre and Performance

Make it Real

Daniel Schulze

Series Editors
Enoch Brater and Mark Taylor-Batty

Bloomsbury Methuen Drama
An imprint of Bloomsbury Publishing Plc

B L O O M S B U R Y
LONDON · OXFORD · NEW YORK · NEW DELHI · SYDNEY

Bloomsbury Methuen Drama
An imprint of Bloomsbury Publishing Plc

Imprint previously known as Methuen Drama

50 Bedford Square	1385 Broadway
London	New York
WC1B 3DP	NY 10018
UK	USA

www.bloomsbury.com

**BLOOMSBURY and the Diana logo are trademarks of Bloomsbury
Publishing Plc**

First published 2017

© Daniel Schulze, 2017

British Library Cataloguing-in-Publication Data
A catalogue record for this book is available from the British Library.

ISBN:	HB:	978-1-3500-0096-4
	ePDF:	978-1-3500-0098-8
	ePub:	978-1-3500-0097-1

Library of Congress Cataloging-in-Publication Data
A catalog record for this book is available from the Library of Congress.

Series: Methuen Drama Engage

Cover design by Louise Dugdale
Cover image: Ontroerend Goed, The Smile Off Your Face (2005)
photo © Virginie Schreyen

Typeset by Integra Software Services Pvt. Ltd.

To those who have no part

Contents

Acknowledgements

*Ein Mann muss seinen Händen Arbeit geben,/womöglich
unbewusst./Die Glut frisst sich hinab auf seine Finger zu.*

(Sedlmayr 2014: 7)

'A man must give his hands work,/perhaps unconsciously./The blaze
guzzles down towards his fingers' – states the poem above. This work
is very much a work of my passion. It took its beginning from curiosity
about authenticity and the relation between reality and representation.
Through the entire process of working on this book I have been extremely
lucky to never have lost my passion about it, and despite long hours
and difficult processes I have never been bored by my work. Quite the
contrary: I was lucky enough to have found blazing embers that could
eat their way towards my fingers. Therefore, while of course difficult, this
project has always been a work of joy. It has occupied me for the better
part of four years, and it is obvious that without the generous support,
input and encouragement of a number of people I could not have
completed it. I am very grateful to all of them and wish to name a few.

First of all, I want to thank Gerold Sedlmayr. I cannot imagine a
mentor with more dedication, supportive comments, wit and wisdom,
who so readily devoted a substantial part of his time to me and who is –
on top of that – a brilliant writer and wonderful human being – *thank
you*. Second, I wish to thank Gloria Berghäuser, whose intelligence
in discussion has enlightened me time and time again and whose
emotional wisdom, encouragement and great soul have been a fixed
star for me for more than three years. Then obviously a huge thank-you
goes to my parents, Ute and Ulrich (†) Schulze, without whom I would
not be where I am today, and to my brother, Michael, of whom I am
endlessly proud and who is one of the most authentic persons I know.
I also wish to thank my cousin Bianca Brachmann and her husband
Ralf for their encouragement and support.

Then I want to thank a number of people who have influenced me academically. There is no one who has done more for my artistic and academic education than Alan Read, who is a brilliant thinker, and whose willingness to fight for radical equality is a beacon light of inspiration. I also wish to thank Wolfgang Funk, who gave me invaluable insights on authenticity and who generously shared his unpublished work with me. Furthermore, I wish to thank the incomparable Jan Suk for being a hot house of creativity, cheekiness and brilliant thinking. I also want to thank Anette Pankratz for our strong and inspiring discussions around theatre. Last but not least, my thank-you goes to the Society for Contemporary Drama in English and, specifically, the graduate forum as represented by Clare Wallace, Eckart Voigts and all participants.

Mark Dudgeon and Emily Hockley guided me through the editorial process with diligence, competence and friendliness, and Mark Taylor-Batty and Enoch Brater, co-editors of the Bloomsbury Methuen Drama Engage series, have given me valuable input and have made this book much better. I am grateful for their help.

Finally, I wish to thank all my friends, specifically the 'Superfreunde', as well as Korbinian Erdmann, Johannes Knoll and all other friends – too many to name. Thank you for bearing with me and putting up with my whacky ideas. Obviously a big thank-you also goes to all my colleagues at the University of Würzburg, and the proof readers and very dear friends: Matthias Krebs, Florian Cord, Andrea Stiebritz, Jennifer Leetsch and Philip Jacobi.

Würzburg, May 2016

1

In Search of Authenticity

Make it Real

−Coca Cola slogan 2005 (The Coca Cola Company 2012)

On 21 November 2014, Forced Entertainment streamed a live, twenty-four-hour version of their durational performance piece, *Quizoola!*. The event came with a Twitter hash tag (#quizoola24) and sparked lively debate among audiences. The entire performance circles around tiredness, exhaustion and possible glimpses of moments of truth. Twitter user Performance@Salford realized this, and tweeted that Forced Entertainment's questions were of 'reality, of art, of humanity, of intimacy, of remoteness, of our ability/inability, of hope and monsters' (Quizoola24 Twitter Feed). Here, spectators and performers alike seem to be in search of something more genuine than the economy of make-believe of theatre, or, as Tim Etchells tweeted: 'we cant find each other − we are slipping past each othr, we misunderstand each othr − losing as well as finding [*sic passim*]' (Quizoola24 Twitter Feed). What is evident in both tweets is the almost desperate struggle and search for human connection and for something that is felt to be genuine and lasting. However, this much-desired something seems evasive. *Quizoola!* is but one example of theatre and performance works of the past decades, which are in search of this desired state. It comes under various labels such as authenticity, truth or the real. Evidently, these concepts are very much sought after by both practitioners and audiences. The following pages will show that authenticity has been a major factor in theatre and the performing arts for the past decade or so. It has been worked, played and tampered with in aesthetic experiments.

Thus, this book sets out to investigate authenticity in the performing arts today, namely its aesthetic strategies, in terms of production and reception, as well as its politics. The study will situate the phenomenon in a broader cultural context. The central claim is that it is an expression of a structure of feeling[1] which has superseded Postmodernism with its irony, detachment and pastiche. It instead reconstructs concepts of *telos*, engagement and closure. Many have tried to find an adequate terminology for this structure. The suggestions range from 'Hypermodernity' (Lipovetsky), via 'Altermodernism' (Bourriaud) over to 'Digimodernism' (Kirby) and 'Metamodernism' (Vermeulen, van den Akker) (cf. Funk 2015: 3). All terms have their material and terminological advantages and disadvantages, and frequently also common features, such as an emphasis on individual production and reception. This study will use the term 'Metamodernism', as proposed by Vermeulen and van den Akker. It is, however, not meant to be a definitive act of nomenclature, which may safely be left to a later period in time. It simply provides a temporary label, a shorthand if you will, to describe the current state of affairs. The nitty-gritty of this discussion is the thorough description and analysis of the phenomena of expression that give rise to this new structure of feeling.

This chapter will lay the foundation for the analysis in part two of this study by surveying the field of authenticity from a number of angles. First of all, it will explore the current cultural landscape and point out strategies, practices and artefacts that are significant for the structure of feeling after Postmodernism. The second section will undertake a short historic survey of authenticity and its development. By way of this genealogical approach in a Foucauldian sense, the concept of authenticity and the discourses surrounding it, such as sincerity, or mimesis will be elaborated on and contextualized. After all, authenticity is by no means a new phenomenon. It has surfaced repeatedly in various periods and guises, and it is remarkably hard to grasp. This is specifically so with respect to theatre, which must always be viewed in close relation to the society it springs from. The following thoughts may briefly illustrate this.

If we go back to the origins of European theatre, namely the Attic city states, we soon become aware that while our evidence of both plays and performance practice is often scant (cf. Fischer-Lichte 2013: 74; Schaper 2014: 45), theatricality and role play permeated almost all areas of life from politics, to the military, to courts of law (cf. Hall 2010: 62). This time is very much performative in many respects and not dissimilar to our own, which has also been called a performatist epoch (cf. Eshelman 2001). All dramatic activity of the time, specifically the Athenian annual City-Dionysia, must be regarded in the broad cultural 'context of all civic/religious rituals and ceremonies of which it was part. Fifth-century Greek theatre was woven into the fabric of civic/religious discourse' (Zarrilli et al. 2009: 61). Consequently, in classical Greece theatrical truth, religious sincerity and political earnestness intersected in the form of role play and performance. All these activities carry strong overtones of authenticity; however, it is difficult to grasp this rich performative texture from a purely literary basis. The abstract analysis with which the remaining thirty-four plays of the classical period are frequently studied today, and which only started almost a century later with Aristotle's *Poetics* (cf. 2009: 67), cannot do it justice. In the lived culture of the period, where ritual, religious activity, acting and public policy intersected, theatre itself can be seen as an event which 'flows from and constitutes life within the *polis*' (2009: 65). The plays and performances were in touch with reality and current debates. A good example is certainly Sophocles, whose plays – specifically the Theban trilogy – were 'highly relevant to the public concerns of a *polis* community' (Sommerstein 2000: 47). This is, however, true not only on the level of content but also in terms of protagonists on stage. In contrast to Aeschylus, Sophocles 'placed increased emphasis on individual characters' and his 'personages are complex and psychologically well motivated' (Brockett 1995: 18). This early (faint) glimmer of realism becomes even more pronounced with the tragedies of Euripides, whose 'realistic exploration of psychological motivations was sometimes thought too undignified for tragedy' (Brocket 1995: 19). His characters frequently interfere with the divine order: they question the gods' justice because they often cause misery and unhappiness (1995: 19). It seems likely that Euripides even brought in 'realistic strokes in characterization, dialogue, and costuming' (1995: 19). But even more to the point, Euripides' atrocious acts of say adultery and child murder (committed by women) had a strong influence on the audience. People felt 'that there was something about Euripides presentation of such stories which deeply disturbed many people but which they could not quite specify' (Sommerstein 2000: 56; cf. also Hall 2010: 70–73). It is specifically this thing which they 'cannot specify' that leans itself to notions of authenticity in the form of shock in the face of human abysses. Authenticity certainly had a place on the level of both content and form in the performances of classical Greek drama. It is regrettable that we have so little information about acting styles and materiality of performances in the period, which could further elucidate these effects. However, there are hints that theatre was at least *perceived* as authentic and moving to a high degree. A striking example is the story of the famous actor Polos, who in the late fourth century BC played the title role in Sophocles' *Electra* and used the ashes of his own recently deceased son to disperse among the audience and allegedly 'filled the place not with the appearance or imitation of sorrow, but with genuine grief and unfeigned lamentation' (Gellius in Zarrilli et al. 2009: 66). Here, the reality of bereavement and performance intermingle to produce an extraordinary effect on the audience. It is certain that the reality of the performance, be it stylized or realist, has always moved audiences and has been perceived as authentic.

This is also true for later periods such as the Renaissance, when theatre took a new upswing in Europe. While we cannot be sure about the exact style of acting say in Shakespeare's England – some claim that it was 'formal' (e.g. boys playing women, little set and props), and others claim it was 'realistic' (e.g. Hamlet's advice to the players, contemporary references to realistic characterization given by actors such as Burbage) (cf. Brocket 1995: 164) – it is safe to assume that similar effects of authenticity were achieved. After all, Renaissance England is also a performatist epoch in which role play at court or in the street, and the spectacle of public executions and acting on the stage intersected (cf. Easo Smith 2001: 71–74), and in which the boundaries between fact and fiction were not clearly marked out, as Philip Sidney's *Defense of Poesy* shows. To paraphrase Shakespeare's famous quote: theatre mirrors life and vice versa. The characters inhabiting his plays are humans of flesh and blood, who are fully fledged and developed in their motives. In performance – about which we know a little more than about ancient Greece – many of them must have appeared authentic or even real to the audience. Great villains such as Iago or Richard III certainly forged a special kind of bond with their audience when they transcended the stage in asides and soliloquies, thus making the audience their silent interlocutor or accomplice, and many contemporary accounts testify that the audience was strongly moved by the actors (cf. Brocket 1995: 164). However, this does not necessarily determine a naturalist style of acting. 'The most that one can say is that the better actors represented well contemporary conceptions of artistic truth' (1995: 164). It is evident that every period and culture will have their own notions of what is to be held as authentic or true, but whatever these notions may be, within their own rationale they are powerful. This goes to show that while styles and forms of theatre may vary over time, what remains constant is theatre's affective power. It is the result of an immediate co-presence of audience and performer (cf. Fischer-Lichte 2012: 55) and theatre's ephemeral nature, which makes it a fleeting pleasure that is only available and alive in the moment and thus authentic and true (cf. Schaper 2014: 51–52).

This special capacity of the theatre became even more pronounced with the nineteenth century's turn towards realism as exemplified by Stanislavsky's technique and Chekov's plays (cf. Brockett 1995: 440–441). A pinnacle of this development is surely Zola's Naturalism, which virtually sought to eliminate 'all distinctions between art and life' (1995: 432). This development, however, should be regarded critically in terms of authenticity because it seeks to put life on a one to one scale on stage, thereby diminishing the aesthetic distance between the two. Tomlin has argued, along with Žižek, that for theatre to gain efficacy, a certain distance or even tension between reality and its representation, which is always tainted by ideology, needs to be kept in place (cf. 2013: 4–6). Thus there is a dialectic at work that is spurned by a culture's structure of feeling and its artistic expressions, meandering between aesthetic distance and verisimilitude. Today, when we have lost a lot of the ontological grounding that characterized former centuries, this dialectic has become far more difficult to grasp than when realism was in full swing. In a time marked by social media, global interconnection and an ever faster-moving media environment, authenticity has become a vital preoccupation for many, because it carries the promise of some tangible outside and essentialist reality.

> The current meanings of 'authentic'/'authenticity' – as genuine, truthful, immediate, undisguised, unadulterated, certified, guaranteed, binding – can be conceived of in terms of an interplay between two developments: on the one hand, 'authentic' and 'authenticity' are taken as synonymous with terms from philosophy and aesthetics of the 18th and 19th centuries (sincerity, naivité, truth). On the other, the shades of meaning for 'authentic' and 'authenticity' are drawn from metaphors or abstractions originating in juridical, philological and theological discourses (authorized, in reference to an author, certified). (Knaller 2012b: 25)

Thus our current culture of authenticity and its manifold meanings have to be navigated with care and have to be viewed from as many perspectives as possible. Only then can a thick image of contemporary performance cultures and authenticity arise. It is the aim of this chapter to deliver such a thick description of authenticity's development and its place in contemporary culture.

I will follow Funk (cf. 2015: 6) by not attempting to give an all-valid definition of authenticity. Instead, I will use Funk's useful concept of authenticity as a black box which can never be fully understood in its workings, but whose effects can be studied (cf. Funk 2015: 55–56). However, while I agree with Funk that the workings of 'the black box authenticity' can never be fully understood, I believe it is possible to highlight some of its constituent parts. In other words, it may be possible to see some of the fixtures and fittings of the black box more clearly, while their interplay remains undisclosed. The second section will, in conclusion, offer an appropriate terminology for the study of authenticity, building on the works of Knaller, Moore and Selwyn, and Funk. The study will then offer a short contemplation of the status of a work of art in relation to its ontology.

Part two of this chapter investigates the aforementioned new structure of feeling by offering ways of explanation for its development. Drawing on theories by Walter Benjamin, Jean Baudrillard and Fredric Jameson, it offers one line of explanation (among many others that could be made) for the emergence of this new structure of feeling. The aim in this exercise is to situate authenticity in its cultural context and to draw up a model that may explain the hunger for authenticity and authentic experience in contemporary culture. In this sense, all the performances under discussion in the second part of the book are an expression of the aforesaid change in culture. They can in no way claim exclusivity and are certainly an eclectic sample, but, importantly, a whole number of other examples from other areas of cultural production could be named (e.g. television and literature) and will be pointed out where appropriate.

This chapter concludes with a brief inspection of the subject under discussion: theatre after the millennium. It will situate theatre in the context of authenticity and the related concepts of truth and mimesis. The central argument here is that theatre's fakeness evolves out of the intrinsic ontological connection between lying and acting, that is performing. Furthermore, it will be suggested that, through the emergence of written forms of drama, theatre from the fifth century BC onwards (cf. Zarrilli et al. 2009: 61) began to lose its status as genuine or real. Again, both lines of theory here offer an idea of the connection between theatre and authenticity. They are by no means exclusive and many others seem conceivable. The discussion of theatre and authenticity serves not so much to resolve all questions of the development of the phenomena under discussion once and for all. It is rather to be seen as encouragement for thought and further investigation into this field. It is a point of departure for discussion.

A state of affairs

It is no exaggeration to claim that for the past two or three decades a feeling of fakeness and deception in almost all areas of cultural production has surfaced. Mair and Becker find our society to be characterized by fakeness in a fast-paced media environment of chat shows and reality TV where the 'real' (whatever that may be) has been replaced by pretending and acting as-if (cf. Mair & Becker 2005: 8–10). Whether this is an accurate perception or just a gut feeling can safely be ignored at this point, because what matters is not necessarily a real increase in fakeness but the *perceived* increase, which will in turn influence cultural practices. Ralph Keyes follows this argument and establishes himself as a severe cultural critic when he remarks thus: 'I think it's fair to say that honesty is on the ropes. Deception has become commonplace at all levels of contemporary life' (Keyes 2004: 5). While his examples at times seem questionable,[2] it is evident that contemporary culture is frequently perceived as inherently fake or even mendacious. Thomas Docherty, building on the philosophy of Gianni Vattimo, argues that the extreme presence and simultaneity of the *Jetztzeit* in the age of multimedia precludes us from having experiences which we perceive as true (cf. Docherty 2003: 27). A number of scholars, most eminently Jean Baudrillard, have analysed these cultural tendencies and their theories will be discussed in detail. For now, it is enough to note that the perceived superficiality and fakeness of contemporary culture leads to an increased wish for genuine experience, or some sort of reality that is perceived as not fake – in a word: authentic. Straub elaborates that '[authenticity] is a visible force in mass entertainment and popular culture and it resonates both with audiences and readerships' (Straub 2012: 16). Thus, the perceived fakeness in everyday culture gives rise to practices of authenticity. The trend towards authenticity can, however, be perceived not only in everyday life and culture but in the arts as well. Susanne Knaller locates the subject as the central theme in a number of contemporary works of visual art and claims that art has taken a playful approach towards documentation, reality and fiction (cf. Knaller 2012a: 56–57).

In literature, Funk makes out authenticity (in his terminology: metareference and reconstruction) as a central feature of much contemporary prose (cf. Funk 2015). Other scholars have made similar observations; specifically, it has been claimed that documentary forms of writing have regained prominence in the past decades (cf. Domsch 2008). Haselstein, Gross and Snyder-Körber also locate a return of the real in testimonial literature or trauma literature because this type of work is thought to be beyond representation, that is 'real' (cf. Haselstein et al. 2010: 16). Susanne Straub names Jonathan Franzen's *The Corrections* (2001) and J. Safran Foer's *Everything's Illuminated* (2002) as well as fake memoirs as examples (cf. Straub 2012: 15–16). She maintains that the popularity of trauma, survivor and minority literature must be regarded as an expression of nostalgia on parts of the readership: 'These texts compensate for the readers' perceived lack in their own lives, lives which appear to be deprived of first-hand experiences' (Straub 2012: 17). James Frey's autobiographical novel, *A Million Little Pieces* (2003), treating his recovery from drug addiction, is a prominent example. It made it to the top of bestsellers lists until it became known that the whole story was made up, again seemingly confirming that all the world's a fake (cf. 2012: 16).

Convergent developments are ubiquitous in the field of television (cf. Fiesbach 2002: 20, 33). Reality television shows such as *Big Brother* or, more recently, *The Real World* have flooded the market since the late 1990s and in the early decades of the millennium. They are, as Shields observes, paradoxically named because they rarely are real (cf. Shields 2010: 107). In fact, most reality formats are scripted to a greater or lesser degree and television stations have started creating formats which pretend to be 'real' but are in fact scripted and staged with amateur actors. Liz Tomlin has consequently diagnosed a fetish in the cultural mainstream regarding the 'authenticity of the "real life stories" of "ordinary people"' (Tomlin 2013: 196). The ever-more growing number of such formats again fosters a feeling of medial superficiality and fakeness. The *BILD Zeitung*, Germany's largest tabloid paper, bluntly asked in 2014 what was still real on German television (cf. Steck 2014).[3] Mair and Becker see the felt proliferation of fakeness as the central reason why people long for a reality removed from the media (cf. Mair & Becker 2005: 105). Television, thus, while pretending to be as real as can be, in fact furthers the perception of a world that consists of fakes and simulations. Jean Baudrillard is the theorist who readily springs to mind when investigating this field. For him, the aesthetics of reality television are a type of mediated *verité* experience that is based on 'a sort of frisson of the real, or of an aesthetics of the hyperreal, a frisson of vertiginous and phony exactitude, a frisson of simultaneous distancing and magnification, of distortion of scale, of an excessive transparency' (Baudrillard 2010: 28). In other words, such longing for authenticity – without recourse to anything genuine – will produce disorientation, which leads to the emergence of a kind of schizophrenic nostalgia, more fake-authenticity and eventually more kitsch (cf. 2010: 7).

The hunger for authentic experience is present in many areas of cultural production, not just in art, literature and television but also in everyday practices. As Baudrillard has it, a culture that lacks robust everyday experiences, which are perceived as authentic, will reinvent simulacra of authentic everyday experiences (cf. Baudrillard 2010: 13). Florian Gross makes just this observation when he claims that there is a growing trend among the white middle classes to seek authenticity in all walks of life (food, furniture, clothing, art, restaurants etc.) (cf. 2012: 238). People consume 'authentic' exotic cuisine, wear 'authentic' clothes and have 'authentic' holiday experiences (cf. Culler 1988: 61). However, this branch of 'hipster- and fake-authenticity' is not concerned with an original but just produces kitsch, very much in Baudrillard's sense (cf. Gross 2012: 238).

> Need an adjective to describe bars and restaurants with ethnic, historical, or outdoorsy themes; or new items of clothing or furniture that have been distressed, weathered, stone-washed, and otherwise pre-aged for the purpose of looking like it's been used or worn, for years, by someone who works on a farm/with his or her hands; or urban hipsters who adopt or otherwise admire what they imagine to

be the non-white (or ethnic white), urban/rural (i.e. non-suburban), working class, and 'outsider'-in-general style of life; or anything and everything re-enacted, 'authentically reproduced,' and Disneyfied in general? Try: fake-authentic. (Glenn 2010)

How does theatre then fit into this picture of a cultural landscape? Even though often thought to be almost by definition fake and unreal because actors pretend to be somebody who they are not, some thinkers have attributed strong features of authenticity to theatre. According to Alan Read, theatre has in the twentieth century been the one place that had the highest chance of being perceived as real precisely because it so obviously carried the signs of its own fakeness.

> [T]heatre was the last human venue in as much as its objects were measured, not for their potential to act, but for their impotential to be realised. Literally – realised, to become in some way more real, more than palpable and present [...]or at least just a bit 'less fake'. (Read 2008: 4)

Even so, this perception of theatre as real in ontological terms does not necessarily do justice to its perception and to its subject matter. For decades, practices of fragmentation, pastiche and deconstruction have pervaded the stages. 'In postdramatic theatre, it seems, language is used, not to wield an invisible and ideological authority as in dramatic theatre, but rather to expose its own indeterminacy' (Tomlin 2013: 65). The term 'postdramatic', as coined by Hans-Thies Lehmann, refers to a type of plays and performances originating roughly between 1970 and 1990 (cf. 2008: 27). What they, according to Lehman, have in common is a rejection of story (*fable*) in favour of images and individual association (cf. 2013: 16). However, the performances that I would like to investigate begin – as it were – where postdramatic theatre ends, both in terms of chronology, starting somewhere in the late 1990s, and also in terms of content. Postmodern drama, specifically with its notion of character as fragmented and ever fluctuating (cf. Tomlin 2013: 81), then, produced performances which were fragmented, pastiched and open. Birgit Schuhbeck, however, claims that the category of the authentic has returned to the theatre and the practices above have been largely abandoned.

> After decades in which plays were marked by association, citation and intertextuality, nowadays we appear to experience a comeback of a kind of play that puts the focus on logic, psychological motivation and straight-forward narration. [...] Theatre turns towards 'real' people with real problems. (Schuhbeck 2012)

Weidle makes very similar observations on the grounds of the popularity of documentary drama in Great Britain (cf. 2011). The examples above make it clear that the idea of authenticity is strongly present in contemporary culture. How authenticity fits in with other phenomena of a time characterized by superficiality, fragmentation and simulation is a puzzle for Haselstein and others.

> Modernism is nostalgic for authenticity, or utopian about the cultural practices that might some day make authenticity possible. Postmodernism, as Linda Hutcheon (cf. *Irony's Edge*) and many others have argued, abandons nostalgia for irony, consigning itself either with *juissance* or resignation, to the realization that everything is pseudo reality (Daniel Boorstin), simulacrum (Jean Baudrillard, *Simulacra and Simulation*), or pastiche (Fredric Jameson). Authenticity does not make much sense in a culture of copies. The self, once assumed to surpass presentation, turns out to be a performer; the well-designed artefact reveals itself to be a commodity; rebellion is just a pose. (Haselstein et al. 2010: 13, italics in the original)

In a culture that indeed consists of simulation to the degree that Baudrillard describes and which is perceived as fake by wide parts of cultural practitioners, the category of the authentic should long have become obsolete – a museum piece at best. However, the widely felt presence of phenomena of authenticity speaks a different language, leaving Baudrillard and others with a problem: if authenticity is present to such a high degree, the category of simulation cannot be upheld. Baudrillard might argue that the phenomena described above are also merely part of kitsch and nostalgia in an environment of simulacra. This book claims, however, that the practices described go beyond simulated experience. Some of them, as will become apparent in the analyses, are genuinely real and free of any context of simulation. The real should in the course of this study be understood in opposition to fiction, that is, anything that exists or has occurred in the factual world. It often surfaces in the guise of authenticity. In academia this has been a subject of fruitful debate for a number of years. 'Given the number of recent publications on authenticity [...], one can argue that authenticity has gained momentum in literary and cultural studies as well as in related disciplines during the last decade or so' (Straub 2012: 10). Authenticity is an important factor in today's culture. It is the first strong clue that the postmodern age of simulation and fragmentation has been replaced with mechanisms of authenticity and, thus, possibly even new forms of essentialism. I am not arguing in favour of dismissing Postmodernism and its practices altogether. On the contrary, it is clear that many forms of postmodern practice have achieved great merit and are still in practice. Indeed, it is these forms that have shaped the current structure of feeling. But, it is evident that new practices, while still conscious of the old ones, have superseded them (cf. Kirby 2009: 6). They have built, as it were, on the sandy foundations of Postmodernism a new and more stable house.

The decay of authenticity

In the following section, I intend to give a brief account of authenticity's evolution. In his monograph on the history of authenticity, Daniel Dietschi stresses that terms such as 'authenticity' must always be regarded, used and defined within their specific historic discourse and meaning because they have undergone profound changes (cf. 2012: 28). However, I do by no means seek to give a complete account of authenticity's development – quite the contrary. As Dietschi also remarks, a study with a broad subject such as authenticity must always be eclectic of sorts, seek out key issues and relate them (cf. 2012: 11). It is then not the aim to (re)write a history of authenticity but, by way of a genealogical approach in Foucault's sense, highlight key moments in the development and understanding of authenticity and related concepts. It is an exercise in gaining a broader understanding of authenticity and in giving the term more scope.

Highlighting only key moments is, however, not only indebted to a Foucauldian approach but also inscribed in the very concept of authenticity. To write a complete history of authenticity seems a futile exercise because 'authenticity' is a term that becomes only prevalent in certain periods and then is confined to marginality again. Funk maintains that authenticity becomes prominent at crucial moments in time (cf. Funk 2015: 38). Specifically, he finds that in periods of drastic change where the relationship between experience and representation is renegotiated (cf. 2015: 79), authenticity and its adjacent discourses (sincerity, veracity, etc.) tend to reclaim the spotlight. Writing a history of authenticity is, in a sense, always writing a history of key moments. This section is titled 'the decay of authenticity' to imply that authenticity has somehow diminished over an undefined period of time. Funk calls the history of authenticity a 'history of loss' (cf. 2015: 22). It is no exaggeration to say that authenticity, or rather the longing for it, always goes hand in hand with a profound feeling of having lost something. This something may variously be called sincerity, truth, reality or whatever the *mot en vogue* may be. Thus, the history of authenticity today is in part always an uncovering and sometimes also a bit of guesswork in what the thing is that (seemingly) was lost (cf. Taylor 1991: 4).

What I want to do in the following is try and highlight conceptions of authenticity with specific focus on the aspect of loss. In other words, by seeking out what was perceived as lost, I try to excavate what it is authenticity is ascribed to have. The periods under investigation roughly follow the same pattern which other scholars of authenticity in their accounts have used before.[4]

Antiquity

The word 'authentic' is derived from the Greek word αὐθεντικός (*authentikós*), which has a number of meanings. The semantic field revolves around the notion of being true, real or genuine, literally meaning 'self-consummating' (cf. Kalisch 2000: 32), in other words, something, which is whole and complete. The later Latin word *authenticus* acquires a much-less cloudy meaning; it refers to documents believed to be written by authorities themselves (cf. Dietschi 2012: 18). Consequently, it becomes evident that the notion of authenticity in Greek antiquity refers to a state of being complete or being whole. A notion of loss, which authentic could be opposed to, is not necessarily prominent yet. In Latin then, the focus shifts from a notion of wholeness in a broad sense to the very narrow notion of not being a forgery – for example an official document.

Dietschi maintains that authenticity was not an issue for philosophers or common people in classical antiquity. His chief witnesses are Plato and Socrates, who are both inspired by a notion of transcendence, a place of inner knowledge which is inspired by truth itself (cf. 2012: 20–21). The divine light of perfection shines in and through every human being, which implies that authenticity is a core value, present everywhere. This view is contested by Aleida Assmann, who locates a fundamental split between seeming and being in Western culture, beginning with Plato. She cites his dialogue *Phaedrus* as an example.

> Throughout the text, the dialogue is structured by the polemical opposition of seeming and being, which is paralleled by that of exterior and interior. This opposition is underpinned by the normative distinction between a real truth and a false simulation of truth. (Assmann 2012: 39)

Assman makes a very good point, because a great portion of Plato's philosophy is based on his system of *ideas*, which embody everything that is eternal, divine and perfect (cf. Plato 2000: 597a). The tangible appearance of *ideas* in the world is then necessarily inferior (cf. 2000: 600e). The *idea* is self-fulfilling in the best sense of the word, while any materialization of the abstract *idea* in the world needs a facilitator and is inferior. In this case one may very well argue that in Plato's system there is a trace of something being lost: the perfection of every *idea* is lost in its materialization. However, loss in this case is not felt as something personal or something which renders life in its completeness impossible. Charles Taylor claims that authenticity is strongly connected to the loss of an orderly system in which man was embedded and had his place (cf. Taylor 1991: 3). Such an orderly system, however, was still firmly in place in antiquity. Being authentic was not understood in terms of individualism, but rather the collective and one's place in the divine order were foregrounded (cf. Guignon 2004: 12–24). The famous Γνῶθι σεαυτόν (*gnothi seautón*) on the Apollon temple in Delphi had nothing to do with modern-day notions of finding one's inner self but meant just that: find your place in the divine order of things (cf. 2004: 13).

The conclusions to be drawn from the origins of authenticity are then the following: the notion of being whole is one that has its origins in antiquity albeit wholeness was not understood in individual terms but rather as finding one's predestined place in society and the cosmic order. Authenticity was thus not a high value or subject of debate because the place was given naturally and more or less easily recognizable. The divine system of order granted a good foothold for judging reality from fiction, truth from lying and authenticity from inauthenticity.[5] In short, authentic signifies something which is perfect (self-consummating). This idea of perfection and self-fulfilment breaks apart with the dawning of modern science and the destruction of theories of divine order – a process that stretched over centuries and which Taylor has called 'the "disenchantment" of the world' (1991: 3).

Renaissance

This disenchantment began to show its features around the Renaissance. The foundations of the very system on which authenticity in the antique understanding of the term was built, that is a divine order and man's place in it, became shaky. The scientific discoveries of the time (e.g. those of Copernicus,[6] Galileo), the religious revolutions (of Luther, Calvin) in the sixteenth century and ultimately the realization that many things such as society were manmade and could be altered by man destabilized traditional social and psychological orders. In short, the anthropocentric worldview and the divine order, symbolized by the Roman Catholic church, came into question (cf. Guignon 2004: 27–33). The old feudal order, which was firmly rooted in divine right and theology, had become porous as well (cf. Machiavelli, and later on Hobbes). At the same time as this disenchantment and scientific rationalization of the world set in, another convergent development took its starting point, namely the foregrounding of individuality, rather than collectivity. Dietschi maintains that subjectivity is clearly a phenomenon which starts in the Italian Renaissance and then quickly spreads all through Europe (cf. 2012: 52).[7] Some first, coy attempts at trying out subjectivity can be found in many literary works of the Renaissance. The example most readily employed is of course Prince Hamlet, who embodies all sorts of doubts and speculations and is lost for a place in the world and a role to play in it. However, not a phrase by Hamlet but by Polonius is most commonly cited as key example for the search for authenticity. The notorious 'to thine own self be true' (*Hamlet* I.3.78) is employed by many critics as the prime example of an emerging concept of authenticity (cf. Assmann 2012: 39; Funk 2015: 23; Potolsky 2006: 73). One must, however, be careful, not to read a contemporary understanding of authenticity into Polonius' phrase. While it seems convenient enough that Hamlet speaks about 'that within which passes show' (*Hamlet* I.2.85) and Polonius advises his son to be true to himself, one must keep in mind that if such a thing as authenticity existed in the Renaissance, it was still only tentatively tested out and not a fixed concept. Furthermore, as Funk remarks, Polonius' primary objective in counselling his son is not that he be in touch with his inner core but that he be truthful and sincere and most importantly not false towards other people (cf. 2015: 24). He is thus still rooted in a more or less feudal understanding of the self, which stresses the importance of the encounter with the collective. Moreover, a whole number of other characters in Shakespeare's plays which are firmly rooted in an undisturbed theological system could easily be named (Henry V. for instance springs to mind). Additionally, while authenticity or concepts similar to it were debated, a word for authenticity did not enter the English language until the eighteenth century, when it also entered German and French, hinting at its necessity at the time and its insignificance before (cf. Dietschi 2012: 18). Thus, while Hamlet is not necessarily an example of convenience, it shows that questions surrounding authenticity, such as notions of the self, or neighbouring concepts of sincerity were debated and tested out but certainly not fully developed.

For Lionel Trilling, the Renaissance is schizophrenic in this way. On the one hand, he argues that feigning and dissimulation – the very opposites of authenticity – gained prominence, exemplified in Shakespeare's dramas or Machiavelli's political writings. On the other hand, the doctrines of Protestantism demanded an approach of sincerity in all situations of life (cf. Trilling 1972: 13–22). He therefore proposes to investigate authenticity in two guises. First, he establishes 'sincerity' as a category, which is taken to mean being truthful in relation to others (cf. 1972: 11). He remarks that 'sincere' in the sixteenth century when it first entered the English language meant 'not tampered with, or falsified, or corrupted' (1972: 12). This is presumably the advice old Polonius wants to give Laertes: do not lie or be treacherous, be honest to yourself and other people. Sincerity here is the very social value which is connected to a higher order of meaning and justice. As the second, and in the Renaissance only vaguely defined, concept, Trilling names authenticity. According to him, it resists definition but suggests 'a more strenuous moral experience than "sincerity" does, a more exigent conception of the self and of what being true to it consists in, a wider reference to the universe and man's place in it' (1972: 11). 'Authenticity' is then indeed something close to what we understand by the term today – a sort of inner core, a *prima causa movens*, the one place of the true self on which any outer appearance is based and to which one must return at times. The older concept of sincerity, which one may even link to the Γνῶθι σεαυτόν (*gnothi seauton*, i.e. 'know thyself'), is slowly questioned by the emerging phenomenon of authenticity. Funk proffers that *Hamlet* is to be read as a meditation on what it means to be authentic or not authentic (cf. 2015: 24). Hamlet stands on the brink of the modern world and grapples with his own newly found subjectivity and decentredness.

The self as autonomous instance, according to Funk, begins to arise in the Renaissance (cf. 2015: 25). With the emergence of the subject as an autonomous instance, the collective place gradually erodes. The subject finds itself alone and faced with numerous questions of ontology. This new autonomy demands definition and asks for an authentic core: 'To be, or not to be; that is the question' (*Hamlet* III.1.56). With the unity of self and world lost, the individual is thrown back onto itself. Consequently, one would rather have to ask: 'Who to be or not to be?'

From Enlightenment to Romanticism

The simple question, 'Who am I?' becomes even more prominent in the decades of the Enlightenment, where the focus on rationality and science – even towards the mind itself (Kant) – becomes ever more present. Trilling suggests that the gradual evolution of a literary public also helped speed up this process. Along with Rousseau, he finds that literature challenges the notions of both sincerity and authenticity. The evolving public sphere and the status of literature are frightening and threatening to the subject, because one is constantly in contact with mental processes of others whereby one's own consciousness becomes fragmented (cf. Trilling 1972: 61). In other words, with the evolution of a public sphere of discourse, readers gain insight into the world of thought of other people as never before. Through an increased circulation of fiction, possible versions of a self can be viewed and tested out by proxy. Subjects, one could say, learn that different roles are possible. Rousseau is very aware of the danger of playing different parts and, for that same reason, rejects theatre as a medium of catharsis: How could affect purge us of affect, and how could putting on another face where the self completely vanishes be beneficial to a wholesome human being (cf. Trilling 1972: 64)? Rousseau then is one of the first and most prominent advocates of a subjectivity that could be named authentic. Authenticity, in our contemporary understanding, is also connected to individuality. Rousseau, both in the *Contrat Social* (1762) as well as in *Emile* (1762), contrasts society and individuality, the state of nature and civilization, natural, good impulses and rational reflection (cf. Guignon

2004: 56–57). In this view, true authenticity can only be achieved as an individual, not in a collective. Guignon, along with Jean Starobinski, finds the moment of conception of authenticity in Rousseau's emphasis on subjective truth (cf. 2004: 69). In his *Confessions* (1782/89), Rousseau admits that he may make errors of fact (objective truth) but will remain true to his feelings at the time of events. In other words, he will with utmost veracity narrate what he believes to be his life story (subjective truth). This concept of subjective truth seems to be the beginning of authenticity as a subjective quality in our modern understanding (cf. 2004: 69). One does no longer need to be true to facts and towards other people (Polonius) but rather to one's own feelings, memories and perceptions. Truthfulness (or might we say personal authenticity?) trumps truth, and individuality trumps collectivity. What is more, Rousseau's state of nature and the ideal of the *homme naturel* are then also the first instant of a longing for the 'golden age' of authenticity, the state of nature: the being-one of the self (cf. Dietschi 2012: 8). According to Rousseau, the ideal authentic being has been disturbed by civilization but there is the possibility of recovery through nature (cf. Dietschi 2012: 22–23). Here, we clearly find a situation of a (perceived) loss of an original and desirable state, which truthfulness can possibly ameliorate. The longing for authenticity comes hand in hand with a longing for a golden age. Authenticity, it seems, becomes the cure-all pill for a world which is increasingly complicated, rationalized and fragmented, in which the only terra firma is Descartes' *cogito ergo sum*.

Naturally, this form of doubt *in extremis* soon experienced a strong backlash. In a way, Rousseau, with his conception of truthfulness and his insistence on a state of nature, laid the foundations for Romanticist thinking. The Romantic ideals of genius, genuineness and originality are based on the idea of a state of nature and are also heavily opposed to the rationality of the Enlightenment (cf. Dietschi 2012: 91). Through an emphasis on emotion as opposed to reason, on nature as opposed to culture and on the cult of the genius and originality, the concept of authenticity was formatively shaped in Romanticism (cf. Guignon 2004: 51). Guignon finds the first important property of Romanticism to be 'the attempt to recover a sense of oneness and wholeness that appears to have been lost with the rise of modernity' (2004: 51). It is a truism that Romanticism can *cum grano salis* be conceived of as a backswing of the pendulum, from Enlightenment rationality towards emotion. In Romanticism,

> there is the nostalgia for an earlier state and the intimation that by turning inward and hearing the inner voice of the true self, one might make contact with the great groundswell of Nature from which we have sprung. There is the idea that our access to the source of our being is achieved not by cognitive reflection, but by *feeling*. And there is a conception of freedom as liberation from socially imposed constraints. (Guignon 2004: 59, italics in the original)

Guignon's statement might as well have been taken from a review of a contemporary spirituality and self-help book, which goes to show how deeply felt and powerful the reverberations of Romanticist thinking and, by proxy, Rousseau's ideas are. By stressing truthfulness rather than truth (Rousseau) and emotion rather than rationality (Romanticism), the late eighteenth and early nineteenth centuries established a system of thinking with wide-ranging consequences. Mankind is forced to rethink its own ontological status and is by and large alone in this undertaking (*sapere aude*). The term 'authenticity' first comes into play during the eighteenth century, and is formatively shaped in the eighteenth and early nineteenth centuries. Its qualities, some of which have lasted until today, were established then. Namely, these are: individuality rather than collectivity, and a foregrounding of emotion and truthfulness rather than rationality and truth.

Modernity

The development, which had begun in the late eighteenth and early nineteenth centuries, only sped up and gained more momentum in the middle to late nineteenth and early twentieth centuries. Through the industrialization and the division of labour, social and spatial mobility increased, furthering a feeling of loss and decentredness. But crucially, science also undertook it to destabilize the concept of a stable and unified self. The subject itself came into question. The godfather of this development is certainly Sigmund Freud, with his theories of the human mind. However, a number of other sciences also participated in the 'disenchantment of the world' (Taylor 1991: 3). Darwin's theories on the evolution of species cannot be underestimated in this context as they made it plain that man was not by any means the crown of creation but just one mammal among others. The consequences of this insight are far-reaching. Freud recognizes that science had dealt three 'wounding blows' to mankind's image of itself:

> In the course of centuries the naïve self-love of men has had to submit to two major blows at the hands of science. The first was when they learnt that our earth was not the center of the universe but only a tiny fragment of a cosmic system of scarcely imaginable vastness. This is associated in our minds with the name of Copernicus [...]. The second blow fell when biological research destroyed man's supposedly privileged place in creation and proved his descent from the animal kingdom and his ineradicable animal nature. This revaluation has been accomplished in our own days by Darwin, Wallace and their predecessors [...]. But human megalomania will have suffered its third and most wounding blow from the psychological research of the present time which seeks to prove to the ego that it is not even master in its own house, but must content itself with scanty information of what is going on unconsciously in its mind. (1963: 16, 284–285)

What Freud describes here is, by and large, what has been elaborated above, namely the gradual destruction of an orderly teleological system where mankind could locate a fixed place for itself at the centre. Freud's deconstruction of the subject becomes one of the signposts of a felt loss of wholeness for the modern subject (cf. Dietschi 2012: 14). Whereas Rousseau could still postulate an inner core to which he could at least be truthful, mankind was now made painfully aware that even the vague unit which one calls the self is a construct and to a large degree shaped by factors outside of one's control. The very core of the human self, which some centuries ago had been somewhat of a safe haven in an increasingly disparate and complicated world, was now convincingly deconstructed. Subject and identity as autonomous institutions were put into question (cf. Dietschi 2012: 11). It is very understandable that such a development is more than frightening for the modern 'subject'. One of the defence mechanisms against this shattering of the world is a longing for a world where the inner core and the subject's place in the world were still intact.

> One of the characteristics of modernity is the belief that authenticity has been lost and exists only in the past – whose signs we preserve (antiques, restored buildings, imitations of old interiors) – or else in other regions or countries. (Culler 1988: 160)

Thus, a version of the past is invented and nostalgia for a golden age evolves. Eighteenth-century neo-gothic building style or the paintings of the pre-Raphaelites may serve as a case in point. Trilling sees the organic in all its forms as a characteristically modern value where, it seems, machines have taken over (e.g. 1908 Marinetti's *Futurist Manifesto*) and a longing for this past ideal state is proliferated (cf. 1972: 127–129). It seems justified to say then that the developments, which had begun in the Renaissance and had accelerated in the age of reason and Romanticism, found their first pinnacle around the beginning of the twentieth century. By way of a general tendency, one can say that it is modern civilization itself which brings forth the notion of authenticity. The scientific revolutions, the division of labour, the discoveries about mankind and its place in the world have all contributed to a profound feeling of loss and being lost. Authenticity is the counter-movement to these profound feelings of uncertainty and instability.

Postmodernity

In the decades starting circa from the 1950s, the developments described above became even more pronounced, with new concepts of (poststructuralist) thinking and eventually the culture of postmodernity. Thinkers such as Erving Goffman proffered that life and all the 'authentic' roles of the subject were only performative (cf. 1959). Others, such as

Roland Barthes (cf. 1977) and Jacques Derrida (cf. 1976), questioned the stability of language itself. Whereas modernity had questioned the self, now that vaguely defined entity became an isolated island, as it were, with no proper means of intersubjectivity or communication. But what is more, political and social developments of the twentieth century also deconstructed the hope to (re)build some utopian state or golden age by human means. Derrida, in a very illuminating essay, takes up Freud's notion of the 'wounding blows' and ascertains that the twentieth century saw the fourth and most damaging blow to mankind's conception of itself.

> There is the temptation to add here an aporetic postscript to Freud's remark that linked in the same comparative history three of the traumas inflicted on human narcissism when it is thus de-centred. [...] Our aporia would stem here from the fact that there is no longer any name or teleology for determining the Marxist coup and its subject. [...] The Marxist blow is as much the projected unity of a thought and of a labour movement, sometimes in a messianic or eschatological form, as it is the history of the totalitarian world (including Nazism and fascism, which are the inseparable adversaries of Stalinism). This is perhaps the deepest wound for mankind, in the body of its history and in the history of its concept. [...] For we know that the blow struck enigmatically in the name of Marx also accumulates and gathers together the other three. [...] The century of 'Marxism' will have been that of the techno-scientific and effective decentering of the earth, of geopolitics, of the *anthropos* in its onto-theological identity or its genetic properties, of the *ego cogito*. (1994: 6, italics in the original)

Whereas earlier generations, despite the destruction of an orderly world and a unified subject, still had a longing for a golden age – or rather the hope to (re)build any such state – the postmodern subject is deprived even of this possibility. The failure of the great ideologies of the century made it clear that mankind was unable to create any form of a better world by its own means. With this possibility gone, Derrida suggests, mankind's narcissism is dealt a lethal blow. In other words, while mankind was once only lost for a firm place and greater meaning, now it was even lost for hope. For Derrida, however, this final blow is not a problem. It is rather a necessary, bitter cure, from which new possibilities arise.

> In the same place, on the same limit, where history is finished, there where a certain determined concept of history comes to an end, precisely there the historicity of history begins, there finally it has the chance of heralding itself – of promising itself. There where man, a certain determined concept of man, is finished, there the pure humanity of man, of the other man and of man as other begins or has finally the chance of heralding itself – of promising itself. (1994: 11)

It is only through the loss of hope – when mankind comes to terms with the fact that the subject, the world, the languages we speak and basically everything around us are constructed and in themselves meaningless – that a new and true history can begin. While Derrida and his supporters see this as a liberation for mankind, others have been far more critical. Fredric Jameson, one of the fiercest advocates against this way of thinking, believes that poststructuralism has led to a loss of affect (cf. 1991: 16), as well as to a loss of historicity, leaving mankind only with empty husks of texts that are deprived of any meaning (cf. 1991: 18). Assuming that for the layman in postmodern society, postmodern theory is perceived as scary rather than liberating, it becomes evident that the search for authenticity – in other words, a flight from the unwelcome truth of fragmentation and uncertainty – is the only viable option. Society and one's environment are perceived as fake, medialized and lacking first-hand encounter. Therefore, any offer of authenticity in its various guises will meet with great popularity. Matthew Potolsky diagnoses that '[t] he lure of the authentic is an implicit acknowledgement that we live in a world of fakes and simulations, that the real is a vanishing quality needing the protection of a museum' (2006: 155). But not only the real seems to have disappeared in postmodern life but also the notion of truth has become more and more obsolete. With the de-centred self of Postmodernism, there is no one true instance of the self; there is no longer any sort of core to be true to (cf. Guignon 2004: 120). This leads Liz Tomlin to the conclusion that authenticity in postmodernity is perceived as a myth and that 'there is significant rejection of the notion of a singular, coherent and essential self and a turn instead to multiple and constructed identities' (Tomlin 2013: 81).

The de-centring of the self is furthermore also expressed in a certain estrangement from natural processes. According to Carl Rodgers, this is rooted in a number of factors such as genetic technology, computer technology, control over weather and resources. Consequently, humanity is more and more drifting away from their natural origins and this creates a sense of loss in a complex world (cf. Dietschi 2012: 107). This leads on the one hand to a renewed upswing of nostalgia, 'a longing for the all-powerful, the wondrous, the holy, and the authorless object' (Jan Berg in Hulse 2012: 63) and on the other hand to a widely felt 'sense that lives have been flattened and narrowed, and that this is connected to an abnormal and regrettable self-absorption' (Taylor 1991: 4). The postmodern subject feels far-removed and isolated from nature and its own origins, sentenced to live in a world which is perceived as fake and superficial. Jameson describes this environment vividly as the 'cultural logic of late capitalism' (1991). He argues that specifically the economic, capitalist system of the West has led to 'a society where exchange value has been generalized to the point at which the very memory of use value is effaced' (1991: 18). Charles Taylor makes similar observations when he points out that cost-utility calculations pervade all areas of postmodern life (cf. 1991: 5), leading to a (felt) loss of freedom in both a political and an economic sense (cf. 1991: 8–9).

Finally, the use, quality and quantity of media and communication saw the most rapid changes in the late twentieth and early twenty-first centuries (cf. Kirby 2006). This fast-paced media environment also contributed to the rise of authenticity as a postmodern value: 'Authenticity is increasingly valued in a society in which new forms of media and new forms of mediation rapidly gain importance and have started to pervade virtually every aspect of life' (Funk et al. 2012: 10). More will be said about mediatization and the phenomenon of second- and third-hand information later on. For now, suffice it to say that the desire for authenticity reflects the felt lack of first-hand experience. However, as Funk points out, the promise of authenticity is a double-edged sword because it is itself a mediated construct (cf. 2012: 10). Authenticity in postmodern and contemporary society thus becomes a very cloudy concept that can find application in almost any context. Most prominently, it figures in a large number of popular-psychological and self-help books as a sort of congruence between self and world (cf. Dietschi 2012: 47). However, the quest for personal authenticity may even further a feeling of being lost. The quest for authenticity, according to Taylor, only leads to focused introspection, isolation and loneliness (cf. 1991: 29). In a similar way, Jameson has suggested that the lack of any 'deeper logic' of Postmodernism leads inevitably to self-referentiality and superficiality (Jameson 1991: xii), which abolishes any notion of authenticity (cf. 1991: 12). While Derrida might more positively phrase this as 'autopoiesis', Taylor argues that true authenticity in the shape of self-definition can only be achieved in dialogue with 'significant others' and through 'horizons of significance' (Taylor 1991: 66–67). It is obvious that a poststructuralist would disagree on his notion that there *has* to be significance. After all, the whole point of, say deconstruction, is that there is not one signification but that each one is a situational construct. Taylor's fear is that 'anthropocentrism, by abolishing all horizons of significance, threatens us with a loss of meaning and hence trivialisation of our predicament' (1991: 68). Derrida's simple answer to this reproach might be: 'Yes, so what?' Effectively, two irreconcilable positions collide here. Taylor – possibly along with popular opinion – finds that a 'pure doctrine' of poststructuralism cannot be upheld. On the other hand, Derrida claims that it is precisely poststructuralist theory that will liberate mankind from the shackles of ideology.

Returning to authenticity, the decay of authenticity in postmodernity should be evident. If one follows the strict cultural and analytical concepts of poststructuralism, one would have to concede that authenticity does not exist and neither does it play a role.

As Baudrillard's simulacra, Derrida's *différance* and Jameson's critique of postmodern superficiality attest, art and theory in postmodernism have effectively put an end to any meaningful distinction between inner and outer personality, surface and deep structure, essence and representation. (Funk 2015: 28)

However, as has been pointed out (cf. Knaller 2012a; Mair & Becker 2005; Taylor 1991), conceptions of authenticity and a longing or even nostalgia for authentic experience and order, which seem to have structured earlier centuries, are very present in the culture of today. Thus, the concept of authenticity becomes a sort of fetish in a society without reference points. It is marketed and advertised and, in Jameson's sense, also becomes a commodity (cf. 1991: x); but fundamentally, the phenomenon is only created because of a need for it. 'I believe that in our culture of simulation, the notion of authenticity is for us what sex was for the Victorians – threat and obsession, taboo and fascination' (Turkle 2011: 4). Turkle, by evoking Foucault, hints at the construction of authenticity. This construction, however, has very real consequences. In a society where people demand the real or authentic, the genuinely real may actually not be genuine enough anymore. She gives the example of Disneyland's Animal Kingdom, where visitors complained about the real animals not being as good as the robotic ones (cf. 2011: 4). Authenticity in postmodern popular culture then would be a prime example of a Baudrillardian simulacrum: entirely fake but with very real effects (cf. Baudrillard 2010: 3). Furthermore, if we return to Turkle's suggestion that authenticity is discursively created in contemporary culture, it is interesting to consider two further propositions. Goffman claims that our lives are performative (cf. 1959) and McKenzie proposes that performance has become ever more prominent as a practice in contemporary culture. He maintains that it will be 'to the twentieth and twenty-first centuries what discipline was to the eighteenth and nineteenth that is, an onto-historical formation of power and knowledge' (McKenzie 2001: 18). If we accept this line of thought, it becomes apparent that authenticity is created, performed and developed, and once it is established it becomes a social (unquestioned) reality. It becomes a social reality in the face of a void of meaning, reference, *telos* or whatever the *mot de rigueur* may be.

Alienation: An explanation

While Postmodernism was extremely critical of any *grands récits* or general explanations (cf. Lyotard 1984), today it may be possible again to attempt ways of general explanation. In the following, I intend to give one possible trajectory of the current prominence of phenomena of authenticity. By linking two theories, I will try to give a more precise account of the cultural developments which lead to the proliferation of authenticity. The contention in this case is that the demand for authenticity is fuelled by a process of alienation that occurs in relation to the work of art and in the role of consumers. The attempt, however, comes with a *caveat*: it is by no means the only or the definitive explanation. There are a large number of other possible approaches, aspects and thinkers that have contributed to this field. So the following discussion is one exemplary, explanatory account, and it does not claim universality.

Authenticity today seems to be one of the highest values in society and yet also one of the most elusive ones. Most of our information about anything, speaking in Niklas Luhman's terms, is generated by the media and consequently is second-hand; from the information available we create our own version of reality that is deemed 'authentic' (cf. Mair & Becker 2005: 101–103). In the same way, a large number of scholars agree that the postmodern subject constitutes itself through performance, that is through performing roles that have been learned in the course of medial consumption and socialization (cf. Eshelman 2001; Mair & Becker 2005; McKenzie 2001). Reality then is more and more experienced as representation and staging rather than authentic (cf. Fischer-Lichte 2000: 23). In the dramatic arts, this phenomenon can be found as well, and performances which employ mechanisms of authenticity have been hugely successful (cf. Lane 2010: 64; Schulze 2013). The reason for this development towards a structure of feeling in which authenticity is performed can be seen in a process of alienation that started in the first quarter of the twentieth century.

Walter Benjamin, whose theories have recently been enjoying great popularity (cf. Funk 2015: 27), claims that a piece of art had traditionally been endowed with an aura of uniqueness. In his essay 'The

Work of Art in the Age of Mechanical Reproduction' (1936), he states that this 'aura' falls prey to the invention of mechanical reproducibility.

> Even with the most perfect reproduction, *one thing* stands out: the here and now of the work of art – its unique existence in the place where it is at this moment. [...] The here and now of the original constitute the abstract idea of its genuineness. [...] *The whole province of genuineness is beyond technological (and of course not only technological) reproducibility.* (Benjamin 2008: 5–6, italics in the original)

The genuinely real, in other words, the 'aura' of a piece of art, can never be copied. At first, the term 'aura' seems very ephemeral and elusive; however, Benjamin goes on to describe that the 'aura' should be understood in quite concrete terms. In his view, art is rooted in the ritual making of objects and in worship.

> Now it is crucially important that this auric mode of being of the work of art never becomes completely separated from its ritual function. To put it another way: *The 'one-of-a-kind' value of the 'genuine' work of art has its underpinnings in the ritual in which it had its original, initial utility value.* No matter how indirectly, this is still recognizable even in the most profane forms of the service of beauty as a secularized rite. (2008: 11, italics in the original)

The aura of the piece of art embodies its cultic value (use value) but also, as it were, the performance of making it. That is to say, the concrete action of a unique human being who produced and used the one-of-a-kind object is still present in it, even centuries later. The aura enacts both the metaphysical, cultic reference of an object and its continued existence over time. It reminds the beholder of a time that had some metaphysical system in place, but it also connects the beholder with times past. This is the crucial point of distinction between an original and a fake: the original object establishes a human relation, something that is felt to be real and that at the same time elicits the experience of time and mortality in the beholder. An original establishes a chronotopian moment which is able to link the experience of time and presence of the artist to that of the beholder. It brings back to mind one's ontological status and thus connects the ideas expressed in the artwork to the higher meanings of time, mortality and eventually life. This relation between artisan and beholder, this conversation over time and space, however, is disturbed with the arrival of mass (re)production. Copies of paintings, prints of manuscripts and, for theatre, the arrival of film bring about the death of the original.

> The artistic performance of the stage actor [i.e. what he or she *does* artistically] is presented to the audience by the actor in person; of that there is no doubt. The artistic performance of the screen actor, on the other hand, is presented to the audience via a piece of equipment, a film camera. The latter has two consequences. [...] Guided by its operator, the camera comments on the performance continuously. [...] The second consequence is that the screen actor, by not presenting his performance to the audience in person, is deprived of the possibility open to the stage actor of adapting that performance to the audience as the show goes on. (2008: 17–18)

Film as opposed to theatre destroys the 'aura' of the playhouse by, first, preselecting the images an audience will see and, second, by disabling any human interrelation between performer and audience. Moreover, while a stage play is necessarily different every night, a film will always be exactly the same, each night in hundreds of venues. The spectator in the theatre who was empowered to influence the performance by booing, cheering or heckling and who was free to gaze upon whichever detail they wanted is now reduced to a passive consumer of a uniform product that no longer has an 'aura', nor an artist who can be seen as a virtuoso (cf. Schulze 2015). In a convergent development, functional shifts in the role of audiences are also under way.

> For centuries the situation in literature was such that a small number of writers faced many thousands of times that number of readers. Then, towards the end of the last century, there came a change. As the press grew in volume, making ever-increasing numbers of new political, religious, scientific, professional and local organs available to readership, larger and larger sections of that readership (gradually at first) turned into writers. It began with the daily newspapers opening their 'correspondence columns' to such people and it has now reached a point where few Europeans involved in the labour process, basically, could fail to find some opportunity or other to publish an experience

at work, a complaint, a piece of reporting or something similar. The distinction between writer and readership is thus in the process of losing its fundamental character. That distinction is becoming a functional one, assuming a different form from one case to the next. The reader is constantly ready to become a writer. (2015: 22–23)

Benjamin effectively predicts the 'blogosphere' in which the roles of producer and consumer are indeed merely a question of chronology, not ontology. Taking both of Benjamin's propositions into account, one arrives at the conclusion that the modern public has been overburdened with two conflicting demands: on the one hand, to be passive consumers of a uniform, mass-produced good, and, on the other hand, to become producers of such goods at any time. The conflict arising from these demands is to be passive and active at the same time. In this system of contradicting demands, it is no longer talent that matters but persona, or, in other words, performance – the absolute adaptability to situation and circumstance (cf. 2015: 23). For Benjamin then, the first half of the twentieth century is characterized both by a loss of authenticity which leaves audiences extremely unsettled when negotiating the conflicting demands, and, at the same time, also renders performance and appearance more important than 'being'.

> For Benjamin, the artwork's loss of aura symbolizes the alienation of mankind from itself, which has often been cited as symptomatic of the modernist condition and which can be traced back to the theories of Darwin and Freud as well as to the cataclysm of World War I. (Funk 2015: 28)

The loss of authenticity that Benjamin describes, however, did not stop there. It even accelerated over the following decades, culminating in the information age and the web 2.0 reality of today (cf. Kirby 2009: 6). But even earlier, poststructuralist thought and later Postmodernism had exacerbated this development. If Modernism had left audiences uncertain about their role and undermined authenticity, Postmodernism questioned the very validity of the concept itself. One of the best examples for such postmodern doubt is offered by Jean Baudrillard's theories on simulacra and simulation. He maintains that the category of the 'real' has become obsolete in an age in which the media create images that are not rooted in reality anymore. These images are just 'models of a real without origin or reality: a hyperreal' (Baudrillard 2010: 1). For him, the very proliferation of texts in all forms and shapes just masks the absence of any genuine content. In this hyperreality, the category of the real no longer exists because there no longer is any relation between sign and referent (cf. 2010: 6). Consumers of any text or cultural product then find nostalgia to be their only viable option.

> When the real is no longer what it was, nostalgia assumes its full meaning. There is a plethora of myths of origin and of signs of reality – a plethora of truth, of secondary objectivity, and authenticity. Escalation of the true, of lived experience, resurrection of the figurative where the object and substance have disappeared. Panic-stricken production of the real and the referential, parallel to and greater than the panic of material production: this is how simulation appears in the phase that concerns us – a strategy of the real, of the neoreal and the hyperreal that everywhere is the double of a strategy of deterrence. (2010: 7)

What then remains for consumers and producers alike, if authenticity and the real are no longer available, is to go down the same route that the sign has gone in Baudrillard's theories: simulation. By way of nostalgia, of longing for some ideal and obscure past in which authentic experience was still possible and the sign was still rooted in the real, audiences create their own version of an (imagined) authentic past. 'Everywhere one recycles lost faculties, or lost bodies, or lost sociality, or the lost taste of food. [...] One reinvents penury, asceticism, vanished savage naturalness: natural food, health, yoga' (2010: 13). Or, as Kirby has it, the 'aesthetic of the apparently real [...] proffers what seems to be real ... and that is all there is to it. The apparently real comes without self-consciousness, without irony or self-interrogation, and without signalling itself to the reader or viewer' (2009: 140).

The postmodern subject thus creates its own reality by performing the role it thinks still reflects the genuine and the authentic. Reality is experienced as staged, a mere representation that has no depth (cf. Fischer-Lichte 2000: 23). And the self is acted out in a performance of make-belief (cf. Mair & Becker 2005: 118–122). McKenzie has stressed the importance of performance for the twenty-first century (cf. 2001: 18), just like Eshelman, who speaks of a 'performatist epoch' (2001: 5). For McKenzie, performance is a form of discipline. We enact the roles that have been generated by a system without depth or genuine reference and thus comply with power structures in Foucault's sense. In other words, we have lost the idea of a unified and authentic self that would have somehow been rooted in the real. Instead we enact roles generated by nostalgic fantasies of an authentic past. These roles in turn are learned and shaped by the needs of a capitalist, consumerist, media society. We behave according to the role models of production and consumption. Performance indeed is power and discipline. Seen in a more positive light, one could argue with Liz Tomlin that aesthetic returns of the real are a counter-movement against Postmodernism. Drawing on Jameson and Paul Mann, she argues that that which had seemed inconceivable in Postmodernism becomes the very form of resistance against the death of the avant-garde in the period – the only innovation left. Thus the real took its rise because it was precisely the thing which had been abolished (cf. 2013: 27).

Not only theatre audiences but also the general public by this stage must have lost all points of reference and be ready to act out and change roles ever more quickly. However, it has also been claimed that because of this ontological uncertainty, or rather confusion, a great longing for something that is not a simulacrum, something that is genuinely real and authentic, has arisen. Bernard Williams, following Baudrillard, has remarked that nostalgia is a genuine part of this experience.

> Indeed, the whole point of authenticity as a characteristically modern value has lain in the attempt to regain in some reflective form the unexpressed certainties which are supposed to have structured the pre-modern world. (Williams 2002: 183)

However, it needs to be mentioned that Baudrillard's theories have been heavily criticized. While they seem somehow intuitively appealing,

Horst Ruthrof – for instance – has remarked that Baudrillard has no clear methodological foundation for his claims; nor does he bring forward concrete instances of what he claims to have found: 'He has no semantics with which to argue the case. All we can say in his defence is "Nice Metaphors"' (Ruthrof 2000: 65). These 'nice metaphors', however, make it understandable that his theories have been received so widely. It is also a matter of debate whether all forms of authenticity indeed disappeared in the second half of the twentieth century. All that can be affirmed is that much of the theory of the past decades had in mind to abolish the idea of certainty. Similarly, Dennis Dutton, already in 1990, was dismissive of Baudrillard's theories: 'To the list of charges I would add [...] that, when it [his writing] isn't unintelligible, almost everything Baudrillard says is either trite or somehow vaguely or badly – false' (235). The main line of criticism has always focused on Baudrillard's tendency to work with sweeping generalizations that lacked a sustained and structured analysis, and that his examples are limited to the narrow field of television. Even his editor is highly critical when he writes,

> Baudrillard's writing up to the mid 1980s is up to several criticisms. He fails to define his major terms, such as the code; his writing style is hyperbolic and declarative, often lacking sustained, systematic analysis when it is appropriate; he totalizes his insights, refusing to qualify or delimit his claims. He writes about particular experiences, television images, as if nothing else in society mattered, extrapolating a bleak view of the world form that limited base. He ignores contradictory evidence such as the many benefits afforded by the new media, for example, providing vital information to the populace (as in the Vietnam War) and counteracting parochialism with humanizing images of foreigners. (Poster 2001: 8)

Furthermore, even if one acknowledges, as Mark Poster does, that Baudrillard's work is valuable for understanding 'the impact of new forms of communication on society' (2001: 8), one would still have to ask a more fundamental question. Baudrillard constantly operates with, along and around the category of the 'real'. While he of course proclaims the death of the real and fails to define it, one would have to acknowledge that the category of the real in some form or other still exists, as even Baudrillard cannot operate without it (cf. Norris 1990: 182). While Baudrillard's analysis may be flawed in a number of ways, its wide reception and intuitive appeal may still be helpful because they point towards a structure of feeling that has become very uncomfortable with the category of the real. The media and television age has brought about a state of affairs that incorporates many aspects of the theory Baudrillard describes (even if the Gulf War *did* actually happen). Such a felt lack of the genuine, the real or the authentic is crucial in the development of the performances under discussion in this study.

As this study will show, audiences are keen on bringing back the idea of truth, the real and authenticity, and not just as a way of performance but as a genuine human experience. While theory may have abolished truth and the real altogether, they have never ceased to play a role in people's lives. Audiences and consumers are apparently not happy with the abyss of uncertainty and medialization, and have sought to retrieve something that is authentic. Ihab Hassan, for instance, undermines some of his own earlier writings when he demands the reinstatement of truth, even with a capital 'T' (cf. Hassan 2003, 2004). His approach is largely pragmatic in that he postulates truth as a factor in people's everyday lives and that, consequently, it must have a place in theory, too (cf. 2003: 205). Truth in this sense is longer necessarily an absolute, but rather a function of the audience's perception. For Hassan, it is clear that such a function can only be built on human interaction, which for him is based on the authentic experience of trust. Consequently, he calls for an 'aesthetic of trust' in artistic production. But what could such an aesthetic look like?

Mapping the field: Authenticity and the real

Before turning towards a closer inspection of 'authenticity', it is important to clarify the term further. I intend to use authenticity as a reconstructive ascription made by an individual. Authenticity is performative; at the same time it enacts a very tangible social reality and influences all kinds of cultural practices. How can this performance then be understood in contemporary culture and how can it be defined or studied? What is its relationship with neighbouring concepts such as truth and mimesis? The following section maps out the theoretical territory for this study. It makes three central claims: first, it argues that authenticity is a backlash against postmodern rationality and doubt. It has already been alluded to that contemporary cultures are in many ways not dissimilar to Romanticism in so far as they bring back notions of *telos* and stability in the guise of authenticity. However, as will be shown, this backlash is not a simple destruction of the house that Postmodernism built but rather a renovation which is very sensitive to postmodern style and structure. Second, it proffers that authenticity is often consciously created, specifically in the performing arts, as an aesthetic tool; it is both a strategy of creation and reception. Third, it argues against Funk that unmediated experience is possible while it may still evade linguistic communication. Funk claims that 'there can be no such thing as unmediated experience, no conscious existence before or beyond representation' (2015: 16). As the analyses in part two will demonstrate, there are performances and aesthetic means which induce a visceral understanding and experience of performance. I argue that this understanding is indeed unmediated: a sort of *hors de texte*. However, for obvious reasons, it evades verbal description and is therefore locked in the subject's cortex. Consequently, I try to circumnavigate the experience and describe its surroundings, while the thing itself cannot be named with words, lest it loses its immediacy.

An understanding of authenticity

I am aware that such claims as stated above do not sit well with a number of contemporary theories and theorists, and it is true that, at first glance, it sounds like I am trying to reinstall everything that Postmodernism had worked so hard to deconstruct.

Is authenticity thus a versatile alibi for taboo concepts such as 'truth', 'origin(al)' or 'real', all of which threaten to re-evoke the spectre of essentialism? [...] The question that scholars need to ask is how they can account for the persistence of such apparently essentialist needs and demands in a postmodern world, where they are commonly depicted as staged or performed. Authenticity concerns our view of the artists, the artwork and the artistic act of creation. In other words, it concerns the human subject, the object world it inhabits – and the ties that link the two, i.e. literature, film and the visual arts. In which ways can the authentic then be reconsidered, at a time when the necessary philosophical and epistemological grounds are no longer available? (Straub 2012: 18)

It is certainly curious that a concept with such absolutist connotations as authenticity should be the focus of many contemporary academic debates and should be so present in popular culture. I will try to highlight some of the features of authenticity today and try to discern how – as Straub points out – the concept can be grasped when appropriate philosophical concepts are no longer available. In his seminal work, Wolfgang Funk has provided a very lucid discussion of authenticity and its place in today's culture, specifically in literature. He consciously avoids a modern-day definition and confines himself to highlighting key features by way of eight theses on authenticity (cf. 2015: 6). Some of these have been discussed already; some of the other ones will be inspected more closely in the following. As Funk has delivered a very convincing approach to authenticity, this study will, by and large, follow his foundations, although some alterations and adaptations to a theatrical context are in order.

Authenticity the paradox

When trying to define prominent features of authenticity, one is soon faced with a paradox inherent in the concept itself, which voids attempts at a definition. The first one to comment on this phenomenon is Jonathan Culler. He describes authenticity as a sought-after quality in the world of today by the example of tourism, and finds that tourist landmarks and sights gain their authenticity not out of themselves but through description as such. 'The "real thing" must be marked as real, as sightworthy; if it is not marked or differentiated, it is not a notable sight [...]. The authentic is not something unmarked or undifferentiated; authenticity is a sign relation' (1988: 161). The quality of authentic experience, food, clothing or custom must be named as such in order to be perceived accordingly. At the same time, authenticity, almost by definition, stakes a claim to being unmediated, genuine or real, that is, the thing itself. Thus, a fundamental contradiction arises:

> The paradox, the dilemma of authenticity, is that to be experienced as authentic it must be marked as authentic, but when it is marked as authentic it is mediated, a sign of itself, and hence lacks the authenticity of what is truly unspoiled, untouched by mediating cultural codes. (1988: 164)

Authenticity is only perceived, when marked as such (mediated) and thus becomes the very thing it desired not to be. It claims to be the real, unmediated thing but only by entering the symbolic dimension of language does it obtain its quality of genuineness. This paradox leads Funk to conclude that authenticity is both, its own antithesis and the ultimate simulacrum (cf. Funk 2015: 36).

> Although frequently used in a similar sense, authenticity's relationship to truth is in fact dialectical. Truth can be only positively stated inside the symbolic frames of reference [...]. Authenticity, on the other hand, claims to surpass these confines of human-made reference and to hint at a reality beyond representation. In consequence, it can by definition never be fully subsumed and incorporated within structures of meaning. (Funk 2015: 14)

In other words, as soon as one tries to give any verbal account of authenticity, the concept collapses like a soap bubble. Authenticity is an elusive phenomenon and it is to a good degree self-referential (autological) because it creates and marks itself (cf. Knaller 2012a: 59). It obtains a 'paradoxical position between subjective legitimisation and objective certification' (2012a: 70). It is obvious that scholars who seek to describe authenticity are then at a loss, because description renders authenticity inauthentic, or, it may be that only through description (marking) an inauthentic object becomes authentic. Moreover, people seeking to be authentic or live an authentic life are faced with the same dilemma; they live according to the rules of their authenticity but the judgement to be passed is from society around them (cf. Trilling 1972: 11). Authenticity seems to be an exercise in marking something as authentic and for that mark to find general acceptance. Authenticity then is a very real phenomenon which in strictly logical terms should not exist. 'To put it another way, experience (life) and representation (art) touch in the infinitude of paradox' (Funk 2015: 19).

Authenticity as a black box

Of course, this paradox makes it nearly impossible to define authenticity (cf. Funk 2015: 13–18; Trilling 1972: 11) or even attempt a proper description. Funk has found a very sensible solution to this problem. He suggests not to investigate authenticity directly but to study its outcomes which are very real and can be properly observed.

> Instead of forever chasing illusive representations of authenticity, I will reverse the perspective and examine what happens to cultural and literary terms and notions once they are subjected to the black-box mechanism of authenticity. Authenticity, as it were, shall be known by its fruits, that is, by investigating how it impinges on concepts with which it comes into contact. I contend that it can be described as a catalyst which collapses what are traditionally considered to be binary oppositions or at least complementary ideas. (Funk 2015: 55–56)

In a second move, he also sensibly opts for studying not only the fruits of authenticity but also the strategies creating it and the discourses surrounding it.

> As it evades direct terminological access, it can only be detected in the impact it has on other discourses and concepts. This black-box character of authenticity, in turn, is a prime cause for its construction as both postmodernism's ultimate symptom and its most significant other. (Funk 2015: 64)

In other words, while the phenomenon itself is as elusive as the previous pages have suggested, its effects may very well be studied. Funk's use of the 'black box' metaphor for this approach (cf. 2015: 55–56) also makes visible another quality of authenticity. The black box effect voids all distinctions between fake and original because the black box collapses 'the difference of signifier and signified' (2015: 59) and consequently both creates and presupposes authenticity (cf. 2015: 59). Due to its self-referential nature as an autological phenomenon (cf. Knaller 2012a: 59), the black box authenticity logically undermines discourses surrounding it and also subverts normal discursive dichotomies such as fake and original, essence and construction, reality and fiction (cf. Funk 2015: 55–64). The authentic object is itself a paradox, which embodies both fake and original and thus nullifies these dichotomies. It is true and authentic on the grounds of itself making it so.

Reconstruction as an approach

This terminological and epistemological quicksand can only be grasped with greatest difficulties. Funk therefore argues for a new aesthetic paradigm, for which he 'suggest[s] the term "reconstruction"' (Funk 2015: 5). Reconstruction is the process by which the seemingly irreconcilable epistemological and ontological paradoxes posed by authenticity can be resolved (cf. Funk 2015: 2–4). It is to be understood as a strategy of the recipient who tries to make sense of the work of art. Reconstruction then in turn leads to a perception of authenticity (cf. 2015: 2–4). The recipient tries to reconcile the mutually exclusive dichotomies of, say, fake and genuine, which are both embedded in the same object. Reconstruction is not to be understood as some unified entity, but it rather encompasses all strategies, on part of both the artist and the recipient, to overcome deferral and difference. Concretely, these strategies can range from metareference and real-world reference to mechanisms of intimacy, or corporeal-synaesthetic experience. Through these strategies of production and reception, the performance is perceived as whole and unified, and hence authentic. Authenticity then disables the tensions posed by binaries, which would normally beg deconstruction. Because it is itself a paradox, it can reconcile these poles. The path leading to the ascription of authenticity is called reconstruction.

In literature, Funk proposes that the strategy most readily employed to create the paradoxes of authenticity is metareference (cf. 2015: 51, 53). Artworks touch upon the real world, by breaking the fourth wall or referring to real-world events. This reference then creates a very dubious or, rather, paradoxical ontological status for the work in question. A novel may for instance reference real-world events or characters may become conscious of their status as fiction. This paradox is where authenticity is effected. 'I [...] argue that the effect of authenticity enacted in and through metareferential literature is the result of processes of reconstruction, which are triggered by the epistemological and ontological paradoxes inherent in metareference' (Funk 2015: 2). In other words, an audience reconstructs ontological sense into a work of art that obviously evades such description. Authenticity may then be conceived of as an audience's strategy of making sense of a work.

Types of authenticity

So far, I have mapped out the territory of authenticity and have shown that it is not a concept which can be directly observed or described. It is only by proxy, that is aesthetic strategies and outcomes, that the black box can be described and analysed. For the description of these outcomes and strategies, some useful typologies of authenticity have been brought forward. Again, I rely heavily on Funk's thorough and well-researched account when I now introduce three of these types, which will prove helpful for the analysis of the performances.

Susanne Knaller distinguishes between two kinds of authenticity along the criterion of 'who validates the authenticity of something'. Her term 'subject authenticity' denotes the concept of an authentic personality or an authentic life, in other words, authenticity which is validated by oneself. 'Object authenticity' (referential authenticity) on the other hand describes authenticity, mostly of an object, which is based on some fixed criteria and based on validation by some expert or other authority (cf. Funk 2015: 18–19).

Allan Moore has proposed the category of 'third-person-authenticity', which 'occurs when a performance succeeds in conveying the impression to the listener's experience of life being validated, that the music is "'telling it like it is' for them"' (Moore in Funk 2015: 20). Moore's terminology is primarily laid out to analyse musical performances and popular music (cf. Moore 2002: 219) but it also proves useful for analysing theatrical performances. After all, both forms of live performance to some degree rely on similar strategies and activate an audience on a visceral level. Moore is also quick to point out that authenticity is not an inherent quality but is inscribed by the audience (cf. 2002: 220). Thus, the terminology can be very fruitfully used with Funk's concept of reconstruction.

Finally, Tom Selwyn coined the terms 'cool' and 'hot authenticity'. His line of distinction is similar to Knaller's: cool authenticity is the quality of a work of art or any object which can be ascribed by an authority, referring to the quality of something being real or genuine as opposed to being fake (e.g. a genuine Vermeer). Hot authenticity in contrast focuses strictly on subjective criteria: it is an ascription of the individual, made in the moment and more through emotionality than rational reflection (cf. Funk 2015: 20–21).

Mimesis

When studying theatre and authenticity, the concept of mimesis also quickly shows its face. The question of mimesis is old and more or less of an ontological nature. It comes down to negotiating the relationship between reality and its representation – specifically in art. While I do not intend to reopen the discussion on issues such as whether all fiction is inherently fake or a lie,[8] a brief discussion of mimesis will contextualize theories of authenticity and situate the performances under discussion in a broader context.

Despite sharp attacks from Wilde to Barthes, colloquially realism still remains the central interpretation of mimesis in Western art, as Potolsky argues (2006: 111). This interpretation, however, disregards a long and much more sophisticated discussion on the subject. Plato was the first one to reject mimesis in art altogether. He precisely understood art as an imitation of nature, which leads to inferior copies and as a last consequence would also violate the divine order.

This was the point of agreement I wanted to reach when I said that painting – and imitation in general – operates in an area of its own, far removed from the truth, and that it associates with the element in us which is far removed from intelligence – a liaison and friendship from which nothing healthy or true can result. (Plato 2000: 603b)

Aristotle took a much more lenient stance on the subject. For him, it was evident that art did not imitate but conveyed truths. It did not just play on affect, as Plato had supposed, but spoke to the rational mind by conveying experiences of truth (cf. Potolsky 2006: 32–34). His concept of catharsis, which Plato would have dismissed as well, may serve as an example, because only through emotional access to people's minds is reflection enabled, which leads to the betterment of the soul (cf. Potolsky 2006: 43). In other words, through experiencing someone else's fate, truths about life can be understood. Plato and Aristotle have effectively already marked out the two diametrical positions on mimesis: art as imitation of truth and art as representation of truth.

While for centuries, in art imitation was the dominant *modus operandi*, with the dawning of the Romantic Age, this practice slowly subsided (cf. Potolsky 2006: 67). One of the most prominent advocates of art as creative and opposed to imitation is surely Immanuel Kant, who saw a 'complete opposition between genius and the spirit of imitation' (Kant 2013: 113). The artistic genius which does not imitate but is fundamentally creative is a concept whose long shadow can still be seen even today. Taylor argues that art (aesthetics) and authenticity become fundamentally intertwined with the arrival of the ideal of the genius: the artist who no longer just imitates (*mimesis*) but creates something new and authentic out of himself (*poiesis*) (cf. Taylor 1991: 62–63). For Agamben, the concept of authenticity embodies the very notion of close to the origin, of something which cannot be reproduced (cf. 2008: 61). In the eighteenth century, the work was still considered as whole because the division of intellectual and manual labour had not yet taken place – it was still authentic (cf. 2008: 61). The situation today is, however, quite different. With the wholeness of the work destroyed, after ready-mades (industrial to art) and pop art (art to industry), how can art obtain something original again, Agamben asks (cf. 2008: 64).

But is it actually art's aim to be original? After all, the relationship between art and life has always been a dialectical one. Art influences life and vice versa. Originality is then also purely situational in a constant play of thing and representation. Surely the most famous defender of this conception is Oscar Wilde, who wrote that '[a]ll bad poetry springs from genuine feelings. To be natural is to be obvious, and to be obvious is to be inartistic' (2008: 1052, 'Artist as Critic'). In Wilde's aestheticism, art does not simply have the status of imitation but is seen as the original invention. In his dialogic essay 'The Decay of Lying', he makes the bold statement that life imitates art far more than art imitates life (cf. 2008: 982). Wilde's character, Vivian, declares that art is the process which schools our eye for beauty; it teaches us how to look at nature and when to find an image beautiful. 'Where, if not from the impressionists, do we get those wonderful brown fogs that come creeping down our streets, blurring the gas-lamps and changing the houses into monstrous shadows?' (2008: 986).

Human ingenuity and creativity are then what shapes nature and its perception, not the other way around. Nature does not shape our perception of beauty but our creative endeavours shape our perception of nature, which is seen as a complete human construct with little ontological essence for itself. As if to rub salt into Plato's wounds – and it is probably no accident that the text is organized as a dialogue, just like Plato's – Vivian contends that nature, as the original role model, is very often inferior to the products of artistic creation.

> Yesterday evening Mrs Arundel insisted on my going to the window and looking at the glorious sky, as she called it. [...] And what was it? It was simply a very second-rate Turner, a Turner of a bad period, with all the painter's worst faults exaggerated and over-emphasised. (2008: 986–987)

In this system of thought, art's status is elevated from supplementary and imitative to being the original creation. Art is perceived as an independent mode of action that creates its own way of perception and thus its own legitimacy. This mode is ontologically not part of creation but rather creates itself and thus is authentic in the original Greek meaning of the word as something that is 'self-consummating' (cf. Kalisch 2000: 32). It therefore does not need to be true because it will create its own truths, which are only measured by aesthetic quality not by factuality (cf. 2000: 992). The only gauge is aesthetic pleasure, not any form of factual accuracy, truth or imitation.

Wilde was not the only one to come to the conclusion that art occupies a status radically different from reality. Nietzsche had a very similar view. For him, the world with its inconsistencies and uncertainties (epistemologically and ontologically) can only be accounted for in aesthetic terms: 'The only criterion which accounts for us is the aesthetic criterion' (1979: 13), he noted already in the 1870s. Whereas for Wilde art is a sort of game that entertains and at best allows insight into matters of one's life, for Nietzsche art has a much more existential purpose: it is the only way to make sense of the world.

> This proposition must be established: We live only by means of illusion; our consciousness skims over the surface. Much is hidden from our view. Moreover, there is no danger that man will ever understand himself *completely*, that he will penetrate at every instant all the laws of leverage and mechanics and all the formulas of architecture and chemistry, which his life requires. However, it is quite possible that the *schema* of everything might become known. That will change almost nothing regarding our lives. Besides, this is all nothing but formulas for absolutely unknowable forces. (Nietzsche 1979: 18)

The ideas laid out here in Nietzsche's early writings become the cornerstone of his philosophy. In his nihilist system of thought, nothing can have a claim to absolute veracity, truth or factuality. Phenomenologically, none of our senses can be trusted at all, and it is not unlikely that any truth, if it exists, will never be discovered. Nietzsche links the will to art to falsehood – to a flight from truth, even the denial of truth. Art is for Nietzsche not a vehicle for truth but a purveyor of necessary illusion (cf. Broadhurst 1999: 31). Therefore, lies are permissible by all means and an understanding of the world is only possible in aesthetics terms, that is through sensual perception, while at the same time accepting all limitations of this way of structuring the world. For him, it would not even make a difference if anything like a 'great truth' became known because the fundamental way of understanding the world as a human being remains an aesthetic one.

Wilde and Nietzsche have both given crucial impulses to the study of art's ontological status, that is mimesis. It becomes clear that art's status will always have to be viewed in terms of finality; that is art's purpose will influence its ontological status and vice versa. This implicitly also hints at the fact that art, like any cultural product, is tightly interwoven with many other current social factors, ideas and practices. Today, however, where '[i]mitation, mimesis, and the implied representation of nature all relate to a conception of poetry and literature that has long been discarded' (Behler 2000: 76), this debate seems obsolete. In the twenty-first century, it would appear, there is no longer a great dispute about rhetoric and fiction as being mendacious (cf. Jay 2010: 44), because

> there is no external standard by which fictionality can be judged as true or false. As in the case of prayer, which Aristotle – and much later Derrida – noted was a type of speech that was neither true nor false, fictionality differs from lies, which depend on that very distinction. (2010: 44)

In this way, Nietzsche can be seen as the godfather of Postmodernism and deconstruction. Where an absolute truth or absolute centre is abolished, truth and lying lose their validity as absolutes and become situational or discursive. The relation between art (representation) and world is not one of imitation, as Derrida has pointed out:

> Mimesis here is not the representation of one thing by another, the relation of resemblance or of identification between two beings, the reproduction of a product of nature by a product of art. It is not the relation of two products but of two productions. And of

two freedoms. The artist does not imitate things in nature, or, if you will, in *natura naturata*, but the acts of *natura naturans*, the operations of the *physis*. (Derrida 1981: 9)

In other words, where imitation presupposes a stable relation between an object and its representation, poststructuralist attitudes towards mimesis presuppose a state of flux. Mimesis is seen as a dynamic relationship between objects, their representations and the decoding subject. Accordingly, Derrida explains that mimesis is

not the imitation of an object by its copy. 'True' *mimesis* is between two producing subjects and not between two produced things. [...] [T]his kind of *mimesis* inevitably entails the condemnation of imitation, which is always characterized as being servile. (1981: 9)

Consequently, art's claim to truth in the guise of mimetic qualities has become obsolete. Postmodernism is then practically in accordance with Wilde and Nietzsche in that art must be judged purely on aesthetic grounds. As David Shields succinctly remarks, 'There's no longer any such thing as fiction or nonfiction; there's only narrative. (Is there even narrative?)' (2010: 110). Therefore, mimesis cannot be understood as simple representation or imitation of nature, but will in the course of this study be understood as an aesthetic relationship between perceiving subject and artist or artistic object, which may elicit sentiments of authenticity.

Reconstructing the fragments of postmodernity

Funk, along with Cornelia Imesch, proposes that authenticity becomes especially prevalent in periods of cultural transformation where the relationship between experience and representation is renegotiated (cf. 2015: 23, 44). The ubiquitous presence of authenticity indicates that possibly the past two decades are such a period of change. Therefore, contemporary culture, specifically the years from circa 1990 to 2010, need a closer inspection.

The period from circa 1960 to the mid-1990s can be understood as 'postmodernity'. Postmodernism then are the practices which characterized this period, such as deconstruction, irony, detachment and the like. They are often deeply interwoven with poststructuralist thought. Now, I want to suggest that a new era of cultural production has emerged. This period is characterized by a new structure of feeling, for which a label has yet to be found. This structure of feeling grows out of Postmodernism and supersedes it. That is to say, postmodern doubt, fragmentation, irony and deconstruction are still very present in the collective consciousness; however, they are not the prevalent strategies anymore. They serve as a backdrop to new modes of production, which seek to overcome the fundamental decentredness which had characterized Postmodernism. Some of its central practices can be characterized as expressions of reconstruction. They in turn lead to the emergence of authenticity.

Postmodernism had been, almost from the start, accompanied by substantial criticism, both of its cultural practices and its central theories. Recently, this process has accelerated. One can say that 'postmodernism [...] has fallen out of fashion. Its decline, had been a long time coming [though]' (Funk 2015: 2). Fredric Jameson had doubted quite early whether Postmodernism was in fact a genuine structure feeling in Raymond William's sense (cf. 1991: xvi). Like Habermas, he was not convinced of the concept and argued that the postmodern reopened 'the question of the modern itself for re-examination' (1991: xvi). Was modernity then really an unfinished project as Habermas has it and Postmodernism just a misguided expression of it? Jameson finds that poststructuralist theory in postmodern time has abolished some of the fundamentals necessary for human culture. One of his main points of critique is a loss of historicity. 'In faithful conformity to poststructuralist linguistic theory, the past as "referent" finds itself gradually bracketed, and then effaced altogether, leaving us with nothing but texts' (1991: 18). In his view, many postmodern practices are just thinly veiled attempts to cover up for this lack. For instance, intertextuality in Postmodernism, according to him, is 'a deliberate, built-in feature of the aesthetic effect and as the operator of a new connotation of "pastness" and pseudohistorical depth, in which the history of aesthetic styles displaces "real" histories' (Jameson 1991: 20). As a Marxist thinker, history is of course a central category for him. Therefore, he argues that Postmodernism is merely modernity, or, more specifically, the economic system of modernity which has gone wild. Economic thinking, according to him, permeates all areas life and is not just confined to the sphere of business anymore. Culture itself becomes a commodity: 'The culture of the simulacrum comes to life in a society where exchange value has been generalized to the point at which the very memory of use value is effaced' (Jameson 1991: 18). In such a system, art will evidently also lose its special status and become one commodity among others and just as 'depthless' as any other sign. But what is more, the notion of authenticity cannot be upheld in a culture characterized by mass production and exchange value. For Jameson, the flat image surfaces of computers and televisions are the herald of a system of representation where authenticity has vanished.

> Such machines are indeed machines of reproduction rather than production, and they make very different demands on our capacity for aesthetic representation than did the relatively mimetic idolatry of the older machinery of the futurist movement. (1991: 37)

Aesthetic representation (art) then becomes just as flat and meaningless as any other text. For Jameson it is clear that Postmodernism must be regarded 'as the cultural dominant of the logic of late capitalism' (1991: 45). Jameson mourns the loss of the values of modernism (cf. 1991: 63) in favour of a present that is, in his view, inferior to it. Whereas for Jameson Postmodernism is, by and large, an offspring of an all-pervasive economic system and thinking, Ihab Hassan suggests a different approach. He claims that Postmodernism should not so much be regarded as a cultural practice but rather as one strategy of interpreting the present.

> [P]ostmodernism [is] a collective interpretation of an age. More than an artistic style or historical trend, more than a personal sensibility or zeitgeist, postmodernism is a hermeneutic device, a habit of

interpretation, a way of reading all our signs under the mandate of misprision. (Hassan 2003: 201)

This view seems not too far from Jameson's because it implicitly acknowledges that modernity is still present and has developed into the cultural system which we see today. It is only the reading strategies that have changed. In other words, for Hassan, it is a different attitude that characterizes Postmodernism, not necessarily different practices. Hassan condemns this attitude which he finds to be characterized by passivity and suggests that other ways of reading are possible: 'I want [...] simply to suggest that postmodernism could be understood as a kind of autobiography, an interpretation of our lives in developed societies, linked to an epochal crisis of identity' (Hassan 2003: 202). He does not elaborate on what sort of crisis he means, but some readily spring to mind: globalization, the digital revolution, a global capitalist system and so on. This state of crisis then calls for a remedy to the malaises of *deferral* and *difference*. It goes to show that Postmodernism is not (yet) a stable system for human life and culture.

> Paradoxically, it might even turn out to be postmodernism's most lasting achievement to have shown that eventually even an endless free play of signifiers will *not* be able to deliver us – as individuals and as a society – from an inherent pining for closure. (Funk 2015: 4)

In other words, it appears that the fundamental practices of Postmodernism had proved to be unsustainable or at least unwelcomed in everyday culture. Jameson also found that Postmodernism had eroded some of the concepts fundamental to modernity, which at the same time seemed to be fundamental to human thinking.

> [B]esides the hermeneutic model of inside and outside [...] at least four other fundamental depth models have been repudiated in contemporary theory: (1) the dialectical one of essence and appearance [...] (2) the Freudian model of latent and manifest [...] (3) the existential model of authenticity and inauthenticity [...] (4) [...] the great opposition between signifier and signified [...] depth is replaced by surface, or by multiple surfaces. (1991: 12)

Such fundamental categories then in turn were also found lacking in everyday life, not only in theory and criticism. Constant states of detachment, irony or apathy did not go harmoniously with human experience of life. This is not to say that these concepts have lost their validity. Quite the contrary: they are theoretically as valid as ever, but they have proven impractical in everyday life. I am aware that the link between Postmodernism as culture and poststructuralist theory is not a direct one. Nonetheless, the two have been fundamentally intertwined from the start. Alan Kirby, another critic of the postmodern, has pointed out that the very evident decline of postmodern practices might also 'involve the demise of poststructuralism and post-1960s Franco-American cultural theory' (2009: 27). Recently, a number of new practices have found their way into art, theory and everyday life which were fit to slowly erode Postmodernism. Funk, as well as Jacobi (cf. 2016: 29–30), and also Kirby (cf. 2009: 151) see the millennium and the attacks of 11 September as defining moments.

> The turn of the new millennium as a general caesura and the attacks of 9/11 in particular represented a disruption in the collective imaginary, the ultimate impetus, as it were, to force the postmodern moment to its crisis and relegate it to history once and for all. (Funk 2015: 2)

Whether Postmodernism will be relegated to history once and for all remains to be seen and is still contentiously discussed (cf. Kirby 2009: 6). It seems more that no one wants to forget Postmodernism but rather take what has been proven useful and disregard what is excessive. Specifically, Funk suggests that deconstruction 'eviscerates this communicative process by revealing and parodying its unspoken hierarchical and relational structures' (2015: 5). He thus acknowledges the fundamental assumptions of the method such as hierarchical structures and *différance*. They have not been disproven or invalidated; it, however, seems that other practices are more useful in contemporary culture. New reading strategies have evolved. In other words, there is no simple going back to a state before poststructuralist criticism and Postmodernism. The theoretical underpinnings of postmodernity retain their validity. Indeed, 'facets of postmodernism have now found a place, often embedded as "common sense", as that which "goes without saying"'(Kirby 2009: 6). They are not eradicated but simply used less or not at all. At the same time, new practices which seek to overcome fragmentation gain prominence. One example of such practices Funk identifies as 'reconstruction'. Reconstructive texts attempt to close the very gaps that Postmodernism had created and to 'rekindle the connections between the constituents of the act of communication by renegotiating the relations and hierarchies between the individual elements' (Funk 2015: 5). Stephen Knudsen opts for a similar strategy:

> We find utopian ideas of modernism to be suspect – that is the postmodernism I see. But in practice, there is much of modernism that the world cannot detach from. We have been displeased but not to the point of utter detachment. The kind of postmodernism I see now does not need to exacerbate our angst with hyperbole. It no longer needs to make requisite the air quotes of ironic detachment on words like faith and action. It can still lead somewhere meaningful and concrete. I do not think I am alone here. I know I am not alone as others take similar thoughts into the fray to find some better nomenclature in this late phase of postmodernism. (Knudsen 2013)

In the light of these arguments, it seems possible that a new, genuine structure of feeling has emerged. The collective sentiment has abandoned postmodern practices and returned to older notions but, crucially, with the knowledge of Postmodernism in mind as a continuous backdrop. It is a rediscovery of older practices but with a more sophisticated understanding of them. Raoul Eshelman proffers that

> [a]ttempting to find itself through meaning, the subject drowns in a flood of ever expanding cross-references. [...] Every fixation of meaning is dispersed through cross-connected forms; every use of form links up with already existing meanings; every approach to an origin leads back to an alien sign. Searching for itself, the subject quickly ends where it began: in the endlessly expanding field of the postmodern. (Eshelman 2001: 1)

In a way, one can describe this structure of feeling as conscious of the constructedness of almost every aspect of human life. It freely acknowledges that essentialism in all its forms has been disproved. However, after some decades of living without these forms of reference and with poststructuralist theory firmly in mind, it may now be possible to handle essentialist concepts again. I repeat: this is not simply a return to a blissful golden age before Postmodernism, but a development which builds *on* Postmodernism. In practical terms, this leads to a

> switch from a mode of endless temporal deferral (*différance*, process) to the one-time or finite joining of opposites in the present (paradoxical performance, Gans's ostensivity) [... and a] Transition from metaphysical pessimism to metaphysical optimism; the metaphysical point of orientation is no longer death and its proxies (emptiness, kenosis, absence, dysfunctionality) but rather psychologically experienced or fictionally framed states of transcendence (resurrection, passage, nirvana, love, catharsis, fulfilment or plerosis [*sic*!], deification etc.). (Eshelman 2001: 9)

Metamodernism

Many terms have been proposed for this new structure of feeling (cf. Funk 2015: 3–4). All have their descriptive advantages and different emphases, but none of them has stuck so far. Funk therefore opts to not side with any one of the going terminologies (cf. 2015: 4). Possibly it is not even useful to try and find a label for an ongoing process. However, in order to spark debate, a clear description and even a label will prove helpful in order to refine concepts and encourage further discussion. It can be comfortably used as shorthand for contemporary structures of feeling without allowing it to become set in stone. In order to sharpen the concept, and make plain what is meant by this shorthand, I want to display the concept of 'Metamodernism' in more detail.

> When we use the term 'meta', we use it in similar yet not indiscriminate fashion. For the prefix 'meta-' allows us to situate metamodernism historically   beyond;   epistemologically   with;   and   ontologically

between the modern and the postmodern. It indicates a dynamic or movement between as well as a movement beyond. More generally, however, it points towards a changing cultural sensibility – or cultural metamorphosis, if you will – within western societies. (*Notes on Metamodernism* 'Editorial October 2010', Anon. 2010b)

Metamodernism is therefore an apt description because it denotes a relation to both Postmodernism and Modernism and yet allows for the freedom to reconstruct. It does not seek to wipe the slate clean but works with its material and goes beyond it.

Fundamentally, one can then say that Postmodernism as a cultural *modus operandi* is dead, specifically, if one takes a look outside the field of academia at everyday practices (cf. Kirby 2006). Many of its fruits and merits still live on in theory and practice, but as a structure of feeling, as an apt mode to describe the motivations, practices and mental structures of art practitioners, it is indeed dead. There are a number of examples from the past two decades which support this proposition. In the visual arts this has long been observed. As Jessica Fischer wittily remarks, '[l]ast year Lucian Freud (*1922), Richard Hamilton (*1922) and Postmodernism died. All three have had major impact on British art and are partly products of it' (Fischer 2012: 58). She calls Postmodernism '"one of the most contentious phenomena" of recent history, with its 70s and 80s architecture, art and design in particular' (2012: 58) and sees the retrospective at the Victoria and Albert Museum in 2012, titled *Postmodernism: Style and Subversion 1970–1990*, as its final gravestone. Other art critics have made similar observations. Hal Foster already saw an end of postmodern irony and a *Return of the Real* (1996) as early as the mid-1990s. In theatre, similar tendencies have been pointed out. Birgit Schuhbeck claims that after years of post-dramatic theatre, dramatic theatre has made a fulminate return.

The 'dramatic drama' tries to convey a concept of unity. The mosaic structure of postmodernism is not appropriate anymore to represent the current developments in culture, the 'new' theater feels the need to turn to seemingly 'old' traditions like mimesis, and the pristine urge to tell stories. The stage is not an open (postmodern) stage, rather it serves as a virtual closed space. Fiction is separated from reality again. (Schuhbeck 2012)

Kirby claims that it was mainly the digital revolution of the late 1990s and early 2000s which fundamentally changed the relation of author, reader and text (cf. Kirby 2006). Whereas Postmodernism essentially dealt with television, contemporary culture is fused by a focus on the creative recipient in an online environment (cf. 2012). More examples from other fields could be named, but it already seems evident that Postmodernism is over and artists as well as audiences have found modes of production that bring back exactly those concepts that Postmodernism had intended to burry.

> And new generations of artists increasingly abandon the aesthetic precepts of deconstruction, para-taxis, and pastiche in favor of aesthethical notions of reconstruction, myth, and metaxis. These trends and tendencies can no longer be explained in terms of the postmodern. They express a (often guarded) hopefulness and (at times feigned) sincerity that hint at another structure of feeling, intimating another discourse. History, it seems, is moving rapidly beyond its all too hastily proclaimed end. (Vermeulen & van den Akker 2010: 2)

The name that Vermeulen and van den Akker propose for this new phenomenon is 'Metamodernism'. 'Metamodernism' is not only to be understood as yet another cultural or artistic theory but the term encompasses a whole number of changes in all areas of everyday life and cultural production. It is a genuinely new structure of feeling (cf. 2010: 9). It is characterized by a pragmatic approach that is fully aware of postmodern theory and also knows that concepts such as 'truth' or 'meaning' have been convincingly deconstructed. Yet, it is also aware that everyday life and pragmatism have shown their necessity. Thus it reinstates these variables in a very undogmatic way, knowing fully well that they can never be reached. 'For indeed, that is the "destiny" of the metamodern wo/man: to pursue a horizon that is forever receding' (2010: 12). Of course, associations with sentiments of Romanticism readily spring to mind, and Vermeulen and van den Akker acknowledge that a new form of Romanticism is one trademark of Metamodernism (cf. 2010: 8–9). The significant feature is that Metamodernism takes ideas from both Modernism (*telos*) and Postmodernism (apathy/irony) without ever settling at one point. It oscillates, as it were, between the two poles.

> One should be careful not to think of this oscillation as a balance however; rather, it is a pendulum swinging between 2, 3, 5, 10, innumerable poles. Each time the metamodern enthusiasm swings toward fanaticism, gravity pulls it back toward irony; the moment its irony sways toward apathy, gravity pulls it back toward enthusiasm. (Vermeulen & van den Akker 2010: 6)

Metamodernism then is the quest for the blue flower; it allows for authentic experience, while knowing that in strictly logical terms this may not be possible. It also accommodates realist, utopian, deconstructivist, enthusiastic and apathetic positions under one roof. Metamodernism supersedes Postmodernism when it happily announces the arrival of a new meaning that can never be found but that should enthusiastically be sought. In the visual arts, such practices of reconstruction have been observed for a while.

> Artists such as Olafur Eliasson, Gregory Crewdson, Kaye Donachie, and David Thorpe, and architects like Herzog & de Meuron no longer merely deconstruct the commonplace, but seek to reconstruct it. They exaggerate it, mystify it, alienate it. But with the intention to resignify it. With the intention to create within the commonplace an uncommonspace. (*Notes on Metamodernism* 'Editorial August 2010', Anon. 2010a)

In theatre, reconstruction has also made its appearance. It shows its face through authenticity and confrontations with the real. Audiences are very conscious of a theatrical situation of 'as-if' but they play along and are willing to become lost in their quest for authenticity and the real. They partake in an exercise of reconstruction. This phenomenon goes beyond simple suspension of disbelief because spectators are aware of the constructedness of the situation but are still keen on authentic experience. Individuality and specifically individual experience are key to understanding this phenomenon. Meaning here is no longer generated for a large audience as a collective but on an individual basis. Metamodernism allows for authentic experience that is not parody or nostalgia but is genuinely real while everyone knows that it is fake. This is the central point: because audiences are aware of concepts of fakeness and simulation, even of their own performative self, they are now able to gain authentic experience in this fake situation. It seems that audiences have negotiated the schism of being active and passive at the same time that Modernism imposed on them and also the loss of all reality that Postmodernism provided them with.

The fakeness of all theatrical production becomes a virtue because it puts individual Truth in the centre of attention. It has been remarked that '[f]iction appeals to us because it can do things real life cannot. […] Fiction can be so moving precisely because it is unlike real life' (Sierz 2011: 48). In this fictionalized context, meaning is found on an individual level. Sierz has claimed that 'the audience is a vital element in the creation of meaning. It is even tempting to say that the meaning of a play lies in the experience of the audience' (2011: 6). This is very similar to Kirby's diagnosis of contemporary culture, which for him places supreme value on the active, creative recipient rather than the author (cf. 2006).

In Metamodernism, all meaning and truth are individualistic. For such an experience the mechanisms of authenticity and also intimacy bear crucial relevance. Metamodern theatre is individualistic, intimate and genuinely real, if only on an individual level. It knows and serves an audience member's hunger for authentic experience.

Theatre, drama, performance: Live art

So far, 'theatre' has been used as a sort of umbrella term to describe a number of subcategories. I would now like to rephrase this term as 'live art', because it denotes more precisely what I mean. Theatre in its everyday use still carries connotations of a picture frame stage and a play by a single author. However, many contemporary pieces of live art do not fit such a mould because they take place in non-theatrical settings and often have several authors. Furthermore, European theatre, as was shown above, is very strongly rooted in the tradition of the written word, but I want it to be understood in a wider sense. Zarrilli and others claim that the written word caused a literary revolution when it found its way into ninth-century Athens (cf. Zarrilli et al. 2009: 60). Poets quickly began to adapt their craft and changed their dramatic works structurally: what had originally been the voice of one actor who would declaim to the lyre now evolved into dialogue. This crucial point marks the beginning of the written European tradition of theatre. It also led to an

> abstract analysis of speech itself. In this sense, writing in the fifth-century Athens enhanced some forms of oral communication since speeches were given extempore – no orator would ever speak from a prepared text. For the Greeks [...], oratory and reading were social activities. They always read aloud even when there was no audience. Literature existed for hearing not for silent, private activity. Manuscripts were intended for declamation. (Zarrilli et al 2009: 61)

In classical Greece, literature was subordinate to the spoken word and, due to the communal nature of religious festivities, of which the plays were a part, theatre was a social activity. The advent of writing then produced a rift between the live event and the written text, which can theoretically be consumed in the privacy and solitude of one's home. I would argue that in this rift between the written and the performed, a fundamental rift in the perception of this art form appeared, which will resurface a number of times over the centuries. Where the live performance of a memorized text that had never been fixed in writing always had a strong sense of authenticity, with the written text there appears an idea of fakeness. When an actor reads out something that is not his own, the performance can easily be perceived as fake or inauthentic. This scent of fakeness can be interpreted in a very Platonic way: in the oral tradition an actor would hear a text, memorize and then recite it – most likely with minor changes, additions and so on – so that the text was to a high degree his own and unique. The written word ensures, however, that any actor in any corner of the world would speak the exact same words. This is essentially Plato's fear of someone speaking in someone else's voice (cf. Potolsky 2006: 73). The written word as opposed to the oral tradition then may be one of the poisons that killed authenticity.[9] In his essay 'Economimesis', Jacques Derrida also elaborates on the problem of codified language and (authentic) representation. He claims that imitative mimesis is the most naive form of representation and dismisses its artistic means. More useful, in his opinion, are the aesthetic approaches to mimesis proffered by Nietzsche and Artaud (cf. Derrida 1976: 354). Artaud had suggested (but unfortunately never clearly defined) a 'theatre of cruelty', in which there would be no boundary between audience, performers and bystanders. Every person present would be involved in the spectacle on a visceral level. '[T]he spectator must be allowed to identify himself with the spectacle, breath by breath and beat by beat' (Artaud 1958: 140). It is unclear what one should understand by this spectacle, but it seems certain that it would be some form of ritualistic, Dionysiac and even orgiastic and extremely physical event which Artaud pictures. It is obvious that such an event evades the fixed form of a written text and would most likely be perceived as authentic by all persons involved. That is also why Derrida favours this theatre which is not primarily text based. 'The origin of theatre, as it needs to be restored, is a hand raised against the unlawful possessors of the logos' (Derrida 1976: 361, my translation). For him, the written or spoken word is simply the corpse of psychic language (cf. 1976: 363). Therefore, he goes beyond the condemnation of codified (written) texts, but even wants to abolish texts themselves. He seeks to find again that thing which was word before the words (cf. 1976: 363). What fascinates Derrida about Artaud's theories is the unrepeatability of the spectacle. For him, repetition (e.g. in the shape of a text) is the fundamental problem (cf. 1976: 372). A theatre which deserves the label authentic – and, as was seen, this label is already highly problematic – can only be a collective, Dionysiac form of performance/celebration which is not planned, scripted or repeatable. The real cruelty, in Derrida's interpretation of Artaud, then is not the confrontation with extreme states of mind but the unrepeatability of the event. Through its uniqueness, it enacts the concept of death and finitude, which brings participants into painful contact with their own mortality (cf. 1976: 374). Experiments with form and also with the concepts of Artaud have been numerous in the twentieth century. Many tried to close the rift of inauthenticity between scripted text and performance. Jeffrey Alexander argues that everyday performance, and by extension also theatre, has the very potential to do so.

> Performances in complex societies seek to overcome fragmentation by creating flow and achieving authenticity. They try to recover a momentary experience of ritual, to eliminate or to negate the effects of social and cultural de-fusion. Speaking epigrammatically, one might say that successful performances re-fuse history. They break down the barriers that history has erected – the divisions between background culture and scripted text, between scripted text and actors, between audience and mise-en-scene. Successful performances overcome the deferral of meaning that Derrida (1991) recognized as differánce. In a successful performance, the signifiers seem actually to become what they signify. Symbols and referents are one. Script, direction, actor, background culture, mise-en-scene, audience, means of symbolic production-all these separate elements of performance become indivisible and invisible. The mere action of performing accomplishes the performance's intended effect (cf. Austin 1957). The actor seems to be Hamlet; the man who takes the oath of office seems to be the president. (Alexander 2004: 549)

Performance in all its guises then has the potential to be perceived as whole and authentic. However, schools of acting also vary greatly. A Brechtian actress, for instance, will not try to create a complete illusion for the audience to lose itself in; she will rather try to create a certain frame of expectation that enables the audience to actively engage with the issues being debated (cf. Hamilton 1982: 38–39). Matters are very different with a method-actor or, more precisely, an actor using Stanislavski's techniques. Here, authenticity is the ultimate goal of the actor (cf. Hamilton 1982: 44). By endowing the character with as much of her own emotional experience as possible, it is supposed to become a true expression of herself and thus true. These conflicting views[10] of acting cannot be resolved because they exist parallelly and are alternatingly used by practitioners in contemporary theatre. As they have fundamentally different aims and views about theatre and its place in the world, this usually does not become a problem. It is worth noting, however, that acting may be a strong expression of authenticity or it may be just the opposite (cf. Alexander 2004: 548). However, Philip Auslander has made a very convincing case that the idea of truthful acting is strictly never valid because we can only ever compare to other performances of the role or of that actor and would thus never know what the 'real' self is. Truthful acting is always supposition and speculation (cf. Auslander 1997: 29). In other words, only if we presuppose the essentialist notion of an authentic core of, say a character or an actor, the concept of truthful acting makes sense. Acting's claim to authenticity then is also problematic.

The strongest claim to authenticity in the performing arts has, however, not been made by theatre but by performance art. 'Performance art [...] seems to have everything to do with the wish to be credible, to be authentic, to create a work that is as real as possible, that has no screen of protection – anything that is not a simulacrum' (van Mechelen 2006: 128). The idea that performance art is true and authentic while theatre is fake is deep-seated with audiences and also with practitioners. Richard Schechner maintains that performance art evolved out of Allan Kaprow's happenings which had the purpose of making art more lifelike, or more authentic, everyday and real (cf. Schechner 2006: 39). Marina Abramović claims that she never worked in the theatre because she always felt it was too fake (cf. Yablonsky 2011: 1). One can, however, claim that in recent decades performance art has also made a substantial move away from authenticity. For instance,

Abramović was the first performance artist to be honoured with a large-scale retrospective at the New York Museum of Modern Art in 2010 (cf. Biesenbach 2010). In this retrospective, many of her pieces were re-created. One may justifiably ask whether a piece of performance art is still authentic if someone else other than its original creator re-creates it years later. Indeed, one can pose the question if performance art can be repeated at all or if its authenticity fails when it is repeated, even by the same performer. As Osipovich points out, '[a] live performance *as a whole* is [...] unscriptable because it is *as a whole* unrepeatable' (2006: 464, italics in the original). If a performance is repeated, however, does it become a piece of theatre that can be played out every night, as happens in London's West End every day? Does performance art become fake?

Furthermore, Abramović also had her life, death and elements of many of her performances staged by American director Robert Wilson in the autobiographical piece *The Life and Death of Marina Abramović* (cf. Yablonsky 2011: 1–2). Performance art, biography, acting and theatricality become interwoven here in a hodgepodge of authenticity, fakeness and acting. Performance art, which has traditionally been believed to be the stronghold of authenticity, here arguably becomes fake through repetition and theatricalization.

The example of Marina Abramović's work of the past years hints towards the possibility that the boundaries between theatre and performance art have become much more permeable than they used to be. In theatre one can observe tendencies of it becoming more authentic while performance art moves more towards the 'inauthenticity of theatre' (cf. Schulze 2012). Furthermore, many pieces of theatre and performance today cannot be placed within one specific category of theatre or performance anymore.

> The sprawling field of performance theory [...] is still one that needs careful navigation; 'performance' [...] therefore [is] assumed to refer to a theatre event consciously produced for an audience. This may seem like a limiting definition considering the broad scope of performance theory, but it allows us to consider some of the progressive work falling under the category of contemporary drama,

particularly that which is probing for greater flexibility in the role of the theatre audience. (Lane 2010: 13)

The scope of this study then is any performance, as defined above. This may include, but is not limited to, theatrical events that are set in a theatre building and have a scripted text, performances in abandoned buildings, promenade theatre but also invisible theatre and street theatre. In short, the whole canon of 'live art' is within the scope of this study. Theatre and performance can thus be used synonymously while still being distinct from performance art. The term to encompass them all can be 'live art', as proposed by Lois Keidan, who opts that 'Live Art is a way of mapping new performance culture [*sic*] that respects no limits and understands no borders' (in Suk 2014: 55; cf. also Hoffman 2010).

In conclusion, it remains to be said that the concepts of live art and Metamodernism also necessitate new ways of writing about performance. Whereas theatre scholars could traditionally rely on written texts, this is not always the case with contemporary live art. Furthermore, the text, if it exists, is often inferior to the visceral experience of an audience member. The study of the pure text would often not do justice to the performance. Many scholars of theatre have thus developed a different approach to the study of performances.

> Instead [of theatre historiography] there will be new texts, translations, partial re-enactments and re-fashionings, at best the fictional, dynamic products of memories, desires, bodies, imaginings having taken place or to come: what the poet Paul Celan referred to as 'Singbare Rest' (Celan 1995: 100), the 'singable remains'. The return to the event in representation cannot effect recovery of what is lost, but it is in this very irrecuperability that there lies the possibility of an ongoing, unfinishable historiographic project, an enabling 'decomposition' (Wood 2000: 202), a critically, reflexive thinking and working through of memory and history, embodiment and inscription, as process [.] (Williams 2006: 105)

The study of live art must take all these factors into consideration: the event itself, space, bodies, experience, accounts of spectators, remnants of the performance, such as videotapes, photos or written documents. Live art is elusive and unrepeatable. Therefore, all scholarly work in this field must aim for a 'thick description' (cf. Geertz 1973) in the best sense of the word. It must gather as much information from as many sources as possible in order to arrive at the 'Singbare Rest'. In this way it can deliver an impression, a mere glimpse at lost beauty. This leads to

a gradual displacement from the relatively 'solid ground' of theatre studies and theatre history towards a more fluid, and tentative articulations of the shifting 'lie of the land' in an expanded field of contemporary performance and its intersections with philosophy, politics and historiography. (Williams 2006: 106).

In other words, live art must always be studied and understood in terms of the culture it is situated in. Theatre is one expression of Metamodernism and of practices of reconstruction. It stands in a reciprocal relationship to culture. Therefore, not only aesthetics but also crucially politics and philosophy must be viewed alongside and taken into account.

Finally, a short remark about what is to be understood by 'contemporary theatre' is in order. By contemporary theatre I mean all theatrical events that were created or performed within the past two decades and have arguably achieved critical success. Most works discussed in this study are British in the sense that they were created and performed in the UK and by British citizens. However, some performances, such as those by Ontroerend Goed (Belgium) or Walid Raad (Lebanon, USA), have originated in other countries. I have chosen to include them, first, because I believe that they are exemplarily indicative of a culture of authenticity, and, second, because they have been received and discussed widely in the 'Global North'. Globalization has changed everyday culture as well as theatre. National boundaries in terms of style, influences and feedback loops have eroded to a large degree (cf. Schechner 2006: 39). Furthermore, it is often hard, if not downright wrong, to attribute one single country of origin to a piece of theatre. For example, if the writer of a piece is Lebanese, the director

German and the production takes place in France and later on travels to Scotland, where would such a piece have to be located? It becomes evident that artistic globalization has, to a degree, made national borders superfluous. The ever-stronger interconnectedness of the art world and the world in general leads, as may be assumed, to the debate and artistic treatment of common (global) issues. It is one presumption of this study that authenticity takes a prominent place in this global theatrical debate.

2

Intimate Theatre

DAVID: [...] But ... I like to think it [the Russian doll] may stands [sic] for other things like ... Hidden feelings ... One truth which is hiding another truth and another one and another one.

–*Polygraph* (Lepage in Gale and Deeney 2010: 724)

This chapter analyses performances, which closely work with concepts of intimacy and individuality. They put the viewer in the centre of attention, focusing on individual, unique experience and personal narratives as opposed to a commodified, uniform product. The appeal to individual perception, narration and interpretation, which often closely links the life of the spectator to the spectacle on stage, is one fairly prominent strategy of metareference that is able to effect authenticity. The chapter is split into two parts: the first one focuses on the work of British performance group Forced Entertainment in general, and, in more detail, on two of their durational performances. In the second part, the practice of one-on-one (sometimes also called one-to-one) performance, which was hugely successful over the past decade, its strategies of authenticity and intimate bonding with spectators will be given a close inspection.

Forced Entertainment

Founded in Sheffield in 1984, Forced Entertainment (FE) have been one of the towering entities of experimental theatre in Britain for more than twenty years. Although recently a number of critics have questioned whether their work today is still as cutting-edge and as fresh as it used to be (cf. Green 2013; Hoffmann 2010), it is certainly no exaggeration to say that FE have shaped the perception of theatre for almost a generation of theatregoers and practitioners through their experimental and non-hierarchical approach. Green, however, is also quick to remark that despite all non-hierarchical pledges with FE, the artistic director Tim Etchells is firmly at the top of the (supposedly non-existent) hierarchy (cf. Green 2013). Sarah Jane Bailes has called FE's theatrical style 'performance theatre' (following Elinor Fuchs' definition), meaning that it is self-conscious and not available for re-representation; that is it could not be repeated by another group (cf. Bailes 2011: 21). FE have gained notoriety for toying with theatrical conventions and laying the theatrical machinery bare to the viewer's eye. They frequently question some of the foundational concepts of conventional theatre such as make-believe, storytelling and the power economy of audience and performer. They are also 'a company that have built a reputation for aestheticizing failure and making theatrical manipulation so visible it becomes a dramaturgical device' (Damian 2012). The point of departure for FE, as Tim Etchells explains, was an attempt at breaking with theatre as one commodified product among many in the entertainment industry.

> We did not, it seems, want 'a play', which, for us, became a by-word for the homogenised, the pre-packaged, the performance which somehow wanted to deny presence and performance and liveness and insist instead on writing, closure, absence and fixity. We wanted the unstable. The trembling. The thrill of live decisions. The collision of different materials, different narratives. A theatre that placed you in a world rather than describing one to you. Or which placed you in a situation rather than describing one to you. A theatre in which your agency as a watcher was an acknowledged and known part of the performance from the out-set. A theatre that felt more like event. (Etchells 2004: 286–287)

A 'theatre that feels more like an event' already suggests that performances by FE are something to be experienced rather than watched. The role of the spectator in such a work cannot be as easily defined or marked out as in conventional theatrical performances. Spectators can be witnesses, active participants or spectators – at times meandering between these roles. While all of their stage works are 'rehearsed down to the last breath', as Tim Etchells stated in a conversation with me in June 2008, a performance by FE still aims to be something unstable, based on improvisation and the ever-present possibility of failure. Accordingly, Etchells founded the Institute of Failure together with Goat Island's Matthew Goulish (cf. Goulish 2004). The idea was that a system could best be understood when looking at the points where it starts to break. In other words, by allowing for failure, FE aim to scrutinize the underlying structures, mechanisms and hierarchies of theatre itself. It is both an exercise in meta-reflection on theatre and gives the performance a decisively real and humane quality.

The other crucial strategy in FE's work is audience involvement. They aim, as Etchells explains, to '"place the audience in a world" where your agency as a watcher was acknowledged' (2004: 287). The audience is thus not reduced to a state of passive contemplation but they are part of the spectacle, even if they remain quietly in their seats. By acknowledging the audience, and thus acknowledging the theatrical nature of the event, FE allowed the 'real world' to enter the theatre room. The theatrical space is no longer a space of fantasy, suspension of disbelief and make-believe. It becomes a very real place of performance where audience and performers come together with a common purpose but without a fourth wall – a real place of assembly, as Lehman has it (cf. 2008: 12). Each performance consequently has an urgent claim towards the audience, more urgent than a classical proscenium play could have. The works of FE are curiously positioned between the real world and the theatrical world, set in an ontological limbo, neither here, nor there. Etchells explains that FE's theatre 'had to work the territory between the real and the phantasmic, between the actual landscape and the media one, between the body and imagination' (qtd. in Malzacher 2004: 134). FE pursue various strategies and formats in order to achieve such a theatre. Their oeuvre, which also underwent substantial transformations in thirty years of activity, encompasses works, which seem very theatrical and are staged in theatre venues, and others, which may last for a very long time and are often staged in non-theatrical venues.

> Forced Entertainment has different strands of work that they present, ranging from the very theatrical performances – *The Thrill of It All* (2010), *Bloody Mess* (2004), *12 am: Awake & Looking Down* (1993) – all of which seem to have a level of chaos and a suggestion of spontaneity. However, we know that all of these performances are highly rehearsed. The performances make a clear parallel to the form of traditional theater, yet clearly shaking up normal conventions by creating chaos and mess on the stage. *Spectacular* (2008) consisted of two actors standing on a bare stage. The male character wore a skeleton outfit and the female screamed into a microphone, enacting a death scene and trying to provoke a reaction from the male character, who was describing all of the things that would be happening and the scenery that should have been onstage. (Green 2013)

Consequently, it is hard to describe FE's body of work as a whole. The spectrum of performances and formats is broad and thus it is necessary to differentiate, first of all, between stage works, which will be of minor importance to this study, and durational works, which will be in its focus.

Stage works: Emancipated spectators

Two shows may serve as illuminating examples of the 'theatrical branch' of FE's work and its development over time. *Showtime* (1996) is a performance about theatre, its audience and their expectations and roles, but also about death in its various forms (cf. Bailes 2011: 70) – it is a clear example of FE's work in the 1990s. FE's more recent show, *The Coming Storm* (2012), treads on similar ground. Its central concern is, again, the relation of audience and performer. It poses questions about immersion and make-believe, but also, fundamentally, about storytelling and the way stories gain our attention.

Showtime (1996)

Right in the beginning of *Showtime*, a man with a bomb belt strapped to his stomach enters the stage and addresses the audience directly. The presence of the audience is thus acknowledged and any illusions about a fourth wall are immediately destroyed. The performer then quickly begins to berate the audience.

> There's a word for people like you, and that word is audience. An audience comes to the theatre perhaps to see something that if they saw it in real life they might find it offensive. Something that if you saw it in the street, it might make you turn away.... An audience likes to sit in the dark and to watch other people do it. Well, if you've paid your money – good luck to you. (Forced Entertainment, homepage)

It is immediately evident that, as a spectator, one is not encouraged in this performance to sit back, watch and enjoy. On the contrary, the audience is directly accused of sensationalism, of paying money to see things, which they might not dare to look at in the 'real world' or actions they would never commit themselves. In other words, theatre is a thinly veiled excuse for sensationalism and exploitation. That, it goes without saying, goes for 'conventional' theatre, and, as the performer announces, it is not going to happen in this performance. As the show continues, the audience is time and again directly addressed and forced to reconsider their policies of viewing, their own part in the creation of a theatrical work and their status (ontological and epistemological) as an audience member/viewer/witness/spectator/individual.

An actress [Cathy Naden] is interviewed as a pantomime dog, questioned about how her family may commit murder, and then about how she may plan her own suicide, during which time she removes the pantomime head, blurring the distinction between the identity of the actress/human character/ pantomime dog, and that between fiction and fact. The tension created as a result of the ambivalence that surrounds the events manifests itself in a penetrating silence that pervades an auditorium of spectators unsure as to how near a truth they may be, or how effectively they are being manipulated. It is this

ambiguity that gives the performance its power. […] As the boundary
between truth and fiction closes, all beneath a traditional, but makeshift
structure of a proscenium arch, the boundary between the stage and
the auditorium is ruptured and the locus of meaning inverted, as the
performers scream for explanations from the audience as to how and
why, they can and are, watching these events as entertainment – 'close
your eyes, close your fucking eyes and keep them closed. You shouldn't
be watching this' [Gardner: 1996]. (Harper 2000: 93–94)

Of course, this kind of audience treatment readily suggests
Brechtian notions of an audience's[1] function, and FE's strategies are
definitely indebted to his theories. However, while the comparison with
Brecht's theories seems startling, there are a number of, at times subtle
but crucial, differences. Whereas Brecht's idea of an active audience was
of a collective and political nature, firmly held together by a common
ideology (i.e. class struggle, communism), these notions are not
present in FE's work. There are a number of political dimensions to
FE's experimentations with form and performer–audience relation, but
there is never a simple solution offered. In fact, ideology is routinely
questioned and not given privilege as a solution. Furthermore, politics
are negotiated on a far more personal and individual level. Questions
do not revolve around Marxist class struggle but around individual
responsibility. Brecht tried to bring an audience to think and eventually
take positions in a class war. Artaud, in his theatre of cruelty, sought
to activate spectators by abolishing any distance and integrating them
completely into a spectacle (cf. Artaud 1958: 140; Rancière 2009: 2).
Both have this in common: the artificial distance between performers
(active) and spectators (passive) is abolished. FE pursue a similar, but
yet different, strategy. The active role of audiences in FE's work can best
be understood with Jacques Rancière's concept of the 'emancipated
spectator'. For him, '[t]hat is what the word "emancipated" means: the
blurring of the boundary between those who act and those who look;
between individuals and members of a collective body' (Rancière 2009:
19). He fundamentally questions the opposition between passivity/
spectating and activity/performing, and argues that while the spectator

may remain calmly in her seat, she may well take an active part in the production and meaning making of the performance (cf. 2009: 12).

> What makes it possible to pronounce the spectator seated in her place inactive, if not the previously posited radical opposition between the active and the passive? Why identify gaze and passivity, unless on the presupposition that to view means to take pleasure in appearances while ignoring the truth behind the image and the reality outside the theatre? Why assimilate listening to passivity, unless through the prejudice that speech is the opposite of action? The oppositions – viewing/knowing, appearance/reality, activity/passivity – are quite different from logical oppositions between clearly defined terms. They specifically define a distribution of the sensible, an *a priori* distribution of positions. (Rancière 2009: 12)[2]

Viewers are actively not only coding and decoding signs that are presented to them but engaging in a mode of 'active watching', which is a form of thinking, and hence a form of action. Theatre thus becomes political on an individual level: it both relates to the real world and radiates into it. This political dimension is, however, not marked by a collective ideology; it is rather marked by individual ethics. Erika Fischer-Lichte has made a strong case against Rancière's argument, claiming that as an audience member one is always active and never passive because one always decodes, has corporeal experiences and so on; in short, there is no such thing as a passive spectator, even in the most conservative theatrical setting (cf. 2012: 55). Possibly it is more helpful to not see active and passive as dichotomies but rather to think of involvement in terms of a scale along the lines of 'more active' and 'less active'. On this scale of involvement, FE arguably go beyond what most theatre performances do, as they metareference and involve the audience. FE encourage audiences to question their place in relation to a performance. This happens on an individual level, and the performance offers enough room for a wide range of personal sense making.

> In many ways we saw theatre increasingly as a space for projection, a projection occasioned always by blankness, by lack of information,

by repetition, by silence. Constructed through the manipulation and coding of these deliberate emptinesses, the stage is a screen – the viewers both projectionist and audience. The other, before you, can never be known. Only guessed at. Mistaken. Projected upon. (Etchells 2006: 140)

Each audience member brings to the table one's own expectations and experiences and is able to project them onto the performance in a constant ontological negotiation. In other words, a theatre-savvy spectator may renegotiate her own relation to text and story, while a one-off theatregoer may just feel bored and uncomfortable because his presence is acknowledged. In either case, the theatre of FE leaves enough room to become a projection space for an audiences' own expectations. Tim Etchells recognizes this crucial role of activity and personal experience – paraphrasing Peter Handke – when he says that one should have the audience tell the story but make them feel afterwards that they have been told the story (cf. Etchells 2006: 141). Although it is debatable whether Etchell's notion of audience activity is not mere fraud in the sense that audiences are made to feel like they were active when in fact they were not, it is absolutely clear that audiences will at least *feel* more actively involved in the construction of the show or the story. This process of activity is firmly part of Rancière's idea of emancipation. Activity necessitates individual action.

> Emancipation begins when we challenge the opposition between viewing and acting [...]. It begins when we understand that viewing is also an action that confirms or transforms this distribution of positions. [...] This is a crucial point: spectators see, feel and understand something in as much as they compose their own poem [by relating to their own prior knowledge and experience], as, in their way, do actors or playwrights, directors, dancers or performers. (Rancière 2009: 13)

This process of emancipation, of becoming active, is one that is, however, not only found in the theatre. According to Rancière, emancipation begins everywhere, and the theatre space is not privileged: we are all spectators 'who all the time link what we see to what we have seen and said, done and dreamed. [...] Every spectator is already an actor in her story; every actor, every man of action, is the spectator of the same story' (Rancière 2009: 17). It seems that in this statement, Fischer-Lichte and Rancière are not that far apart: activity is inscribed in human activity and is thus a constant process that is not limited to the theatre. In this sense, FE are simply one (artistic) example of emancipation among many other (non-artistic) ones. They strongly provoke their audience to become more emancipated spectators, or possibly more emancipated witnesses.

Another aspect which endows the performance with authenticity is a strategy of metareference. The active audience is constantly confronted with itself and its own life, which becomes part of the performance. In one scene, Cathy Naden looks into the audience and tells individual audience members how they are going to die, with causes of death ranging from traffic accident, to cancer and street violence. She takes a long time for this and seems very relaxed and cool while telling people or while thinking about how they are going to die. Here, the individual witness can no longer be part of an anonymous collective but is suddenly very bluntly faced with her own mortality. The way Naden behaves in that scene leaves it unclear whether she is still in character and whether this is still a rehearsed part of the show or some evil joke or possibly a person with psychic abilities. Tomlin finds this scene to be a perfect example of how

> through a skilful construction, and then removal, of layer upon layer of artifice, Forced Entertainment continually succeeds in leaving its audience with the illusion of something more essential. [...] The most evocative moments in the company's work are achieved when a sense of 'the real' is contrived via a constructed slippage of the performance persona, or surrogate, to reveal a seemingly authentic self beneath it. (Tomlin 2013: 84)

Showtime offers both: a questioning of the audience's status and room for inferring individual meaning and individual stories. Both strategies of audience activation serve as functions that bring in the 'real world'. An audience member suddenly sees herself in the focus of attention and is able to bring and project her own stories to the table. A curious process then unfolds between the outside world of her everyday life, her multitude of roles and personas, and the events in the theatre: they become connected. Through this connection, a first form of authenticity is established. A spectator has to focus on her own role and status and is at the same time given room to infer meaning and closure into the gaps in the stories and to make sense of what she sees. On a second level, FE are also very apt at blurring the traditional boundaries between fact and fiction, between what is make-believe and what is 'real'. For instance, by allowing failure in, one can sometimes not be sure whether a prop was deliberately misplaced, a monologue mucked up or a gesture of failing made. By laying bare the theatricality of their own proceedings, FE open up the possibility that what is happening on stage might, at this moment, just be real, a genuine flaw, a 'fuck up', a failure of the theatrical machine. This confusion of fact and fiction, and of person and persona, also touches the level of content. In *Showtime*, a number of monologues always border on believability; emotions, especially when addressing the audience, might just be genuine anger or frustration.

> In their works, dying is put on stage and performers are pushed to reveal their most intimate secrets, fantasies and desires. They stand naked before us – desperately searching for some dignity or happiness – while we look on, the ever-present spectators, witnesses, voyeurs. (Malzacher 2004: 122)

The performance is real, not in the poetical dimension of the narrative or events, but in the political one of the event. The performance is a real event of performers and audience struggling to find new relations, and to find their own, individual place in the system called theatre. The nomenclature of 'witness' already hints at the fact that there is something more going on than a mere spectacle. A witness, by definition, perceives an event which is real (e.g. an accident, a crime). If the audience is termed 'witness' to a performance, the terminology suggests that something real is being witnessed on stage. This is not to say that the events on stage are real; obviously they are not, but they are *real theatrical* events. The performers seem to struggle, as much as any witness, to come to terms with their place within the machinery of theatre and all too often fail to do so. FE work with the exposedness of a performer on stage with the very mechanisms of coping with the limelight and the attention. As Rancière has it, "'[g]ood" theatre is one that uses its separated reality in order to abolish it' (Rancière 2009: 7). The difference in FE performances is to a good degree abolished, but not through Brechtian alienation or Artaudian inclusion. Distance disappears in the consciousness of being together in the same room, experiencing a common situation of make-believe. Audiences witness the performers' troubles and anxiety and attempts at performance. They take part, together with the performers, in the exercise of theatre – a joint and mutually dependent undertaking. In short, both audience and performer grapple with the harsh reality of this make-believe situation of fakery called theatre. But in this struggle, in this shared space and time continuum, the conflicts and questions each and every one of them poses are very real.

The Coming Storm (2012)

The double strategy of unsettling an audience by shaking its ontological status and its relation to performance and performers and at the same time bringing in the outside world has been one of the stock in trades of FE for nearly twenty years. Looking at one of their more recent productions, *The Coming Storm* (2012), it quickly becomes evident that, while their strategies have not changed much, their audience has changed substantially. It has been 'educated' over twenty years in soul-searching and status-questioning and now seems more apt to cope with FE's style. The show itself is centrally concerned with storytelling, the value of stories, the ways stories are told and the way they are able to hold our attention.

> I think of Forced Entertainment's *The Coming Storm* as navigating such a library [of endless possibility, which can never be conclusively mapped]; in confronting narrative and its exhaustive necessity to mean, in recalling the personal and weaving the fallacy and the fiction into one, and in excavating what a story might be, it maps the possible and constructs a shape-shifting metaphor of anticipation as a contemporary process. (Damian 2012)

Again, the focus is on potential, rather than fulfilment. FE are not looking for closure but for open-endedness. Hardly any of the stories in the show will ever reach a conclusion. And, again, FE invite an audience's personal thought in and more or less force them to question their own sensationalism and their status as witnesses.

> *The Coming Storm* begins with an empty stage; it begins with the cast all lined-up, looking at us, greeting us, waiting for something to emerge as Terry begins to outline the elements that make up a good story. As her words begin to inhabit the stage like those phantoms of meaning that contain all the histories of stories in their fragments, we begin to consider the people onstage as possible agents of these stories; as characters, narrators and witnesses. Narratives emerge, collide, are refused entry only to come back into the space at a later time. When we hear the first story, the story about the shipwreck, the story that begins to wander like a nomad, the story that opens avenues and doesn't travel them, we co-exist in this belligerence. And through the following two hours, we get used to the anticipation, we settle with the unstableness, we look at the debris and think about this waiting game. (Damian 2012)

In effect, the questions posed by the performance appear like recurrent themes from other FE shows: What is a good story? When am I entertained? When am I bored? What is (my own) sensationalism? Why am I keen on emotion and suffering? What is my relation to the performance and the performers, especially if they are conscious of me? The performers try to put the audience in a similar position as in *Showtime* (and a number of other FE stage works, for that matter). As Tim Etchells states,

> The piece reflects this real conflict we have about narrative, and how it organises ideas and material. You can see in the piece that we are compelled and forced by that, and at the same time there's a kind of revulsion from it, and it's slightly dubious because of its seductive power to charm. This is constantly something we want to disrupt. (Tim Etchells in Damian 2012)

Damian considers that

> Etchells speaks of the ways in which narrative is often mistaken or
> passed by as truth, at the same time, something that both ridicules and
> survives that process. (Damian 2012)

The question that must be asked then is whether these, by now, well-
known strategies can still serve their purpose? At the performance I
'witnessed' at Battersea Arts Centre on 24 November 2012, the audience
already laughed, cheered and applauded from the beginning on. It seemed
that many of them had been to a number of FE shows. They seemed to
know what was to come and they were in for two hours of soul-searching,
nagging questions and boredom. They knew that all theatrical conventions
would be subverted. They even seemed to know the questions they would
be posed. Is this still subversive then? Does it still make sense to question
things if the audience expects just that? Frequently,

> [t]he audience can find itself identifying techniques and devices rather
> than being surprised, shocked, or challenged. But, the question still
> remains, are they still challenging the norm if after three decades, they
> are the norm? (cf. Green 2013)

Subversion cannot work anymore, if the audience expects subversion
(cf. Suk 2012). If the strategy of subversion becomes the norm, what
then becomes of subversion? But, more importantly, the strategies of
individual experience, of unsettling an audience and of metareference
in the form of a bringing-in of the real world become blunt weapons.
The strategies that effected a degree of authenticity do, as becomes
evident, very quickly lose their power.

> Often, the audience (especially if they are new to the work) is unable
> to determine if what they saw was *intentionally* awkward or just badly
> performed, what was 'real' or staged (ie. done on 'purpose'); or at what
> point the difficulty of reception subsumed the event of theatre itself.
> (Bailes 2011: 57)

As soon as audiences become used to these strategies, they will lose
their force. They are, almost by definition, transitory and in need of

constant renewal. The moment of doubt whether this is real or not can only be achieved through surprise, which means constant reinvention of technique. Once a product becomes familiar, it does not have the unsettling effect that is able to reach a spectator on a personal level and establish a sentiment of authenticity. Only the singular, the bespoke and individual that is linked to one's personal life is able to produce sentiments of authenticity. Authenticity is a transient and elusive state.

Durational works: Emancipated spectators in action

The transient state of authenticity is very much supported by the inner structure of FE's durational performances. They establish a time frame which undermines traditional economies of attention and commodified theatrical products. Both performances discussed here last six hours in their durational version. In 2013, even a twenty-four-hour version of *QUIZOOLA!* was staged at the Barbican in London (cf. Yates 2013), and in 2014, FE staged twenty-four-hour versions of all their major durational performances and streamed them live to audiences around the world (cf. Schulze 2015). The passing of time, of shared time to be precise, becomes a crucial factor in the aesthetics of the production. Over such a long time, it is nearly impossible (and unwanted) to plan climaxes or another form of dramatic throughline.

> As a viewer you are able to experience the affect of time as it works through the presented ideas. So time becomes felt in relation, between the performer and the viewer, and that can bring with it resonances and realisations around embodiment, memory, mortality, loss, failure that are difficult to access and comprehend. (Heathfield 2004: 79)

In the durational time frame, the spectator is able to become absorbed, in a meditative way, in the performance. At the same time – as will become evident – the content also connects with spectators on an individual level through various strategies of metareference, truth/lying and intimacy. Even the category of 'the real' is allowed to figure in this equation, because large parts of the performance rely on improvisation.

In an improvisation, utterances and actions – however make-believe they may be – happen in the moment and are a spontaneous expression, a reaction within a theatrical game. They are readily available only in the moment and become an expression of the *Jetztzeit* (Benjamin, cf. Docherty 2003: 27). Tim Etchells claims that in contrast to the 'tyranny of [traditional] theatre', '[t]hings can be what they are. Climaxes don't have to be produced, resolutions are not needed' (in Heathfield 2004: 80). The traditional theatre economy of rising action, climax and falling action is subverted and gives way to a democratic juxtaposition of equally valid, precious moments in time. Both shows, while still having a textual basis, make gratuitous use of improvisation. Playing either *Quizoola!* or *Speak Bitterness* is more akin to playing a game of football than to performing a theatrical piece (cf. Etchells 2013). A performer knows the rules of the game, but within this frame must make her performance up as she goes along. The development and outcome of the performance is different every night and open to new impulses. An audience experiences not only equally precious moments in time together with the performers but will also feel that what is happening on stage is real in the sense that it is happening just now, out of the very moment. In this respect, both performances show some resemblance to the Comedia Dell'Arte tradition, which was also based on fixed routines (*lazzi*) and improvisation around a core story (cf. Gordon 1983).

Furthermore, the time structure also opens towards the possibility of the real on another level. A performer who is on stage, improvising, confessing or answering questions for hours and hours, will find it difficult to keep up a certain character, persona or mask. As the actor continues to grow tired, her defences and performance mask will weaken. In other words, as time goes by, audiences can never be sure if the actor is still in character or possibly speaking in her own voice. The audience feels that possibly they are not hearing a character's words but actually see an individual, honestly speaking, answering or confessing on stage. While this phenomenon must always remain ambiguous, because evidently it is never possible to judge once and for all if a performer was 'putting on a show' or if she was truthful, it is evident that a feeling of intimacy, of being close to someone or something real arises. 'So your attraction here is to the possibility of a moment of truth, or the possibility of revealing a true self, not truth itself' (Etchells in Heathfield 2004: 95). However, one can never be sure of this strategy and it may very well be that performers skilfully deceive their audience and trick them into believing something real is happening, while they are still fully in control. Liz Tomlin contends that all the strategies of earnestness and seemingly authentic personas are nothing but deliberate aesthetic choices, designed to produce the very effect of felt authenticity (cf. 2013: 84). Tim Etchells has admitted that audience manipulation always plays a role in their works.

> Yes, but the achievement of this [emotional] difficulty is still extremely strategic and manipulative, within a set of concerns and frames, especially when you compare it to the ways that visibility, exposure, or 'realness' operate in the durational works. Everything that you strategise in order to cause an effect in durational performances is inevitably outweighed by all of the other things that are happening that you cannot control. (in Heathfield 2004: 96)

The performance remains equivocal in this aspect. It is no genuine truth that the performance aims at but the felt possibility of truth. This strategy is able to lay the ground for the possibility of a sentiment of authenticity. In this case, ambiguity is what characterizes the black box authenticity. However, as the quotation demonstrates, many factors play a role in this game: audience, circumstance, performers' skill and mood and so on. A whole number of factors are also out of control for performers and creators alike; but it is certainly no coincidence that intimacy figures so heavily in the durational pieces. It is firmly written into the structure of durational works. FE, and specifically Tim Etchells, have often proven a certain obsession with personal connection and intimacy. Even in an essay, written by him, he tries to establish such a bond with his reader.

> We face each other again, you and I. The one of us reading, the other writing. It's late at night for me now. Tired. In a different city than the one in which I began. I search for you. I search. I search for you, and

these words like eyes flicker as they try to find and get the measure of your face. With one word or phrase, or another perhaps, maybe this one, we make eye contact. There is something that might be called 'electric' – a glimpse, a connection, a charge that passes between us. Then it's gone. (Etchells 2006: 143)

The moment of possible intimacy, of a possible real connection (if it exists), only lasts for a moment. It is transitory, as all successful strategies of authenticity must be. The pendulum at one point swings back towards detachment; it never settles at one point but oscillates between euphoric intimacy and apathetic detachment, without ever settling down.

Speak Bitterness (1994): A community of sinners

One of the first durational works of FE is *Speak Bitterness* (1994), which toured for a long time and is still performed today. The performance revolves around the act of confession: '[t]he essence of *Speak Bitterness* (1994) is a line of people making confessions from behind a long table. Occupying a brightly lit space, the performers take turns reading from the text that is strewn across the table' (Forced Entertainment in Green 2013). The act of confession itself already comes with a number of evocations and connotations. Religion, salvation and redemption readily spring to mind. Judith Butler has discussed the act of confession and refuted Foucault's claim that confession is always an act of control and power (cf. 2008: 170). For her, confession is not a constitutive act (repression), but a performative one where the 'performative force of the spoken utterance' (2008: 163) is able to create a different (aspect of the) self. Confession thus is a creative act that yields very real effects in terms of self and behaviour. But what is more, confessions are also inherently linked to the concept of intimacy. A confession would, in most cases, be made to one single person or just a small group of trusted people. In the Catholic Church, confessions are by definition only made to one person who is, furthermore, sworn to secrecy. The confessee relies on the confessor to maintain secrecy about the confession.

Bringing a confession to a large auditorium then already implies that spectators (or witnesses) are part of a select group that is privy to secret information – a group that is familiar and can be trusted. On the other hand, a confession is seen as the first step towards redemption. By acknowledging one's own frailties, one is forced to acknowledge one's guilt. The confessee, by accepting the embarrassment of public disclosure, comes one step closer to redemption of her sins. Any repentance is preceded by disclosure, be it only to one person or, in this case, to a theatrical audience. The act of confession then embodies simultaneously an element of publicity and intimacy, and an aspect of secrecy and disclosure. In negotiating these two poles, the performance is able to remain ambiguous about its own status but is also able to capitalize on both effects. Of course, we must presume that it is (yet again) obvious to spectators that they have come to see a performance and most likely they do not expect any 'real' confessions to happen. But, as was shown before, they will quickly learn that they are in a very real environment, together with the actors, in a situation of make-believe. There are then textual and structural strategies, which activate the audience and further a feeling of authenticity. This is especially so if one takes Butler's, rather than Foucault's, stance. She claims that in confession, through verbalization, people are able to transform themselves into something new; they find new versions of the self, while of course not finding absolute truth (cf. 2008: 166). Confessing brings a person into contact with hitherto hidden or repressed aspects of the self and at the same time serves to make the deeds in question more real and even tangible. 'The deed is made more real by virtue of its being spoken, it also, at the moment it is uttered, becomes strangely past, completed, over' (Butler 2008: 166). The act of confession can then be regarded either with Foucault as repressive or with Butler as generative and performative. Either way, it is linked to notions of intimacy, in the form of surrender in a repressive power relation or as bringing to light new aspects of a personality. Trust also plays a role in both constellations as does the notion of the real, either in the form of a deed that has to be brought to light or a transformation to be completed.

The following is an excerpt from the script of *Speak Bitterness*.

We thought that Freud was probably right about laughter. We had no moral compass, or if we did have one it had been badly damaged during the frequent electrical storms. We're guilty of heresy and hearsay, of turning our backs to the wall. We saw Arthur Scargill's blue movie cameo. We lied when it would've been easier to tell the truth. When we broke the law about satellites, there was no one to stop us or care. We sent death threats by fax machine and kept a list on a computer of people we were going to kill. We put the bop in the bop shee wop. We loved each other too much. We held each other's hands. We spat in the beer when no one was looking. We're guilty of murder, arson and theft. We crashed the spaceship on purpose. We got drunk too often, we nobbled horses, we made each other bleed. We knew that a professional foul inside the 30-yard box could lead to a penalty but in the 83rd minute we felt there was no choice – some of us went one way and I went the other, sandwiching the bloke and bringing him down hard – the referee was a Hungarian and never saw a thing. We were cold callers, scared of Kryptonite. We were class traitors, cry-for-help shoplifters, we were murderers of sleep. Everything was a movie to us. We hacked and hoodwinked, we wounded with intent. When the food-aid arrived in the lorries we started shoving and pushing. We had nose jobs, chin jobs, eye jobs, tummy tucks and bum sucks. We were bloody fools. We're guilty of that look people have sometimes when they daren't speak their minds. We confess to radium, railways and romanticism. We were jealous of Helen Sebley's personal transformation. We never made the rendezvous. We were deathless, never fading. We ate pet food straight from the can. We dipped our toes in the water and we got our fingers burned we had a truce on Christmas day. In the last years of our rule we deteriorated both physically and mentally – we planned to eliminate even our most loyal supporters. (Etchells 1999: 181)

All confessions are made in random order by the six actors on stage, the tone of voice changes regularly and so does the length and detail of the confessions. There is no prescribed way of performing; nor is there a running order. The script relies on improvisation as much as it relies on the written confessions. Performers are free to use it but also to make up new confessions on the spot.

Speak Bitterness [...] uses the text as raw material through which relationships between the performers themselves and performers and audience might be constructed. The confessions are read, whispered, shouted. They are erased with laughter or hesitation. Confessions come in single lines, in fast-paced exchanges between performers and in long monologues and lists. The performance may appear to be sincere, bitter, preposterous or even absurd by turns. (Etchells 1999: 179)

The piece then is 'an attempt to confess to everything – a vast catalogue of wrongdoings that includes murder, fraud, genocide, eating the last biscuit in the tin, not washing up properly, hiding the TV remote control, and buggery' (Etchells 2004: 272). The catalogue, as can be seen, is vast and extremely disparate. It is this disparity which partly lends the performance its strength. The text plays with what I want to call 'oxymoronic humour'. It juxtaposes very minor crimes (e.g. taking the last biscuit) or things that are not even crimes at all (e.g. holding hands) with very severe misconduct, leading all the way up to arson, rape and murder. This juxtaposition often leads to a very comic effect. Where a spectator may readily laugh about the confession of having put the 'bop in the bop shee wop', she may very well find her laughter abruptly break off when the next performer confesses to being guilty of murder, arson and theft. The juxtaposition of such mismatches needs reconciliation by the audience, who find it by way of reconstruction. They, in other words, fill the gaps of the mismatched confessions by linking it to life. Life itself poses as a role model for this reservoir of mismatches. In the 'real' world the funny and the horrid frequently stand side by side. An audience can thus make sense of the disparity by seeing it as mirroring everyday life. The performers frequently play with these mechanisms, not only by juxtaposing oxymoronic confessions, but also by varying in tone, volume and timing of their confessions. A performer may well say in a happy voice 'we put the bop in the bop shee wop' when another one interrupts her with an angry voice and confesses to a horrible crime. The spectators are thus induced to laugh, but are also kept in an unsettling state where they can never be sure what is to come next or whether to laugh or retain dignified silence.

What is more, the text also uses a number of references to the world outside the theatre. Those can be literary (e.g. 'murderers of sleep'), pop cultural (e.g. 'Helen Sebley') or historical (e.g. dictators). By referencing real-world events, the performance obfuscates its own status. Are the confessions fact or fiction? Are they based on the real world or are they completely made up? Are some of the confessions possibly verbatim material? In a performance streamed live from the Hebbel am Ufer theatre in Berlin, on 18 October 2014, the performers for instance confessed to having lost contact to Malaysia Airlines flight 370, or to having used the dock to make wild allegations about NATO politics on the Balkan. By referencing a very current airline accident and the trial of Slobodan Milošević, the performance turns towards the real world and at least opens up the possibility of facticity.[3] It seems a deliberate choice that the audience should be left in the dark in this matter because it further serves to withhold any safety from the audience. Both strategies activate the audience by way of metareference and by reference to the outside (real) world. They seek to change the performance's status from pure fiction and entertainment to an ambiguous entity in between the realms of fiction and fact. The text serves the performance structure well when it unsettles the audience and begins to blur the boundary between fact and fiction.

The structure of the performance itself takes the same line as the content. During the six-hour performance, spectators are free to come and go at their discretion. They may always take a break and come back later. The spectator is thus empowered and the rigid distribution of the sensible, which prevails in conventional theatres, is broken. Furthermore, the audience space is not dark but always dimly lit. In this way, the symbolic boundary between performers and spectators is further undermined. The audience has the choice, not only to become emancipated spectators in their seats but also to come and go. These decisions are all individual and each person's responsibility for their own actions is foregrounded. There is not really a way of hiding in the crowd, as is usually the case. On top of that, each spectator who leaves and comes back is always visible to the rest of the audience and to the performers, who, however, do not comment on audience behaviour. Consequently, the old distribution of the sensible is destroyed, but a new, no less firm distribution is put into place. In this power economy, individual decisions are foregrounded. Any spectator has to battle with the eyes of fellow spectators resting on her when she decides to stand up or come back into the auditorium. While spectators are free to leave and come back at leisure, the performers on stage will continue throughout the six hours with no intervals. As has been mentioned, this puts performers under enormous duress, both physically and mentally:

> The suggestion that the work is experimental means that some of it will inevitably fail. This is most apparent in their durational work, a challenge on both audience and performers, as performers reach a point where they will shift from performance mode into their natural state. [...] As *Speak Bitterness* was six hours in duration, there would have been points where the traditional concept of performer/audience was destroyed and was replaced by a new relationship and experience. (Green 2013)

This 'new relationship' cannot be fully grasped with Rancière's 'emancipated spectators', because it involves much more activity, even physical activity, and the audience figures more prominently and is visible. As the performance proceeds, they are continually faced with the question whether what they see on stage is real to any degree or simply a show. As the performers begin to show signs of exhaustion and tiredness, the suspicion grows that something real might be happening – that the performers are no longer able to keep up their mask. Confessions may become shorter and less snappy, the interplay may not be as well-paced or witty or performers may simply yawn and appear tired. At this point, the performance again meanders between fact and fiction; person and persona intermingle. The audience has no way of knowing if a confession was just made up on the spot or is actually from the script. Tim Etchells acknowledges this effect when he speaks about the architecture of theatrical performance as opposed to durational works: '[I]n the long pieces, it is much more open to your live, arbitrary, whimsical or perverse choices. It is certainly open to your mood' (in Heathfield 2004: 80). Liz Tomlin, who dismisses authenticity entirely as a myth (cf. 2013: 80), finds that the entire notion of one unified self cannot be upheld in performance and that FE specifically question the concept. Accordingly, performers always either play a character or a fictional self when they pretend to be 'real': 'In both instances, there is significant rejection of the notion of a singular, coherent and essential self and a turn instead to multiple and constructed identities across a wide spectrum of performance models' (Tomlin 2013: 81). While in a postmodern line of thought this is certainly true, I want to disagree with her conclusion. The notion of a fragmented self is not necessarily as present to an audience as it is to a theatre scholar. Many audience members will, in the culture of authenticity, subscribe to such concepts as 'the self'. The performance, as has been shown, goes a long way to open up this possibility and it encourages audiences to actively partake in its construction. I want to contend that from a reception point of view Tomlin's argument does not hold but the performance can rather be read as a meditation on the audience's wish for authenticity and experiences of the real. Tomlin's shortcoming is that she ascribes an inherent purpose of deconstruction to the performance when it could just as easily be read as reconstructive. This becomes apparent if one focuses on the perspective of the audience.

Spectators, if they choose to stay for the entire duration of the performance, are – just like the performers – put under mental and physical duress. Six hours of watching a performance in a concentrated manner already seems challenging, but in *Speak Bitterness*, the frequency of confessions makes this even harder:

> Hundreds of confessions leave the witness [i.e. spectator] with the choice: either to let them all flow through him, or to focus on individual ones and in doing so, to miss others. Active choice and evaluation is his only option – and in this he must fail. (Malzacher 2004: 129)

The spectator is asked to choose which confessions she wants to follow. She has to make choices but in these she can only fail. In this failure, the real is again invited in, but also sympathy for the performers arises. A curious community of people suffering through a very surreal, performative situation arises. Performer and spectator bond over this shared experience. The spectator has little choice in her failure but to remain an active witness and, like Sysiphos, continue to fail. Some confessions may well linger and the spectator may ask herself if she would have to make that specific confession, too. It is in the very nature of confessions that one may think about one's own sins or mistakes. One may laugh at a minor confession (e.g. 'lying when it would have been easier to tell the truth') and secretly acknowledge that one is guilty of that crime as well. At other times one may feel repelled or even be brought into contact with one's own dark secrets or desires. The performers symbolically take the blame for almost every crime or misconduct imaginable. By spelling out each crime, word by word and not whitewashing anything, they inevitably will bring spectators into contact with their own faults and desires. The spectators become emancipated in the sense that they do not simply wallow in semblances but are faced with the reality of their own life, which they link to the performance on stage. *Speak Bitterness* creates a community of sinners, willing to repent. At this point, the reality of each spectator's own life cannot be ignored anymore, and the outside world of one's private life and the community of make-believe become intermingled. Even moral action or a change of behaviour may be effected. It is an at times painful and continuous process of coming to terms with wrongdoings and the dark desires of one's own – or even humanity in general. The audience, either way, is not able to remain in a state of neutrality for long. In

> *Speak Bitterness* [...] the witness is positioned as a supposedly neutral observer, with a clear view of all that takes place, and even though his place from within the brightly-lit audience is legitimate, it is also true that this gaze is taxed beyond its capacities: The sheer amount of what is heard, with every sentence a confession, cannot be processed, neither quantitatively nor qualitatively. In this situation, distinguishing between true and false, meaningful and meaningless, is simply not possible. (Malzacher 2004: 126)

As the audience fails, in the bombardment of confessions and spectators find themselves in a deeply unsettled state of mind, it is the communal experience that may prove a safe haven. Their failure confronts the audience continually with the real, while the content continually screams for a coming to terms with one's own misconducts. The spectator is an active witness whose only way out remains the communal experience. It is the experience that performers and other spectators all struggle with the same problems of fatigue, failure and their dark confessions that may prove a consolation (cf. Malzacher 2004: 124). FE frequently and consciously try to question issues of community and togetherness and specifically the power economy ('distribution of the sensible') at work in such situations.

'I suppose we made a whole bunch of shows that were in their own way reasonably confrontational with the audience, but that feels a bit done for me as a topic now. I'm more interested in the audience as witnesses, there in an encounter with a particular set of material.' In the politics of that act of witnessing however, there's a sense of a range of negotiations too; a particular kind of social contract. 'Theatre seems to me to be an odd thing; you're in a room with some people, and a bunch of them do something at one end of the room and the rest stay there watching in the dark. It's an interesting space, because it's one that asks questions about who we are, and what is happening.' (Etchells in Damian 2012)

In the power relation that is created in durational performances, the audience and the performers share the space of time and make-believe action. This shared moment may again, through all the factors described above, become very authentic for an individual spectator. In *Speak Bitterness*, performers and audience by proxy live through almost all the crimes and wrongdoings of mankind. By taking the blame for every crime known, the performers symbolically cleanse themselves and mankind of the sins they enumerate. But what about the spectators? Are they purged of their sins as well? What was thought impossible at the beginning may happen in this performance. An instant of reconstruction, an instant of community in a shared space, far from ironic detachment, appears. A very real conversation with the self in a community with others ensues. The confession can obtain a generative, almost healing power in Butler's sense. It does not matter at all whether any of the confessions are authentic, or whether performers were themselves or not. Nor does it matter what sort of truth can be seen on stage. What matters is the sentiment of and effect on the audience after the show. They experience moments of truth, of confrontation with the real and their very own selves in moments of community. These effects are all very real, no mater how they were produced.

Quizoola! (1996): The possibility of truth

While *Speak Bitterness* is a performance about confessions, *Quizoola!* is a performance about questions. It centres around two actors on a makeshift stage, surrounded by a circle of light bulbs on the floor. The spectators sit on chairs around them, on the same level as the performers. The two performers take turns in asking each other questions, loosely following a catalogue of around 2000 questions, but, as in *Speak Bitterness*, they are free to repeat, jump or make up questions. The audience is free to stay, leave and come back as they please. However, at the performance I witnessed in Cambridge on 17 February 2008, it was noticeable that at least a third of the audience stayed for the entire duration (apart from the odd toilet break). The performers further wear badly drawn clown make-up, which – along with the light bulbs and a makeshift sign in the background, displaying the word 'QUIZOOLA!' – all give the impression of a performance that is not quite finished, something temporary, premature and makeshift. FE create a conscious distance to classical theatre and expose theatrical mechanisms and at the same time distance themselves from the smoothly running machine of commercial theatre.

The piece was first developed at the Institute of Contemporary Arts in London (ICA) in 1996 as a forty-five-minute show and was subsequently expanded into a six-hour duration version (cf. Yates 2013). It has been touring up until today and is surely one of FE's most successful performances. On 12 April 2013, and 21 November 2014, mammoth twenty-four-hour versions of the performance were staged in London and Sheffield respectively (cf. Gratza 2013; Schulze 2015).

These performances were also broadcast live online over the entire duration. The one from London had 4500 viewers from fifty-eight countries; it trended number one on Twitter with 1.8 million tweets tagged '#Quizoola!24' (cf. FE homepage 2013). These figures show the broad and continued popularity that *Quizoola!* has with audiences, but they also point towards the broader phenomenon of mixed-media performance and digital performance. Kirby has sensibly pointed out that the audience's participation is frequently constitutive of such artworks (cf. 2006). The viewer at home who 'clicks, presses, surfs, chooses, moves, downloads' (2006) becomes constitutive of the artwork itself. Accordingly, there were two performances being created: the one live at the venue, and an online performance that took place through Twitter exchange. People repeated their favourite lines from the performance, stated where and with whom they were watching or sometimes also commented on the performance. This online performance then must be regarded as an artwork in its own right. And so far, there is too little research on cyber theatre, livecasting and so on (cf. Barker 2013; Schulze 2015: 324–325).

The performance itself, in terms of structure and content, relies on strategies similar to other durational works. However, the structure and nature of a game of questions and answers gives the performance a very different dimension.

Do you have your own bike?
How old are you going to get?
Do you like me?
Do you like yourself?
What is your most recent memory?
What is the average snowfall for this time of year?
What is the average number of lovers for a woman or a man?
What is the average number of keys people lose?
Which is the strongest a steel chain or a fibre rope?
Who holed up in Gotham City?
Which is the smallest a neutron or a proton?
Which is the worst a half truth or a partial lie?

[...]

Do you believe that Elvis is alive somewhere, living in hiding and far
    far away?

What's the legal definition of rape?

Do you think a lot at night?

[...]

Is it true that you're lost and don't know where to turn?

If you spoke another language would you still be you?

What happens to the food that we eat?

How do houses breathe?

What happens when the soul leaves the body?

What is Ohms [*sic*] Law?

What is Newton's Law?

What is Boyle's Law?

[...]

How old are you?

How old are you going to get?

Do you have your own bike?

Do you always do as you are told?

Do you like me?

Do you love me?

Why do you like me? Do you like yourself?

What are trees?

Where is the name of a thing?

Where do dreams come from?

[...]

What is your favourite sexual position?

Do you believe in destiny?

In your opinion is history created by great men or by the inevitable
    moments of social forces? (Etchells 1997: 20–21)

The catalogue of questions can be understood as somewhat of a
foundation on which the actors are free to roam and improvise.
The only set rule is that just one person may ask questions and the other
person has to give answers. Lies are permitted but they must sound
truthful; that is absurd answers are not permitted. Roles and characters

can be changed and are changed frequently over the course of the performance. *Quizoola!* obviously also relies heavily on improvisation and it is telling that Tim Etchells refers to the performance as a game rather than a theatrical event:

> You can prepare for Quizoola! in the same way as you can prepare for a football match – by training, by understanding the rules, by discussing tactics and strategies, by feeling good with your team. But you can't rehearse a football match. Because a proper game has to be played, not performed. (Etchells 2013)

The audience becomes witness to this game of questions. The rules are never stated but are very quickly grasped by spectators. The whole performance then indeed resembles more the situation in a football match, because while the rules are known and the general tendency can be guessed, the action may take dramatic turns, be boring or change within seconds. A spectator very quickly becomes aware of the fact that what she sees is happening just in this moment. It is a real situation of theatrical improvisation. While the content and the game may be theatrical, the action of improvisation is genuinely real. Tim Etchells has proposed that 'there is a tentativeness to this process [of improvisation], an organic rhythm of failure, discovery, consolidation and eventual collapse that a spectator feels (knows, intuits) is real' (Etchells 2006: 141). In other words, audiences are very aware of what is going on between the performers and follow their journey through the game. The whole performance is of course theatrical and a form of make-believe. The process or action, however, is very real. Spectators can see that performers are working hard to play the game and failure is always an option. This is also one of the prominent strategies which elicit a sense of authenticity in the spectators.

> [T]he spectacle of seeing people struggle to come up with an answer on the spot, occasionally slip up only to bounce back again, show their weaknesses and thus lay themselves open to our scrutiny makes for compelling viewing. (Gratza 2013)

A spectator sees and intuits that she is watching a process of live creation, of whimsical, sometimes emotional choices that performers make. In this game of improvisation, again, there is no dramatic throughline, no in-built climaxes or dramatic cohesion. Just like in a football match, an hour of the performance can be all from hilarious, to extremely sad, to absolutely boring. Whatever happens within the frame of improvisation, including all actions and events, is of equal worth. As Etchells states, 'I am very attracted to things that are what they are, and I am very attracted to moments where what's happening is what's happening' (in Heathfield 2004: 90). The moments he describes then also give rise to a sentiment of the real. Theatre is regularly marked by dramatic cohesion and climax. *Quizoola!* subverts this convention and the whole event much more resembles events in everyday life, which can be anything: exciting, boring, funny or sad. The 'real life' has no dramatic throughline. *Quizoola!* is much closer to real life than it is to its theatrical relatives. Theatre's artificiality is undermined and replaced by the possibility of the everyday, which effects a feeling of authenticity. Furthermore, all utterances and actions are displayed in an unconnected fashion. Just as in *Speak Bitterness*, the selection of questions, the tone of voice and so on lead to laughter on which the audience immediately chokes again, when straight after something serious is discussed (oxymoronic humour). The oxymoronic humour has two functions. It serves to unsettle and put the audience in a state of unease, where they can never be sure what to expect next. This state prepares them for an active role as an emancipated spectator. But what is more, it is again a strategy that links the performance to real life where the juxtaposition of the funny and the sad, and the beautiful and the horrid has become commonplace in the media and everyday life. The performance gains another shade of reality.

So far, the structural mechanisms discussed are not dissimilar to those of *Speak Bitterness*. When it comes to material aspects of the performance, however, *Quizoola!* differs fundamentally. Confessions in *Speak Bitterness* are simply made or shouted out into the auditorium. They stand on their own, communication among the performers is rare and very limited. In *Quizoola!*, we see an active and highly fluid conversation between two individuals. This alone gives the performance a much greater range of possibilities, improvisations and paths to follow. Many of the questions already presuppose stories that remain untold. For instance, the question 'Why did you cry last night?' presupposes that the addressee did cry and that the asker knows about this. Presuppositional stories imply narratives that are never told. These blanks are filled by the audience in their heads. They thus personalize the theatrical event and also employ reconstructive strategies. A myriad of such 'presuppositional stories' arise over the course of the performance and, more often than not, are never resolved. *Quizoola!* leaves a whole number of gaps and blank spots in the various narratives. The characters of the performers are sometimes constant and sometimes change over time. An audience is left with a number of irreconcilable details in their mind. If a performer, for instance, answers to the question 'What is my name?' with 'Terry', but five minutes later the same person answers with 'Peter', a contradiction arises. The audience is left with two possibilities: either to judge one or both statements as a lie or to find a solution for the seemingly paradoxical. If the spectator opts for a solution, a strategy of reconstruction is employed. Similar to the paradox of authenticity, the mind of the spectator seeks to reconcile the mutually contradictory facts. She thus creates a higher-order character that she may rightfully call her own. Each spectator will have a different version of what they believe to be true or to be the character or performer in their own head. By making choices of reconstruction a very individual and personal character arises, which is facilitated by contradiction and gaps in storytelling. As Etchells has proffered, it is up to the audience to create a story or a character out of the disparate and sometimes contradictory information they have at hand: 'The public is the maker of the piece, in their heads. Watching is an act of projection' (Tim Etchells in conversation with me, June 2008). The audience becomes active and has to be active in order to make sense of the performance. However, a spectator may also opt for a statement to be a blunt lie. The concept of question and answer alone seems to hint at the problem of truth and lying. Any answer in the performance can always be a lie. 'Lies and mistakes can tell as much about a person as "true" answers. Lies can be convincing lies, transparent lies, skilfully sold lies, incompetent lies. True answers can sound like untruths' (Etchells 2013).

Quizoola! is constantly a game of truth and lying, sometimes of skilful and convincing lying, sometimes of bold lies. It is up to each spectator to judge the veracity of a statement. But again, spectators are left in the dark as to what to believe and what not. The performers frequently do not adopt a fixed character, which a spectator could more easily judge, but they meander between different characters and personas. Thus, it is always possible that something is true or untrue. It is then not truth that matters but the possibility of truth: Could this still be credible or do I doubt the performer? Etchells writes as follows in his 'unpublished notes' on *Quizoola!*: 'Quizoola! is not interested in "true truth", but perhaps in versions of it. Quizoola! makes one essential demand – PLAY THE GAME' (Etchells 2013). Spectators may then very well direct their silent questions about lying and veracity at the performers themselves. And – as in other durational works – time is the decisive factor. After hours and hours of performance, one can never be quite sure how near a truth or possibly a genuine person one has come. Actors tire, begin to lose concentration, shift in their attitude and (seemingly) blunder out facts they had not intended to disclose. The audience keenly observes these processes of gradually losing one's stage persona and the real person shimmering through. 'So your attraction here is to the possibility of a moment of truth, or the possibility of revealing a true self, not truth itself' (Heathfield 2004: 95). It is worth noting that one is only after a 'possibility of a moment of truth', not truth with a capital 'T'. This fleeting moment of a possibility of truth is then again something which is perceived as authentic. It is a (seeming) glimpse at something real in an ocean of fiction and lies. Etchells believes that in such moments: 'I think what's possible … is that you, as an audience member, encounter those other people, the performers, in an extraordinarily complicated and intimate way. I think there's something very valuable about that' (in Yates 2013). The valuable moment here is nothing but the metamodern longing for a moment of truth, of unmediated experience, of something authentic and real. But a spectator can never be sure of this. She can only conjecture and project her own wishes upon the person on stage. This marks a very communal moment because, as a matter of fact, neither may the performer be conscious if she is just putting on a show nor know if she is genuine. '[T]he durational works are very exposing for the performers; they place them under sustained scrutiny, and they can be physically exhausting, taxing the performer's memory, focus, ability to stay alive and connected' (Heathfield 2004: 80).

As the boundary between person and persona begins to vanish, the performer herself may enter a state somewhere between performance and real life, bordering between fact and fiction, where tiredness and exhaustion have taken their toll. Tim Etchells has commented that, after the twenty-four-hour version, he was not even sure anymore of what he had said.

> You know you've been talking for hours and hours without a break, but quite what was said can seriously evade you – a feeling akin to that following long conversations in general, perhaps, especially late night, complex or emotional ones. (Etchells 2013)

'Complex' and 'emotional' are good adjectives to describe the situation in such a performance. *Quizoola!* is to a good degree about 'staying up all night and collectively marking time' (Gratza 2013). The audience and the performers go on a journey together, battling time and fatigue, looking for moments of possible truth. They thus encounter each other much more closely than a conventional theatre audience would encounter the actors. They are active and constantly need to judge truth and lies through strategies of reconstruction and are activated through oxymoronic humour. The possibility of truth, or even a faint promise of a true moment, constantly lingers over the performance.

But the questions may also serve another purpose. Many of them will reverberate within the audience's mind and they will, just in the way that they secretly confessed in *Speak Bitterness*, begin to ask themselves a number of those questions. All questions in the performance are directed not only at the other performer but at the audience as well. At first, just like the performers, spectators will try to be smart or witty or lie to themselves (e.g. 'What would I have said?'). But as time goes on, they may also drop their own mask and begin to ask themselves more searchingly. This again brings the active audience in contact with their own life and their selves. It builds a bridge between the events on stage and their own lives. It brings in the outside world and thus connects the performance to the real. However, the performance, both in structure and content, always remains ambiguous in aspects of truth/lying, person/persona and audience-spectator relation.

> *Quizoola!* rests on their [*sic*] being an ambiguity to its status – is it performance, interrogation, or some private lovers [*sic*] game. If there is real tiredness or real panic on behalf of the questioned, or real embarrassment, if there seems to be real anger or real interest or real exasperation from the questioner then, I feel, we are getting closer to the heart of the piece. In performance terms this demands something quite extraordinary – an ability to be oneself, to expose oneself, to stay human-scale and intimate, whilst at the same time thinking of performance, thinking strategically and, for all the 'honesty' of it, be [*sic*] acting in a quite substantial way. The only rule (if one can make any rules at all in this) might be to say that as soon as the thing feels stable or decided in its status then it is failing. (Etchells 1997: 11)

Ambiguity and instability are the key features of this performance with the possibility of 'the real' ever present. The emerging performance is then characterized by a sense of community that is yet ruptured again, free of classical connotations of collectivity in the sense of uniformity. In this community, every spectator experiences, thinks and acts as an individual and in connection to their individual life. *Quizoola!*, just like *Speak Bitterness*, consciously uses the structure of the catalogue to break its conventions and effect individual, intimate and authentic communication.

> If *Speak Bitterness* is a catalogue of all possible confessions, then *Quizoola!* is a catalogue of possible questions [...] It's not so much the content of any particular confession, story, question, etc. that's of

interest but the nature of the catalogue itself – its boundaries, its built-in agendas, its formal extremities, its *concerns* – is revealed. (Etchells 2004: 272)

The concept of the catalogue follows the idea of categorization, of order and structure. Using a catalogue as a basis for a performance may seem like an invitation of an extremely rigid power economy into the theatre: performers (active) here, spectators (passive) there. Rancière refers to this 'Platonic[4] state of affairs' as a state where everything has its proper place, everybody has their one occupation, where no other activities or deviations are permitted in terms of thinking, talking or action. 'This is what I call the "police distribution of the sensible"' (Rancière 2009: 42). FE, however, break this distribution by taking the catalogue principle *ad extremum* – effectively to the point of breaking. The vast amount of disparate questions, as has been shown, seeks not to stabilize an audience or allocate a proper place but, on the contrary, to activate and to inspire ambiguity. The performance ruptures categories, connecting disparate elements, and the whimsical development of questions out of the moment shows the futility of categorization and cataloguing. By laying bare the agenda of the catalogue, its power economy becomes porous and may at one point even break. Matthew Goulish, co-founder of the Institute of Failure, asserts that '[a]ny system is best understood by an investigation of its failure' (Goulish 2004: 250).

Of course, it is debateable whether the investigation of failure does not constitute a discursive reabsorbtion of the very concept, thus incorporating it into the very discourse of theatre again and effectively nullifying the effort. Goulish's point is, however, not the categorization or even cataloguing of failure, but the application of pressure up to the breaking point to various systems (e.g. theatre, art, writing, car mechanics). The study of failure enables a better grasp of the limitations of each system and can thus help to develop and transform it. In performance, failure not only connects to the real, as it does in the improvisations, but also disrupts the prevalent power economy of the theatre.

The evil [i.e. the undesirable state of affairs] consists not only in the content of representation but in its very structure. It consists in the separation between the stage and the audience, between the performance of the bodies on the stage and passivity of the spectators in the theatre. What must replace the mimetic mediation is the immediate ethical performance of a collective that knows no separation between performing actors and passive spectators. (Rancière 2009: 62)

While Rancière envisages experimental theatres from the 1920s as a realization of such a collective, it seems justified to say that *Quizoola!* already takes things a step into this direction by empowering the audience, by activating them and by creating community. The rigid structure of the catalogue is broken by an active spectator who does not only decode meaning but connect with the performer and the performance on an individual and intimate level. An active witness is someone who shares her activity in a community with fellow witnesses and performers on stage. One may characterize this experience in terms of Nicolas Bourriaud's 'relational aesthetics' (cf. 2002). Bourriaud understands art – in general and in this case theatre – not in terms of a passive subject-object relation, but as a time of shared, common experience. '[I]t is no longer possible to regard the contemporary work as a space to be walked through […]. It is henceforth presented as a period of time to be lived through, like an opening to unlimited discussion' (Bourriaud 2002: 15).

While Bourriaud is chiefly concerned with visual arts, his theory also makes sense in the context of theatre because a number of contemporary visual artworks are performative and interactive in essence: they create spaces for personal encounters and experiences of community. *Quizoola!* establishes a sense of community and individuality at once within the porous framework of the catalogue that gives rise to a space of intimacy, authenticity and possible truths. It never settles at one point but meanders between the structural and contentual categories. *Quizoola!* is a common and individual experience in the fake world of theatre that is very true on many levels for the individual spectator, or even real.

One-on-one performance: Truth, trust and betrayal

The durational works of FE are not the only ones to create feelings of authenticity and intimacy with their spectators. As *The Guardian's* theatre critic, Lyn Gardner, observes, '[i]ntimacy is a theme that is currently sweeping British theatre' (2009). It has been a major force in a number of performances in the first decade of the new millennium. Most prominently, it features in 'one-on-one performances'. As the name proclaims, these kinds of performance regularly feature just one performer and one spectator. Although the terms 'performer' and 'spectator' may be misleading because many such pieces work to destroy the (active) performer/(passive) spectator relationship. They are about 'testing, manipulating and playing with, the traditional performer/ spectator artwork/viewer relationship' (Zerihan 2009: 3). It is difficult, if not impossible, to categorize them or give some sort of general description as they are so manifold in terms of both structure and content. One-on-one performances can last from one minute to an hour and usually they are site-specific/site-based performances that draw on the aesthetics of live art (cf. Zerihan 2009: 3). The only common characteristic is indeed that these works feature one performer and one spectator. Therefore, the performances discussed in the following are an eclectic survey of a very wide and fast-growing field. The examples here serve to highlight key issues that surface in many such performances. I will briefly try to discern some characteristics and aesthetic strategies and also highlight some critical issues that frequently surround such events. Subsequently, two performances that were hugely influential and successful (both in their own way), namely Oentroerent Goed's *Internal* (2009) and Battersea Arts Centre's *London Stories* (2013), will be analysed in more detail.

Description, examples, first assumptions

The phenomenon of one-on-one performance rose to prominence in Britain and Europe at around the turn of the millennium (cf. Zerihan 2009: 4), and the first decade of the millennium saw a substantial upsurge in one-on-one performances (cf. 2009). Lyn Gardner locates this success in a general trend in theatre. She discerns a new appetite for experimentation. 'These live-art performances reflect a wider trend in theatre. Increasingly, it's felt that large playhouses can't deliver the intimacy of experience that audiences crave – so instead, theatre-goers and -makers are seeking out other spaces and other forms' (Gardner 2005). It is obvious that the ideas of intimacy and authenticity in new theatrical forms and spaces are not as recent as might be believed at first glance. The concept of the one-on-one performance clearly stands in the line of tradition of performance art and happenings. In the late 1950s and early 1960s, theatre and art practitioners had already experimented with form in the guise of happenings and performance art. They

> were fascinated by the collapsing distinction between 'fiction' and 'reality'. Certain artistic works both explored and helped bring about the erosion of the real-fictional boundary. From Luigi Pirandello and Nikolai Evreinov to John Cage, Allan Kaprow, and many of today's performance artists, this interplay of realities has increasingly become a central theme in performance art, film and TV, the internet, experimental theatre, the visual arts, and popular entertainment. (Schechner 2006: 126)

Today, it seems, practitioners and audiences both have a newly found appetite for productions that both have a sense of being real and that speak to spectators on an individual level. Lois Keidan of the Live Art Development Agency remarks that one-on-one performance 'feels more real than real life [...] and because it isn't a mass experience you know that nobody is going to have the same experience as you have. It makes the event unique and it makes you feel special' (in Gardner 2005). One may see this hunger as a counter-movement that stands in opposition to medialized forms of everyday life, where the individual feels removed from first-hand experience. Or, one may detect an increased importance of individualism – which goes hand in hand with the consumption of bespoke goods – in the popularity of one-on-one performance. What is abundantly clear is the popularity of the format in the first decade or so of the millennium.

The significant rise in the amount of One to One performance works being made, especially over the last five years, throws up some interesting questions in terms of *our demand for* together with *artists' use of* this format in contemporary performance, body and live art. (Zerihan 2009: 4, italics in the original)

Festivals featuring one-on-one performances have been staged for three consecutive years at Battersea Arts Centre (BAC) in London (cf. BAC 2013) and in Australia (cf. Wilson 2012), and similar projects are also happening in New York (cf. anon. 2013) and other cities around the globe (cf. Logan 2010). Artistic directors and practitioners may on the one hand be 'jumping the bandwagon' of a successful performance model. But on the other hand, one-on-one performances are not a commercially viable enterprise. They feature an audience of one and thus, by nature, can almost never recoup their costs. The increase in such productions must then be regarded as a real artistic endeavour that seeks to innovate and experiment with theatrical practice. BAC's artistic director David Jubb, when asked about the one-on-one festival, stated that it was BAC's mission 'to explore the future of theatre. It's an increasingly important area, particularly when so many theatre spaces and performances feel as if they lack honesty, intimacy and integrity' (in Gardner 2009).

Is one-one-one, then, with its promises of intimacy and authenticity, the 'future of theatre'? The perceived lack of honesty, intimacy or integrity in people's lives is not only felt on the side of the spectators. Practitioners also seem to struggle with the same issues. One-on-one performance may be an expression of a shared need for intimacy. It is an attempt to tease out more of a performance than is usually the case. Logan quotes British performance artist Adrian Howells', who has produced and performed in a number of one-on-one pieces, comment on this.

> To Howells and others, one-on-one's popularity is a response to the intimacy deficit of 21st-century living. 'We are in an age of rapid technological advance, and are more and more disconnected from ourselves, and other people. We spend huge amounts of time in front of computers, and having virtual relationships via email and Facebook.

But we don't meet people eye to eye, flesh on flesh. And nothing can substitute for the nourishment of one human being meeting another in real time.' (Logan 2010)

It is clear that traditional theatrical aesthetics can only be applied to a very limited degree in this context. Accordingly, Josephine Machon has proffered that aesthetics in such theatrical contexts should be understood as 'the subjective creation, experience and criticism of artistic practice' (Machon 2009: 14). Creation, experience and criticism seemingly merge into one in this definition. The roles of performer and spectator are fluid and mutually intertwined in one-on-one performances. The single spectator has to make decisions and interact with the performer to some degree for the performance to happen. This obviously goes beyond Rancière's notion of the emancipated spectator because every spectator is genuinely active verbally and/or physically in the performance. In one-on-one performances, the 'individual's role in the performance's agency – in terms of cultural politics, erotic encounters, sacred moments, therapeutic interactions and risky opportunities – are brought to the foreground' (Zerihan 2009: 3). The performance is no longer a fixed set of events that happen in a chronological order – as in a West End show – but it is open to and welcomes intervention, improvisation and personal input. 'Participation in the performance event often triggers spontaneity, improvisation and risk – in both parties – and requires trust, commitment and a willingness to partake in the encounter' (Zerihan 2009: 3). Performers and participants are both active parts, and the performance can only happen if both parties participate and want to participate: 'My work has always been about a desire to converse and connect intimately with an audience. [...] When audience participation is used in a group setting, the active participants become performers' (Jess Dobkin in Zerihan 2009: 24).

One-on-one performances thus make huge demands on their audience. Participants must advance a large degree of trust and must be willing to expose themselves to a degree of their choice. This gives rise to a completely different (but not necessarily more equal) economy of power and it raises certain questions as to the ethics of the performance.

Before turning to the aesthetics strategies commonly employed in one-on-ones, and discussing points of criticism, it will be illuminating to take a look at a few examples that can help contextualize the debate. Performance artist Franko B, who has performed a number of one-on-one pieces, stresses that, in his work, intimacy is a matter of trust and confession. In his performance *Aktion 893 – Why Are You Here?* (Glasgow 2005), eight participants were shown to a waiting room where they waited until their number was called. They then went to a separate room where they were asked to undress completely. Then the artist entered the room, fully dressed, and asked the spectator, or rather the participant, why they were here. Participants were then free to talk about any subject they liked. '[I]t's fundamentally confessional, [they] tell me things they never tell anyone maybe it's true, maybe not. Certainly there is the element of therapy or people projecting things onto you' (Franko B in Zerihan 2009: 11).

The element of nudity is certainly crucial to the performance. It surely is embarrassing to most people to be naked in front of a stranger. Nudity alone has connotations of intimacy and apparently people felt free to speak 'the naked truth' or confess something they would not have disclosed otherwise. The performer here becomes a strange mixture of confessor and therapist whom spectators seem to trust intuitively because he is in a position of power. In this special case, people may even feel akin to the situation in a doctor's examination room because they are naked and the other person is not. Like a doctor who professionally examines a subject, Franko B thus gains a form of authority. However, it is clear that this is still a performance – at least it is to Franko B.

> A couple of people [who experienced the piece] said to me 'This is the most intimate moment I've had with anybody that's not my boyfriend'. [I thought] Intimate moment? Where?! [They see] the intimate in coming to a space where you have to take your clothes off – but it's a performance, at the end of the day, it's a construct. At the same time, though, there is this amazing cathartic moment that happens to people, this momentary realisation of 'Shit, this is very intimate, I feel very good'. (in Zerihan 2009: 14)

It is obvious that the perception and ontological definition of the event fundamentally differ between the performer, who deals with eight participants every night, and the spectator, who has a one-time, unique experience. It remains to be seen what intimacy can mean in this context and whether all intimacy is not simply another fake, theatrical tool, a shiny make-believe version of the truth – and so in fact a lie. Other performance artists, such as the late Adrian Howells, have a very different take on their performances. They indeed want to try and connect with their audience. 'I was craving a more authentic, nourishing experience of exchange with another human being and one-to-one performance was able to facilitate this' (Howells in Zerihan 2009: 34). In his *Foot Washing for the Sole*, he washes the feet of one participant. This is done in a very sensual fashion where he caresses the foot, makes contact with the participant and generates moments of intimacy and confession in his conversation. 'This provides a space that is resistant to the spectacular society of representations, through its emphasis on touch and presence, and to the economic domination of mass communication and virtual relationships through its emphasis on physical intimacy' (Tomlin 2013: 180). The goal, according to him, is some form of real intimacy through touch and physical proximity. The question that must be asked in this case is, however, whether this is still performance. What distinguishes such a performance from, say, a paid massage or the work of a physiotherapist? In other words, is there still something that gives the performance an artistic quality or is it simply another professional 'performance' of a service? If one were to place such an event on a continuum with theatre on the one end and performance art at the other, it would surely have to be located much closer to performance art, which usually follows a pattern of actions but does not employ make-believe. Howell's actions are real and also mimic the reality of a paid service, but they promise an intimate encounter and also promise artistic quality. This hints at the fact that most one-on-one performances are hybrids between paid service, performance art and theatre.

Aesthetic strategies

There are a number of aesthetic strategies that most one-on-ones make use of. These can be broadly characterized as a type of relational aesthetics, a certain economy of power and as mechanisms of trust and the real. The concept of 'relational aesthetics' was first suggested and defined by Nicolas Bourriaud, who sought to explain a range of works by visual artists from the 1990s. In his opinion, these works could no longer be conceived of simply as objects that are on some level perceived by a spectator, but they had to be understood as objects that created human relations. In a nutshell, for him, relational artworks provide: (a) moments of sociability or are (b) objects producing moments of sociability (cf. Bourriaud 2002: 33). That is to say, the spectator-artwork relationship is no longer the aim of the artists. The work of art only serves the purpose to produce contact between human beings in a gallery space.

> [T]his generation of artists considers inter-subjectivity and interaction neither as fashionable theoretical gadgets, not [sic] as additives (alibis) of a traditional artistic practice. It takes them as a point of departure and as an outcome, in brief, as the main informers of their activity. What they [artists of the 1990 generation] produce are relational space-time elements, inter-human experiences trying to rid themselves of the straitjacket of the ideology of mass communication, in a way, of the places where alternative forms of sociability, critical models and moments of constructed conviviality are worked out. (Bourriaud 2002: 44)

A work of art in this sense is, for instance, Doris Salcedo's *Shibboleth* (2007): a giant crack that spanned the entirety of Tate Modern's turbine hall (cf. Oddey and White 2009: 8). The crack itself was not important, but the experiences and human interactions it facilitated were. People were looking at the crack, began talking to each other, musing about the object, children played in and around it. The work of art, in Bourriaud's sense, consisted of the human encounters and relations that took place in the space. The project encouraged communication in a place where communication and interaction among strangers is usually not common. Other artists have experimented, and are experimenting until today, with crossover works from the fields of visual art and performance art. The ultimate goal in this is again to create human interaction and to facilitate contact.

> In international exhibitions we have seen [in the 1990s] a growing number of stands offering a range of services, works proposing a precise contract to viewers, and more or less tangible models of sociability. Spectator 'participation', theorised by Fluxus happenings and performances, has become a constant feature of artistic practice. (Bourriaud 2002: 25)

I want to suggest that one-on-one can be understood as another expression of relational aesthetics. Its main aim is to facilitate human connection or even relationships. Whether these are genuine is quite another question (cf. Gomme 2015: 293). However, it is clear that one-on-ones more often than not make use of relational techniques. As Bourriaud already implies when he refers to 'services' and 'contracts', there is a very strong aspect of economization within such works. Spectators buy a certain service (artwork/performance). Art is thus fitted into the capitalist discourse of a service economy, where artistic experience can be bought at leisure and one is only limited by one's own financial means. Whether this is a general feature of the art market today or whether such service-performances betray any ideal of *l'art pour l'art* and artistic liberty is debateable and largely depends on one's definition of art. However, as Rancière has suggested, art is inherently political and must use its powers to display and change inequality and politics. 'Artistic practices are "ways of doing and making" that intervene in the general distribution of ways of doing and making as well as in the relationships they maintain to modes of being and forms of visibility' (Rancière 2011: 13). With this view in mind, one would have to admit that art should subvert concepts of demand and supply, service and payment, contract and performance. Art degrades itself to simply another good among others if it uses the service economy model uncritically.

'I had to explain to people that it's not necessarily a performance any more than it is a personal service, like a masseuse or a hairdresser or, I suppose, a prostitute.' Howells too describes his work in utilitarian terms. 'You go to my shows to get yourself revitalised, recharged, re-energised.' (Howells in Logan 2010)

If the artist becomes a prostitute, what remains is capitalism and payment. The artistic event becomes a commodity that is structured along the lines of exchange value. But furthermore, the contract also puts in place a very firm set of rules, which sometimes are explicitly stated and sometimes unknown to the participant.

[S]cript, score, and performance rules (or lack of) play a large part in the performer/audience dynamics within the work, and in turn who is 'in charge'/'guiding' the experience, and how the performance is structured. [...] [Audiences] need to know what their 'role' is within the encounter, with many people stating that they are worried about 'getting it wrong'. (Zerihan 2009: 68)

The power economy between participant and performer is an equivocal one. If the rules are unknown or the participant is shy, the performer has the participant more or less at her mercy. If, on the other hand, the rules are known or the participant actively embraces the performance, the roles of performer and spectator enter into a state of flux. They are mutually informative and yet, while one may be the guiding person, both parties perform in their own way and in their own right. They both gain a share of 'the sensible'; they both speak in their own voice and participate in the discourse. 'Politics plays itself out in the theatrical paradigm as the relationship between the stage and the audience, as meaning produced by the actor's body, as games of proximity and distance' (Rancière 2011: 17). This game of distance and proximity is a dangerous one because the performer on the one hand demands that the participant be active, but on the other hand does not grant them complete liberty. In other words, one may very well find a voice as a participant, but the rules of engagement in this situation are enforced by the performer. Sometimes they are explicitly given beforehand; sometimes a participant will not know them at all. In such a situation, the performance that pretends to abolish distance and empower spectators by making them participants in fact establishes an even more rigid power structure. Whereas in traditional theatres the power economy and behavioural rules are very clear-cut (e.g. stay silent, applaud when appropriate), in such a situation the participant is thrown into a limbo of uncertainty. Not knowing where to look and how to behave or where her place is, she has to rely on the performer who steers her and steers the performance. Effectively, in many one-on-one performances, the performer is fully in control, while the spectator remains in a state of substantial uncertainty or discomfort. This is partly an explanation for the thrill of one-on-ones and their widely felt popularity. The performance becomes more lifelike: you make choices and see what happens without having a guideline for your behaviour. But it also dramatically shows that participants need a considerable degree of trust in order to experience a one-on-one.

However, as neither performer nor the performance will usually be known to the participants, they must advance their trust. If we want to stay with the economic metaphors: it is a future bond that may yield considerable interest or may default. This situation is then often perceived as a very real danger. The performance could go completely wrong: one could embarrass oneself or be embarrassed in front of others. One-on-one is experimental and dangerous because one never knows what is going to happen and how people will react (cf. Zerihan 2009: 12). This danger is inherent in the concept of trust. 'An aesthetic of trust is, ultimately, a stance toward Reality, not toward objects. At the *far limit* such a stance demands identification with Reality itself, dissolution of the distinction between the I and not-I' (Hassan 2003: 211). A one-on-one performance is an experience of reality. Reality in this sense means not only the contact with another human being but the genuine possibility of failure, embarrassment and a future unknown. One-on-one revives what people could be experiencing in their everyday life (unknown futures, possible failure etc.) but it aestheticizes this experience.

Ant Hampton runs the Rotozaza company, whose show Etiquette has toured the world. He too can't stand audience participation. 'When you've got actors on stage, they're coated with this veneer of the rehearsed performer. No matter how hard they try, they know what's coming next and you don't. For participation to be truly non-exploitative, you need to remove this imbalance – or remove actors altogether.' (Logan 2010)

Therefore, Rotozaza uses two spectator-participants as performers. In *Etiquette*, two participants who might well be strangers are given headphones in a public space, such as a Café, through which they are given instructions on what to do or say. Frequently, other people will not even notice that a performance is going on next to them, as the 'performers' simply look like everyday persons executing everyday actions. Thus participants have a genuine encounter with a stranger that may well be perceived as real or intimate. For instance, Gomme describes a performance of *Etiquette* at BAC's festival in 2010 as a 'commitment to an unknown other' (2015: 296). During the performance she and the stranger acted out a scene from a play unknown to them. Yet, like a precisely timed clockwork they interacted, both according to their own script: 'Sound effects, and occasional lines of dialogue over the headphones, coincide with the gestures we are asked to make (my companion points to the table as I hear a man's voice say "This is the stage")' (2015: 296). In this precisely planned encounter, the participant has to play along, or the performance would fail. Consequently, there is a certain pressure on the participants, a real moment of excitement and possible failure.

> The combination of actual physical engagement and enacting the scene on the 'stage' opens an unnerving sense of raw exposure to a stranger, a closeness [...] I also have a sense of having shared something unique with my companion – our struggle to grasp and follow our instructions, our mutual bewilderment as we occasionally gaze at one another, at a loss to make them out, speaks of a concerted effort to make something happen together, between us. (Gomme 2015: 296)

The possibility of failure and the direct, 'raw' exposure to a stranger will of course be perceived as more or less authentic. The performance enacts an encounter between two genuine human beings. The everyday life of participants is mirrored in the reality of the performance because effectively it is the same experience people could have in their lives but chose to ignore, get used to or consciously eliminate. The theatre space becomes the venue where this aestheticized version of 'Reality' can be purchased and played out. The heightened state of tension that a one-on-one produces seems to reconnect participants with a reality they perceive as lacking. Funk, along with Albert Borgman, argues for the existence of a non-mediated reality as opposed to a superficial media 'reality *lite*' (Funk 2015: 44–45, italics in the original). The one-on-one experience subverts 'reality lite' and brings back genuine human processes and anxieties.

Criticism

Obviously, one-on-one performances have been criticized for precisely these power games, their dubious ontological status and whether they actually can achieve any of their goals. '[J]ust because a One to One is about two people connecting with each other it doesn't necessarily mean that intimacy automatically exists' (Zerihan 2009: 6). Intimacy is very much desired and facilitated by many one-on-ones, but Zerihan correctly points out that a number of factors can prevent such an experience from happening. It is to a very large degree up to the participant and also to the performer's mood or feelings, whether (fake) intimacy arises. Furthermore, one could ask why the intimacy in one-on-ones is so special, and what sets it apart from intimacy that happens in a 2000-seat auditorium.

> But are they really any more intimate than more traditional shows? In both, it seems to me, the idea of intimacy is an illusion, albeit here one taken to an extreme. At their best, these plays can be exhilarating; at worst, they are emotional porn. (Gardner 2009)

Traditional theatre may also be able to deliver very intense and intimate moments that are also felt to be 'real' by an audience member. However, they still provide a clear set of rules and power division, thus protecting their audience. In terms of ethics they often tread on much more solid ground because they do not run the danger of producing 'emotional porn' by exposing spectators or encouraging them to navel gaze their own petty issues. Specifically, if the rules are not clearly laid out before the participant, feelings of uncertainty or anxiety are not unlikely to occur. In terms of ethics, it is questionable in how far an artist may 'use' his 'guinea pig participants'. '"One-on-one" is fascinating an entire new generation of theatre goers. But is it drama at its most gripping? Or a dangerous and exploitative power trip?' (Logan 2010). In other words, does drama, if one removes the safe distance between audience and performer (specifically the physical one), produce any effects that are so much more intense that they justify all the emotional disturbance of the participants? Furthermore, when this dividing line is abolished, spectators have been known to mistake the performance for 'the real thing'. 'There are stories of artists being stalked by audience members who believed there was real intimacy, and of theatre-goers being left genuinely distressed by their experience' (Gardner 2009).

A one-on-one performance usually tries to play it as real as possible. Afterwards, if a participant finds out that the whole event was only a show, a performance that is repeated night after night, she may rightly feel upset or even betrayed. Effectively, if artists try to mislead participants into thinking that something real is happening, they simply lie to them. The lie of 'real intimacy' is a tool for artists to play out their own ideas and fantasies of performance and intimacy. Spectators have a right to the truth or at least to know what they are up for, so this argument runs. In other words, the borders of the fictional world of performance must be delineated. This, of course, leaves one-on-one artists with a dilemma: the abolition of the dividing line between fiction and reality, and between performance and life is their very artistic measure. Consequently, one-on-one performance must remain in this state of paradox. This conflict cannot be resolved.

Finally, a case has been made against one-on-ones on structural grounds. It has been claimed that one-on-one furthers social isolation, one of the very things it tries to battle (cf. Logan 2010). Whereas theatre traditionally has been a communal event, one-on-ones have turned it into just another personalized consumer product. The event is experienced alone and one could summarize the logic of the event along these lines: in order to escape pathologic loneliness, I booked an event for myself (and me only) that will make me experience intimate contact with another human being. One-on-ones, in this view, effectively prefer selfishness over sharing (cf. 2010). They thus perpetuate the logic of possession and exchange value and fundamentally continue to separate people rather than bring them into genuine contact.

Internal (2009): The betrayed spectator

One of the first theatre companies to celebrate wider critical success with one-on-one performance and one that is still prolifically active in this field today is Belgium-based performance group Ontroerend Goed. Founded in 1994, their name roughly translates to 'touchingly good, [or] so good it moves you' (Costa 2011). They have been experimenting with the concept of one-on-one performance, with a specific focus on notions of collectivity, solitude and interhuman relations. The group's founder, Alexander Devriendt, describes the intention for making their piece *The Smile Off Your Face* (2007) – which is still touring today (cf. Armitstead 2013) – as follows:

'The basic idea for that was to change the whole experience of theatre. Normally you're with 100 people: [with us] you're alone. Normally you're immobile: let's make you mobile. Normally you can see: let's take that away.' What resulted was a piece in which audience-members were blindfolded and bound into a wheelchair, then had each of their senses teased before a final, unsettling moment of intimacy with a performer. (in Costa 2011)

While this piece was quite experimental in a number of ways, Ontroerend Goed quickly found what has since become their signature style of one-on-one performance. At the festival in 2009, their performance *Internal* became 'Edinburgh's most discussed show' (Dickson 2009). It has been characterized as 'a mixture of speed-dating and group therapy' (Gardner 2009). The format is quite straightforward: five performers interact with five participants at a time. In the show, each participant was shown to a separate space with one performer where they were

> sitting at a little restaurant table opposite a handsome actor, usually of the opposite sex, who offers a glass of wine, gazes into their eyes, and then begins to make contact, either by asking searching questions about life and love, or by asking if they can hold hands, touch your face, stroke your hair. (McMillan 2009)

The performers started a conversation, trying to build trust, and they always made sure not to talk about themselves too much but to have the participant narrate as much and as personally as possible about her own life. Questions could become very intimate (e.g. 'Would you kiss me?'). After a twenty-minute or so session, the performers and participants all came together as a group and each performer talked about the person they had encountered. They explicitly enumerated what they had found out, what they liked but also the secrets they had been trusted with (e.g. 'What I don't like about her is that she would have kissed me although she has a boyfriend. She's a cheat'). Obviously this strategy came as hurtful or even as a form of betrayal to participants who had advanced trust and honesty towards the performers. After this 'group session', actors danced with the participants, apologized for disclosing their secrets and wrote a nice letter to the participants, telling them again the positive things they had found out about them. The letter was, after the show, posted to their home address. It was signed with the same name performers had given during the performance. Whether this name was their true name or whether it was a stage persona remained open.

The whole performance is designed to mislead participants into believing that something real is happening, for example that they are talking to a real person. Of course participants must be conscious of the theatrical situation; but in an experimental performance, it is always possible that you meet a real character and not a staged version, is it not? The performance is designed to seem like a real encounter with a real person and not like part of a performance. This naturally entails the elimination of all factors that normally denote theatricality and make-believe. The abolition of any audience–performers division is the first step in this direction. Performers frequently made physical contact with participants by holding hands or caressing them. This physical contact was always made only with the consent of the participants and in a sensual, positive and warm fashion. Because of this, for many spectators, it served as a trigger for mental proximity. The whole setting was, furthermore, designed to emanate a sense of homeliness and comfort. The participants were served wine, and they sat together with their performer in a warm and dimly lit room at a small table. The setting thus also induced participants to 'let down their guard' and forget about the theatrical situation. Finally, performers always played (?) or were to a degree even themselves. They introduced themselves by their first names and never did the impression arise that they were reciting lines of prefabricated text, but they always talked directly with the participants and about the participant's life and views. The performers warranted their own trustworthiness anti-reductively (cf. Faulkner 2007: 543–544); that is, the audience believed that there was no evidence of them being deceitful or mendacious in any way. Consequently, the audience was brought into a state of 'willed dependence' (2007: 546) because it advanced considerable trust towards the performers. That is to say, the performers took up the manipulative position of the misleader and thus established a power economy that was firmly on their side. As a consequence of the supposed trust, a number of participants opened up substantially and the effect of both the encounter and the betrayal was profound on them. '[A] girl in my group said she'd cried as a result of what she'd gone through; on the other hand, someone else was enchanted, genuinely touched by the intimacy Internal seemed to offer' (Dickson 2009). The breach of trust is one of the fundamental strategies of the performance and its consequences in terms of politics are profound.

Whilst I would argue that Internal was designed to induce a critical response, there were clearly those who were overwhelmed by its strategies of seduction and were unable, or unwilling, to read the structure of the piece once it was exposed. For those who had a pleasurable experience this would position the piece as compensational in my terms. For those who had a distressing experience this would position the piece as politically disempowering. (Tomlin 2013: 204)

The promise of an authentic moment and the promise of unbounded intimacy with a stranger were very strong siren calls for a number of participants, which they willingly embraced. The performer is a stranger who can be trusted because he is precisely that: a stranger. Just as one would be able to confess one's secrets easier to a professional stranger (e.g. a priest or a doctor), the performance creates the possibility to finally 'get something off one's chest' or give in to one's unacknowledged desires in a safe setting. No one must and will ever hear about this. As we have lost the confessor to theological doubt, he is replaced by a paid performer who creates the illusion of safety and confession, or – as Foucault has it – by the therapist who alleviates our psychological distress (cf. Butler 2008: 161). But was it really an illusion? Did the performers lie to their audience? In the strict sense, they never told them that they would keep their secrets (lie), but their behaviour and the setting surely implied confidentiality (misleading). Deception here is an artistic measure, but to what purpose? Why is this betrayal needed? Macmillan suggests that the piece should be interpreted with Erving Goffman's dictum of 'the performative self' (cf. 1959) in mind. For him, it 'makes us think about truth and lies in such encounters. These actors are probably adopting fictional characters; but then how often are any of us completely truthful in presenting ourselves to others' (Macmillan 2009)? The performers and participants both present themselves in a certain, truthful (?) way to the other. The performance thus mimics real life in the performative sense. In other words, to a large degree, it is the participant who makes the performance. Depending on their input and openness, the performance changes radically.

But one of the things that makes the piece so strange, and also so troubling, is that you're never quite certain who's performing. Or, to put it more precisely, you're suspicious that perhaps it's not the professionals up there in the spotlight, but you. (Dickson 2009)

Dickson is right when she remarks that it is, as a matter of fact, the participant and not the performer who is in the limelight. The show is all about creating personal experience. The betrayal is part of this concept. The show can 'be moving, devastating, almost life-changing' (Macmillan 2009), but it can also be boring, if the participant adopts the same strategy of lying or simply chooses not to disclose anything personal. The thrill and success of the performance is equal to the emotional investment and amount of risk participants put in. If this investment is very small, the show has failed, for both, performer and participant.

Internal can be divided into two phases. First, there is the trust-building phase. In it, feelings of trust and intimacy are created; they give the performance the quality of the authentic. The subsequent phase of betrayal destroys the trust but makes for a very real experience of embarrassment or anger. Any spectator thus has the chance to experience emotional processes that are genuinely real. However, this all depends on their willingness to play along.

[T]he tables are almost entirely turned: the risk lies with us, not them. It's up to us what we reveal, what we don't, which boundaries we allow to be breached, which we defend. We take a gamble, and we deal with the consequences. (Dickson 2009)

Figuring out the level of participation will, however, prove a difficult exercise for the participants because they have no knowledge of the show's rules beforehand and they are not party to the rules of the game, while the performers are (cf. Gardner 2009). Such a disparity in power and knowledge begs the question of abuse and lacking ethical standards.

The company was accused of betraying the trust of its audience, something Devriendt regrets. 'I should have seen that one coming. When you confide something to somebody, I think you [feel a] need to communicate. But it wasn't my intention to be mean about that.' (Costa 2011)

As was shown above, the relationship between performer and participant may be meaningful, but chances are that this perception is stronger on the side of the participant, who may feel genuinely intimate with the performer. Whether the performer in this phase feels the same is uncertain. In the betrayal phase that follows, a meaningful relationship does surely not exist anymore. A certain degree of abuse or unethical behaviour (cf. Logan 2010) is arguably part of the show and it is certain that this show is definitely not [...] for the fragile (Gardner 2009). Both, the amount of emotional pleasure or even satisfaction as well as the degree of abuse completely depend on the participant's willingness to play along and to open up. Each participant is thus responsible for one's own actions but also one's own satisfaction. *Internal* focused on the responsibility of each individual for their actions and the amount of privacy they shared with strangers.

> What Internal revealed was that, after years of passively receiving theatre, audiences are unpractised in disentangling reality and illusion; and that one-on-one's exponents have a duty of care towards participants. 'One-on-one throws up those questions,' says Jubb. 'Who is in control? Who's the author? Who is responsible to whom?' (Logan 2010)

Internal, as many other one-on-ones, creates a space of individual responsibility and tailor-made experience. One chooses one's own show and the amount of danger through the inputs that regulate the potential gains. At the same time, *Internal* is a comment on the current state of affairs when it comes to disclosure, personal information and intimacy. Alexander Devriendt explained that they wanted to show how fast one could build a meaningful relationship with a stranger (cf. Logan 2010). 'Meaningful relation' here seems simply another term for a space of sociability. *Internal* draws on relational aesthetics by promising spaces where the spectator can connect on a face-to-face level with another individual. In this encounter, confessions can be made that seemingly enjoy the protection of professional secrecy. Audiences were mostly willing to open up substantially; they craved intimacy and personal contact. The event was experienced by them as a real, authentic, protected space, where secrets could be voiced, or confessions could be made. However, the end of the performance hits them hard with the 'real real'. This 'real real' comes in the shape of betrayal, which of course is also part of everyday life but is rarely acknowledged. Spectators are thus confronted with sentiments of authenticity twice: once in the guise of fake-authenticity and sincerity and later on with the reality of a genuine betrayal. The use of betrayal is the artistic measure that exposes pseudo authenticity and intimacy. *Internal* gives its audience first a lovely warm bath in feelings of trust, human contact and intimacy, only to give them the 'reality-check' straight after. It is a *caveat*, which stresses that meaningful relations cannot be built in minutes. As Rachel Gomme has pointed out, most one-on-ones are very short (cf. 2015: 289). Indeed, I would go so far as to claim that the very brevity of most one-on-one performances is a prerequisite for perceived intimacy. If they lasted for as long as, say, *Quizoola!*, how could a performer uphold a mask? How could one not enter into an encounter with another human being that goes beyond make-believe? The sentiments of intimacy and authenticity that are fake and destroyed by the performers can only be generated in short duration. This is a clue that audiences do not seek an intimate encounter with another human being (which they could also have in their everyday life), but the aestheticized version of it.

London Stories (2013): True stories?

Another slightly different experiment with moments of intimacy and one-on-one performance was created at Battersea Arts Centre in 2013. '[T]he theatre issued an open call for Londoners willing to share their stories, receiving over 100 responses' (Love 2013). The ensuing festival featured thirty-five Londoners, all non-professional actors, who told their stories to an audience of two.

The stories are fragments excavated from the lives of ordinary people. The genius is in the presentation: each story is delivered by a single storyteller to just two audience members at a time. You move from candlelit room to candlelit room through a maze of corridors as disorientating as the streets of London; along the way you connect briefly with strangers. (Gardner 2013)

The festival was named *London Stories* because the aim was to represent the city with its myriad stories and millions of inhabitants in a cross-cut sample. The stories themselves were as diverse as could be expected, ranging from tales of sickness and loss to stories of triumph, laughter, the everyday and the absurd. Each participant delivered his or her own story to an audience of two people who had never met before but were sent on the way together. Colour cards marked the path they had to follow and every pair of spectators perceived different stories, a different mixture of them and in a different order.

[Y]ou're sent on an odyssey through the vast Victorian town hall. On your travels you'll hear seven true autobiographical stories from seven Londoners, scattered throughout BAC's prodigious accumulation of nooks and crannies. (Lukowski 2013)

The festival celebrated success with audiences and critics alike. *The Guardian* gave the performances three stars and found that 'this simple, brilliant presentation reminds us that the extraordinary is found in the most ordinary lives' (Gardner 2013). Nancy Groves from *Whats On Stage* magazine gave it four stars and called the show 'magical' (Groves 2013). But even more interesting is the user rating at *Time Out* online, where the show received five stars (cf. Lukowski 2013). It is telling that, while theatre critics were full of praise, the non-professional critics (i.e. the online users) gave the show the highest marks. Apparently, the promise of true stories, delivered by real people, was extremely appealing to a broad spectrum of audiences. The offer of seeing something authentic, something real, on stage is attractive to audiences. But what is more, it was also felt that during the performance of these true stories, there were 'the moments where the mask slips and a more genuine connection between performer and audience member might just be possible' (Love 2013). In other words, not only the authenticity of the stories procured an effect but also the individual experience of the stories with just one other person in the room had a major impact on spectators. Similar to Ontroerend Goed's projects, in such a situation of close physical proximity and an individual encounter between only three people, a feeling of intimacy is created. The story, it seems, is just told for two persons and no one else. The act of storytelling here is a very individual one, as the stories are often also very personal, along the lines of 'I trust you and will tell you my story'. In this performance, it is the performer who must advance trust towards the spectators. She must trust that they are worthy of hearing her story. No betrayals take place here.

> Immersive theatre this isn't, despite the show's roots in BAC's critically acclaimed One-On-One festivals in 2010 and 2011. Instead, this is pared-down old-fashioned storytelling at its best from a cast of 35 ordinary Londoners, each with an eight-minute story to relate and a candlelit room of their own to do it in. (Groves 2013)

The event is experienced as intimate, and at the same time – because the stories and the people telling them are real – another element of authenticity comes into play. One is faced with a genuine person, who tells her true story and does not play a role, or does she? The question must be asked whether in this setting people simply tell stories or whether they were coached in their way of telling, or, if the stories were even improved dramaturgically by theatrical professionals from BAC.

> Each performer has clearly been coached to the point they can deliver their tale interestingly and with confidence. But there's not too much polish – several storytellers become very emotional, and you never forget something very intimate is being shared. (Lukowski 2013)

On the other hand, if the storyteller is really just a person telling a story and not conscious of the theatricality of the situation, is this then still theatre? In other words, if one wants to bring 'the real' on stage at a

1:1 scale, is there then still a stage, or is this just an everyday situation? Richard Dufty, BAC's head of producing, commented that their approach to this event had been driven by the desire to strip away layers of artifice from the theatrical event (cf. Love 2013). According to him, "'[a] lot of the performance that we're interested in here is performance that is reaching for the real," he says, quickly adding, "whatever that means'" (in Love 2013). This ominous real, that he is quick to mark with the *caveat* 'whatever that means', is, however, something that has played a major role in theatre and the arts in general. Bourriaud has located this trend in a renewed interest in practices of the everyday. 'Above all, the everyday now turns out to be a much more fertile terrain than "pop culture" – a form that only exists in contrast to "high culture", through it and for it' (Bourriaud 2002: 47). However vaguely defined, the 'real' has a major attraction on art practitioners and, as the success of *London Stories* shows, audiences alike. While the real has been and remains convincingly deconstructed, the authentic has taken its place. Certainly in many people's minds there is not even a difference between the two. Because the real has been made impossible in late capitalism, audiences and practitioners all the more sought and seek to regain it through artistic practices and consumption of authenticity, even if it means putting life on a 1:1 scale (pun intended) on stage. I want to suggest, however, that many practitioners and audiences are conscious of the theatrical situation they are in and they know very well how to distinguish between a true tale told and a true tale.

> For all his talk of honesty, however, Dufty acknowledges that through the repeated telling of these stories, they will inevitably be transformed into a kind of performance. No matter how intently we tear away at artifice, a thin layer will always remain. Despite his instinct to reach for the real, Dufty cautions that 'we shouldn't be naive about ever being able to reach it', adding 'there are always masks'. But this should not stop us from reaching nonetheless. 'Whilst you recognise that getting to absolute honesty is impossible, the pursuit of it is beautiful – the honest, genuine pursuit of it is a beautiful and very human thing.'
> (Love 2013)

This is precisely what *London Stories* does: it offers a 'pursuit of the beautiful' in the guise of the authentic. It does not offer the real thing because the real thing cannot be offered. But audiences are more than willing to go on the metamodern quest for the authentic and the real. The pleasure derived from such an experience is not to grasp an element of the real or the authentic itself, but to permit oneself the thought that the real might have happened, or may happen or may be grasped and if only for a fleeting glimpse. It is the joy of knowing that something real may have happened to this very storyteller in a land far off – called London.

3

Immersive Theatre

And all around, a crowd, far larger than I would have expected –
there must have been more than 200 people there – laughed and
applauded, wandering aimlessly from performance to performance.
[...] Were they spectators or part of the spectacle? It was hard to
be sure.

–*The House of Silk: A Sherlock Holmes Novel*
(Horowitz 2012: 315)

Introduction

Whereas intimate theatre is dedicated to authentic experiences created
by spectators/witnesses on a small scale, through means of intimacy,
this chapter devotes itself to almost the opposite in form and style:
immersive theatre. Immersive theatre is, more often than not, bombastic
and grand. It does not employ metarefrence but rather uses forms of
hot authenticity to draw each individual audience member into a world
of wonder and discovery, where every visitor will go on a tailor-made,
individual journey of exploration. Immersive theatre is a young strand
of theatre, certainly not older than twenty years. Its first appearance in
the theatrical world can be located somewhere around the end of the
last century.

Since the late twentieth century a performance style has emerged
which exploits diverse artistic languages to establish an 'experiential'
audience event via the recreation of visceral experience. Impossible
to define as a genre due to the fluidity of the forms explored, this

performance style places emphasis on the human body as a primary force of signification and utilizes the ever-increasing possibilities in design and technology. (Machon 2009: 1)

As is evident, the performances and styles vary greatly from company to company and sometimes even from show to show. Some performance groups, such as Blast Theory, are heavily influenced by transmediality and digital media, and their shows consequently make use of state-of-the-art technology and virtual realities (cf. Machon 2013: xvi). Others, such as You Me Me Bum Bum Train, employ the device of a wheelchair that transports one single audience member through a number of different scenes and scenarios, in which they are encouraged to interact with the performers or are even 'forced' to participate (cf. Cavendish 2013). Again, other companies, such as dreamthinkspeak, create complete environments, often taking over entire buildings, in which the spectator can roam and explore at liberty (cf. Cavendish 2013; Machon 2013: 19–20). 'Immersive theatre' is an umbrella term under which a very diverse range of performances are placed. It is thus impossible to define it as a whole, but certain shared characteristics may be described (cf. Machon 2013: xvi).

One of the pioneering groups, if not *the* pioneering group, in this field is certainly Punchdrunk, who have been numerously praised for their attention to detail but also their skill of execution (cf. Cavendish 2013; Jones 2013; Machon 2013: 3; Remshardt 2008: 643). Strangely enough, theatre and performance studies seem to have had a rather hard time coming to terms with this new kind of theatre in a scholarly fashion. Too little has been written on immersive theatre, and only two monographs have been dedicated to it so far (cf. Machon 2009, 2013). In other academic fields, however, the underlying principles of immersive theatre have been scrutinized very prolifically and fruitfully. Under the terms of 'presence' and 'immersion', computer science, game studies and communication studies have delivered interesting results (cf. Bainbridge 2011; Grau 2003). The idea of immersion and individual exploration seems to be naturally within the domain of computer gaming where the experience for a single player is key. Immersive theatre is one of the cousins of immersive gaming and it is no accident that Punchdrunk, in 2011, designed an advertising prequel for Sony's computer game *Resistance 3*. In this 'immersive advert', participants were quite literally thrown into the post-apocalyptic world of the play, which had been constructed in the vaults underneath London Bridge Station (cf. Hoggins 2011). This cross-over between advertising, theatre and immersive video gaming is indicative for many facets in terms of ontology and poetics of immersive theatre.

Approaches

The term itself entered the theatrical canon around 2007 and also rose to prominence in that decade (cf. Machon 2013: 66). Before that, critics had been uneasy as to how to define the events they were describing. Most often, the words 'promenade theatre' or 'site-specific theatre' were employed. However, as Dominic Cavendish elaborates, the term

'site-specific theatre' [is] a term already cloudy with imprecision. It sort of meant 'theatrical things taking place in unusual, often unoccupied locations with the audience up on their feet, playing a participatory role', but didn't always involve a cast-iron commitment to the space's ambience or history. (Cavendish 2013)

Gareth White makes a similar distinction, claiming that 'site-specific' should only be employed for performances that work directly with the site's history, structure and so on, and create performances that can only ever be performed there. He suggests that companies such as Punchdrunk or Shunt 'make work that is site-sympathetic: they create the work for the site where it is to be performed, but without responding directly to that site's history or context' (White 2012: 223). Immersive theatre can be conceived of as a combination of both site-specific and promenade work, but superseding them both in its totality. Its central feature is – the clue is in the name – that audiences are completely surrounded: physically and sensorially involved in the event. For Josephine Machon, being immersed in a theatrical event means 'being submerged in an alternative medium where all the senses are engaged and manipulated – with a deep involvement in the activity within that medium' (2013: 21–22). In practical terms this means that audiences will enter a non-theatrical building that has been fitted to embody a different world through a number of media (set, audio, visual, digital, etc.), in which they can roam and explore freely. In most immersive works, there is no guideline as to which path to follow or which direction to take. The traditional separation between audience and performers is minimized and in most cases spectators are able to get very close to the action. '[S]pectators are able to approach and examine the performers, invading their space while they accomplish the complex job of telling and inhabiting a story, but doing so in among the spectators and without the aid of a clearly differentiated space' (White 2012: 225).

Performers 'might grab your hands and run through corridors, initiate dances, separate people from the crowd and take them into a secluded space for a private encounter' (White 2009: 221). Each audience member is not only a passive spectator but is an active participator both in terms of exploration and also in terms of interaction. Immersive events can be on a large scale (epic) or on a smaller scale, or even outdoors (cf. Pringle 2013). Immersive theatre is interdisciplinary, it blurs

> the boundaries between installation, performance, private and public ritual, underground gigs and open-air festivals. Often these events incorporate elements from varied disciplines, including architecture, improvisation, storytelling, spoken and/or physical performance, dance, circus skills, aerial arts, puppetry, sculpture, digital or mechanical animation, gaming sound, film video, audio and/or haptic technologies. (Machon 2013: 97)

In the shows of Punchdrunk, for instance, classical acting, sounds, storytelling and even complete magic shows are employed. As becomes evident, immersive theatre is rooted in a number of different disciplines. The association with notions of Wagner's *Gesamtkunstwerk* or Artaud's theatre of cruelty readily imposes itself, almost like a knee-jerk reflex (cf. Machon 2013: 29–31). It is obvious that immersive theatre is also indebted to a number of experiments with form and content, beginning in the first half of the twentieth century.

> This species of fringe enterprise [i.e. immersive theatre] could lay claim to honourable antecedents. One might look back to the 1960s and 1970s and the hippy fad for pop-up happenings, the emergence of 'installation art' as a category, and the work of Peter Brook, whose pioneering 1968 text 'The Empty Space' issued a clarion-call to recognise that anywhere, indoors or out, can be a 'theatre'. In the 1990s, other notable directors tested the possibilities of scouting for unusual locations and letting select numbers of people roam through their responses to them – chief among them American avant-gardist Robert Wilson and Deborah Warner, the latter creating ghostly apparitions in the former St Pancras hotel and celestial imagery in derelict offices at Euston Tower (1999). (Cavendish 2013)

One can make out other forerunners in Wilson's earlier works, for instance in his seven-day outdoor play *KA MOUNTAIN AND GARDenia TERRACE*, which was staged in 1972 in Iran (cf. Otto-Bernstein 2006: 263), and certainly a number of other theatrical experimentations in the 1960s and 1970s can lay a claim to ancestry here. Josephine Machon argues that immersive theatre is also heavily indebted to Allan Kaprow's happenings, which sought to blur the line between art and real life. She maintains that although many immersive performances are repeated and strictly choreographed, the experience for every individual member would be different even if they saw it ten times in a row (cf. Machon 2013: 31). While it is clear that the idea of blurring the boundary between life and art, or in this case truth and illusion, is present in immersive theatre, I would argue that the comparison between Kaprow's happenings and, say, a Punchdrunk show does not hold up. Kaprow placed great emphasis on spontaneity and the paradigm of an uncertain outcome (cf. Schechner 1970: 155–187). In other words, happenings sought to be entirely spontaneous, unrepeatable and very 'real' in that sense. Most immersive shows which I would sum up under that label, however, are repeated night after night and follow a strict structure and choreography, and, as will be shown, also uphold a strict power hierarchy. The pure chance operation, improvisation and acting-out-of-the-moment, which Kaprow had in mind, is something entirely different. Therefore, happenings should better be regarded as some distant uncle or cousin but not as immersive theatre's older brother. In general, it makes sense to trace a broad, genealogical lineage from installation art, happenings, environmental theatre, Artaud's 'total theatre' over to Grotowski's experiments with activating the audience (cf. Machon 2013: 38–40). Immersive theatre is certainly indebted to all of them while remaining an entirely new entity in the performing arts. This entity, as has been mentioned, can – due to diversity of forms – not be pinned down in one firm definition. Furthermore, many such performances are also diversified in terms of their immersivity. More to the point, a performance by, say, Punchdrunk may be considered to be more immersive than, say, one by Coney or Nimble Fish. Machon, therefore, very sensibly suggests to employ a 'scale of immersivity' along criteria such as space, scenography, sound, duration or physical presence/activity (cf. 2013: 93–100). The more such means are played out in a performance, the more immersive it becomes. The key feature of this kind of theatre is, however, always the notion of being completely immersed in the performance. In other words, audiences may well lose track of time and space while exploring. They are absorbed in the performance. All senses are activated and the entire performance is multi-sensorially experienced as a whole.

Immersive theatre's popularity

Immersive theatrical experiences have been immensely successful and extremely popular in the first decade of the millennium and have even found their way into fairly mainstream institutions. Britain's Royal National Theatre funded no less than two large-scale, immersive shows in 2013 (cf. National Theatre 2013a, b). The following section intends to survey reasons for this success. It will suggest that audiences' eagerness to have multisensory experiences is fuelled by a present that is perceived to be lacking experiences that are found to be 'real'.[1]

Specifically, the section will look at the changes theatre has undergone over the past 200 years and suggest that it failed to respond to audiences' need for authentic experiences. Theatre is here viewed as an expression of a wider cultural phenomenon that can be roughly described as a marginalization of contacts with the 'real'.

> The term 'site-specific theatre' itself 'privileges place' and removes theatre from the ideology of the theatre building and the (negative) associations that accompany it. It places work in direct relationship with the space [...] As we experience the world increasingly through a global mediatised lens, the formation of our identity through a direct relationship with space and locations is severely affected. Individuals are gradually removed from the life and communal arena which sit in a specific space and time, preferring the lure of an online community with a vast reach, but which sports no tangible physical or historical dimension. Site-specific theatre counters this by using locations as a 'potent mnemonic trigger, helping to evoke specific past times related to the place and time of performance and facilitating a negotiation between the meanings of those times'. (Lane 2010 quoting Jen Harvie: 98)

Just as in site-specific theatre, the often evocative locations of immersive theatre serve as a potent stimulus for audiences. Immersive theatre is perceived with the spectator's entire body, which moves through the theatrical space, explores, establishes contact and is both alone and part of a collective. Being immersed in this way readily suggests that the resulting experience supersedes conventional theatrical decoding.

> [W]e talk of 'immersing ourselves' in other experiences – new situations, cultures, environments – as well as conventional artworks like books and films, when we want to commit to them wholeheartedly and without distraction. The implication of the term 'immersive theatre' is that it has a special capacity to create this kind of deep involvement. (White 2009: 225)

Similar to Geertz's 'deep play'[2] (cf. 1972), White suggests that immersive theatre has the capacity to let audiences forget time and space and enter a state where they are completely absorbed by their experience (cf. 2012: 225). In this state of 'deep involvement', traditional mechanisms of distance or even critical reflection begin to diminish or may even become obsolete. The spectator is wholly immersed in her multisensorial experience. This experience is described to be more intense and lasting than just audio or visual stimulation, which happens in traditional theatre. It is clear that this notion will not sit well with a number of critics and it is to a degree highly problematic. A rift opens up here, between body and intellect, and it is already burdened with value judgements. While I do not intend to revisit the 'body-privileged-vs-intellect' debate (at this point), the fact cannot be ignored that audiences and scholars have felt that immersive theatre opens up for a deeper, to paraphrase Geertz again, 'thicker' experience (cf. Geertz 1973). This is not necessarily due to some privileged position of the other senses over mind and eyes, but it simply stresses that audiences in an immersive performance have a whole number more of sensual stimuli at their disposal than they would have in a 'traditional' theatrical performance. The experience resulting must necessarily be thicker than in a spectatorial theatre.

> [T]his style enables practitioners and audience members alike to tap into pre-linguistic communication processes and engages with an awareness of the 'primordial' via such sensually stimulated perception. […] As a result, this style produces a response of disturbances that can be simultaneously challenging and exhilarating, at once unsettling and pleasurable. (Machon 2009: 1)

It remains yet to be seen whether an immersive experience can have any claim to being 'primordial' or 'pre-linguistic'. What is interesting is Machon's observation that such an event may produce both unsettling and pleasurable sensations at the same time. She consequently sees immersive theatre as a prime example of what Kant would call a sublime experience (cf. Machon 2013: 49). Immersive theatre's sensual stimulation has the potential to both genuinely delight and be genuinely disturbing. This capacity then also hints at immersive theatre's sensorial and experiential potential. It creates strong sensorial stimuli, which can become an example of what Walter Benjamin has called *Erlebnis* as opposed to *Erfahrung* (cf. 1969: 163).[3] On another note, immersive also carries the notion of having a privileged experience, or of being very close to something genuine. Gareth White, applying the linguistic theories of Lakoff and Johnson, convincingly deconstructs immersivity to the point where the immersive metaphor signifies that it reveals something that is inside (cf. White 2012: 226). Inside is used by White in a Heideggerian sense, as the uncovering of something hidden, something that is actual. In Heidegger's sense: '[a]rt […] is an event of truth. Heidegger's conception of truth is complex, but it centres on an unconcealment of things in their essence and an unconcealment of this kind is possible in a successful work of art' (White 2012: 232). This form of 'unconcealment' obviously begs the question: Of what? Unconcealment of truth, authenticity, a secret and so on? Whatever it is that is excavated by a spectator in this event, it is something which had not been known before, something obscure but also something that was (consciously) covered and hidden. This mode of spectating is the prevalent *modus operandi* in many immersive pieces, where on the one level one has strong sensorial stimuli, which in turn validate the whole event as overwhelming or authentic. On another, more banal, level, the 'narrative' of the show itself is also apt for such unconcealment. Audiences may get a thrill out of this, as Cavendish argues, because 'in a world where so much is an instantly known commodity, not knowing what's round the corner or how you'll react when you find it isn't just an added boon, it's invaluable' (Cavendish 2013). The uncertainty with which such theatrical discovery is undertaken establishes genuine feelings of sublime pleasure and fear. It serves to create a theatre that is open to more possibilities and even a bit dangerous. Josephine Machon argues that Facebook and similar platforms have alienated audiences from real experiences such as danger or intimacy (cf. 2013: 26). She does not define what she means by 'real' intimacy, and the turn of phrase sounds very essentialist. However, intuitively, this seems to be a useful perception (cf. also Lane 2010: 98). One can rephrase her thought then with the help of authenticity's black box: audiences are in search of authentic experiences, be they intimacy, danger or something else. This is supported by all of the leading practitioners from the field of immersive theatre that Machon interviewed. They all gathered from their audience's feedback that there 'is a genuine wish to make *human contact*' (Machon 2013: 25). They also stress that audiences are so keen on their experiences because they spend so much time online (cf. 2013: 72). The online world of social networks is only virtual and by definition always mediated. Immersive theatre, however, is unmediated, first-hand, sensorial experience. Therefore, many immersive artists, along with Nicolas Bourriaud, see immersive practice as an 'antidote to the alienating experiences of globalisation and virtual socialising and networking' (2013: 121).

Modes of interactivity have been present in a number of branches of the entertainment industry for a number of years. They permeate all areas of culture, from video games to the internet and television (cf. Oddey & White 2009: 8–14). Interactivity here is almost synonymous with individual consumption of a tailor-made product.

> By the turn of the millennium, alongside a growing sense that theatre needed to answer the adrenalin rushes available to the younger generation in the wake of rave culture and thanks to advances in gaming technology, there were inklings of what was about to happen. (Cavendish 2013)

This new way of creating interactive journeys, which had already been developed in video gaming and television for a while, found its way into the theatre, transforming it from a collective experience into something individualistic. 'The new mode of spectating is to focus only on what "I" want to see; on my perception of the world as "I" see it' (Oddey & White 2009: 8). This new mode of spectating was able to attract larger, and often non-theatrical, audiences (cf. Machon 2013: 22) because not only could it deliver the individual journey and mode of spectating that people knew from video games but it could also broaden a spectator's experience because it was multisensorial and thus was experienced as authentic. Audiences became 'excited by work which presents a transgressive blurring of boundaries and that stimulates more than the intellect alone' (Machon 2009: 30). So in conclusion, the reasons for immersive theatre's success can be found in its audience which was trained in interactive experience from other media and at the same time felt deprived of authentic experience, both of which immersive theatre could deliver. However, there is another, inherent logic implied in the rise of immersive theatre just at this time. It can be argued that immersive theatre is almost necessarily rooted in theatre's phenomenological and ontological history. In the following I intend to trace out three moments in theatre's genesis, which are contributive to the success of immersive theatre today.

First, the theatrical spectacle, in its purest form, is a display of a small group or an individual for a large, public crowd. This spectacle can have various purposes, ranging from entertainment to metaphysics or politics. Foucault clearly identified theatre's capacity as a display of power and was very clear that there was a 'theatre sérieux', which served exactly this function (cf. Fiesbach 2002: 30). However, this serious theatre as a display of power, most manifest in the staging of public executions, was gradually abolished. It was hidden away and became marginalized.

> The middle classes, especially the enlightened intellectuals abhorred to *see*, to *really experience*, to be *actually confronted* with the dark, horrible sides of the very realities they were constructing; they were 'thinking' them away by abstract Enlightenment humanism. This corresponded to their obsession with the 'real', the 'authentic', as pertinent discourses from the eighteenth through the nineteenth centuries reveal. (Fiesbach 2002: 30)

In other words, as soon as the 'real thing' had vanished, the longing for a simulacrum of it set in. Or, in Lacanian terms, as soon as the real had vanished or become inaccessible, it became fetishized.

Second, theatre itself also changed profoundly at around the same time, from the mid- eighteenth to the nineteenth century. This becomes especially evident in the audience–performer relation (cf. Gran 2002: 259). Whereas in the Renaissance the audience could and would interact lively with the performers, the theatre space had gradually become much more policed and regulated.[4] Before, the stage and the auditorium had usually both been illuminated and the audience could comment on the performance or even call for good scenes to be repeated (which regularly happened, even with death scenes). The actors not only were aware of the audience but also took in their wishes (cf. Gran 2002: 259). This relationship changed in the nineteenth century when it became common to dim the house lights, plunging the audience into darkness, depriving them of voice and power. Now the economy between performer and audience was a different one. Only the performer could be seen but they could no longer see the audience. This led to a sharp separation between the two entities and it led to monologue where once there had been dialogue. Whereas before there had been lively enjoyment and back-and-forth between performers and audience, slowly but definitely rules and behavioural doctrines crept in and changed the power economy.

> In the theater, the actor was no longer someone who mastered the conventions, but someone who had a great personality – a talent. The actor became an expressive performer who could still show feelings in public, and his expressiveness depended on the size of her/ his own personality. And what of the beholder? He fell silent. Out of fear of showing one personality, the middle class made a virtue of self-control, of holding personality in check. In the breakdown of feudal conventions and with the burgeois personality's entrance into the public sphere, the spectator as a public figure became confused. He does not know how to behave, either in the street or in the theater. The result is that s/he does as little as possible, becoming a voyeur, an observer. In the theater he can no longer boo, cheer or interrupt – only clap at the end. On the street s/he cannot be social because of a lack of effective conventions, and out of fear of revealing the inner self. The result is a breakdown in social interaction in the public theater. It is time to dim the lights in the theater, something that took place concretely in Germany in 1876, at Beureuth [sic], under Wagner's management. Thus the illusion of 'there is nobody out there' was fulfilled, becoming the most important principle behind autonomy in the dramatic arts. Sennett is astute in using the theater as an example of the breakdown of the public sphere. In the theater

this development is clear and concrete. The audience is changed from being socially active to passively contemplative. At the same time, it is possible to enjoy the theater as dramatic art and not take part in its social performance. (Gran 2002: 260)

Audiences in this period became passive spectators instead of active subjects; they lost not only their voice but also their place in the theatre. In other words, the audience vanished somewhere between the house lights and the orchestra pit.

Third, in this process, theatre underwent a similar fate that public executions had undergone years before: it became a safe place, where anything untoward or real, in the Lacanian sense, was not present anymore. The theatre became a sanitized place and fortified itself against inconvenience and risk. Alan Read argues that this regime of safety, this regime of eliminating any danger, becomes most obvious in the metaphorical and actual rise of the fire curtain (cf. Read 1995: 232–236). Whereas theatres had burnt down regularly over centuries (the average life span of a theatre was twenty-two years, due to frequent fires), now the fire chief, regulations and most of all the safety curtain reduced the risk dramatically for the audience and by implication reduced real danger in the theatre (cf. 1995: 232–236). 'Comfort had always been in doubt, but the ultimate discomfort, premature death was no longer to be tolerated by the Lord Chamberlain, who as well as censoring the contents of theatre censored its spaces' (Read 1995: 234). The censorship of the space goes hand in hand with the censorship of content. Whereas in the Victorian Age in terms of content anything deviant was a taboo for the stage, the actual danger also became absent. Theatre became superficial in this sense because it could only offer images of danger, love, hate and life but never any real danger.

Consequently, I want to argue – and I am very aware that these are extremely broad brush strokes – that theatre had sought to eliminate the real from its premises so thoroughly that it was bound to make a return in some form. This is certainly a convergent development with other areas of artistic and everyday culture. However, experiences of the real are apparently something that could not be ignored for too long.

Fundamental experiences of, say, rawness and danger returned to the theatre, obviously still in a very sanitized version. No one is really going to die in immersive theatre, but still for many critics, immersive theatre gives at least an impression of real danger, discomfort and adventure, because it 'seems to lack the heavy hands of health-and-safety and customer service' (White 2009: 220). The popularity of immersive theatre in the beginning of the twenty-first century is then rooted in audiences' lack of authentic experience. Theatre is only one expression of this culture of sanitization, which by now has also become a culture of virtuality. Immersive theatre is a counter-movement against this culture. It promises the 'real' and delivers authentic experience, while still avoiding death, injury or executions. It is the 'absolute fake' (Eco 1998: 31)[5] that is able to deliver 'the real thing'. This is as close a citizen of a democratic, metamodern state may get towards such experiences.

Aesthetic strategies

The re-authentification of theatrical experience is achieved by a number of aesthetic strategies that can be found in many immersive performances, despite their enormous variety in form and content. Scholarly study of these strategies is, however, difficult. As Machon points out, all immersive works are based on physical experience which cannot be put into words easily, or, more precisely, it will necessarily lose its strong, experiential quality when doing so (cf. 2009: 2). Therefore, the following section can at best be an outline of some strategies of authenticity, while the analysis of the two performances of Punchdrunk will attempt to put into words the effects of these strategies. Furthermore, an inspection of immersive aesthetics must also take a broad approach simply because immersive practices draw on a large number of techniques and senses. Machon finds a number of aesthetic roots or concepts that can be made fruitful for an understanding of the mechanics of immersive productions. They are, in other words, each ancestors of one aspect of immersive theatre.

She cites Nietzsche's Dionysian principle, the Russian formalists' concept of defamiliarization (*ostranenie*), Barthes' idea of a writerly text and the 'jouissance' in engaging with the material, but also Cixous' and Irigaray's 'écriture féminine', which demands a more sensual approach to art (cf. 2009: 35–43). Furthermore, Artaud's 'theatre of cruelty', or Barker's 'theatre of catastrophe', as well as Broadhurst's liminality, which is based on Victor Turner's theories, have a claim to ancestry of immersive theatre (cf. 2009: 44–45). While all these theories are useful and traces of them can be found in immersive theatre, none of them helps to give a thick understanding of the experience, because they only ever cover one aspect. Machon consequently develops her own concept of '(syn)aesthetics' to describe immersive experiences. The concept stresses the holistic approach to perception and analysis of immersive theatre. Drawing on her theories of (syn)aesthetics (cf. 2009) and her 'scale of immersivity' (cf. 2013), I want to suggest that aesthetic strategies of a specific performance can best be investigated when grouped into three categories. These are: body, politics and set/ frame. For Machon, 'immersive experiences in theatre combine the act of immersion – being submerged in an alternative medium where all the senses are engaged and manipulated – with a deep involvement in the activity within that medium' (Machon 2013: 21–22).

This definition of 'immersion' makes sense and can be very well applied to most large-scale immersive theatre. It is not clear, however, why Machon would count stand-alone one-on-one performances among immersive theatres as well, as they usually lack the 'deep involvement', which she sensibly demands (cf. 2013: 17, 76, *passim*).[6]

Body

The experience of authentic moments is created in immersive theatre through visceral cognition of set, performers and events. It derives from the complex interplay of sensorial impressions that the spectator has. She moves through the space with her body; she touches, smells, hears, sees and in times even tastes. This is what Machon means by '(syn)aesthetics', the audience perceives corporeally (cf. also White 2012: 229).

> The (syn)aesthetic style allows the explicit recreation of sensation through visual, physical, verbal, aural, tactile, haptic and olfactory means. Here, I do not simply refer to the mere description of a sensual experience but *sensation itself* being transmitted to the audience via a corporeal memory, the traces of lived sensate experience within the human body, activated within the perceiving individual. This **fusing of sense (semantic 'meaning making') with *sense* (feeling, both sensation and emotion) establishes a double-edged rendering of making sense/*sense* making** and foregrounds its fused somatic/ semantic nature. (Machon 2009: 14, emphases in the original)

In other words, the sensations gained from an immersive theatre experience are both semantic and somatic; intellect and visceral perception become inextricably linked to form a greater unit of meaning. It is impossible to give a description of an immersive experience by simply studying anything like a script, neglecting the experience of the spectator in space. Especially in site-specific and immersive theatre 'the aesthetic gap between the world of the stage and the world of the audience [is] reduced to a minimum' (Lane 2010: 2).

> For Punchdrunk's audiences, the restriction of vision, encouragement of movement at different speeds through very different environments, and variations of dense proximity to other spectators with individual encounters and moments of solo exploration, are fundamental to the physical experiences of the performance, and the sensations gathered in these ways cannot be separated from those acquired by watching and listening alone. (White 2012: 229)

Out of this fusion of intellectual and visceral/emotional experience, a *thick experience* unfolds. Only in a second step – after the performance – intellectual interpretation sets in.

> [T]he *experience* of the work is the most important factor in appreciation and impacts on any subsequent intellectual processes of analysis; a visceral cognition via this corporeal memory. It is the fusing

of 'the felt' and 'the understood' in making sense/*sense* of intangible, inarticulable ideas that is crucial to (syn)aesthetic appreciation. (Machon 2009: 21, italics in the original)

Memory is key in the process of describing immersive performances. This obviously goes with all the *caveats* that interpretation from memory begs (cf. Williams 2006). All memories of a performance have necessarily been tainted with imprecision, past glorification or simply errors in memory. But the fact remains that, when taking a (syn)aesthetic approach seriously, there is no other way than to rely on personal memory; anything else would not do the performance justice. But furthermore, the (syn)aesthetic approach also raises questions concerning the divide between intellect and visceral cognition. It is true that the entire *thick experience* must at one point after the event become subject of intellectual reflection to make it fruitful and give it a lasting impact on a spectator's life.

> The experiential impact of (syn)aesthetic performance affects a visceral cognition which leaves its traces on the perceiver's body via the immediacy of a corporeal memory. Put simply, we *feel* the performance in the moment and recall these feelings in subsequent interpretation. (Machon 2009: 55, italics in the original)

Machon argues that such events always leave the participant with an 'embodied memory' (2013: 97). Without any 'subsequent interpretation', the whole *thick event* loses out on becoming a formative event that influences a spectator's life or can be fruitfully recalled. One can argue that this is one of the central purposes of art: to make an impact on people's lives and thinking. If this process does not happen, the performance simply becomes a cheap thrill: a roller-coaster ride that made one scream and the heart pump with adrenalin, but that has no lasting impact. Walter Benjamin already proffered the importance of intellectual reflection on artistic experience in his essay on Baudelaire, in which he introduces a distinction between *Erfahrung* and *Erlebnis*.

> The greater the share of the shock factor in particular impressions, the more constantly consciousness has to be alerted as a screen against

stimuli; the more efficiently it does so, the less do these impressions enter experience (*Erfahrung*), tending to remain in the sphere of a certain hour in one's life (*Erlebnis*). Perhaps the special achievement of shock defense may be seen in its function of assigning to an incident a precise point in time in consciousness at the cost of the integrity of its contents. This would be a peak achievement of the intellect; it would turn the incident into a moment that has been lived (*Erlebnis*). Without reflection there would be nothing but the sudden start, usually the sensation of fright which, according to Freud, confirms the failure of shock defense. (1969: 163)

Benjamin has a very different focus in his essay, but his conceptualization is useful here, too. Immersive theatre provides the concrete and sensate experience (*Erlebnis*), which is overwhelming or even prone to shock. If this *Erlebnis* is not processed later on, it becomes an empty husk of an emotional thunderstorm that has long since passed. However, if conscious reflection is used, the visceral *Erlebnis* will enter a spectator's *Erfahrung* and thus be accessible and employable in the future. The spectator gains from it.

But how does the activation of the spectator's body work concretely in immersive theatre? Sometimes, activation can, quite literally, mean movement. In Blast Theory's *Rider Spoke* (2007), for instance, 'spectators' were given bicycles and a handheld computer, on which they cycled through nocturnal London. Each participant was physically moving through the very real and tangible city, but was also connected to other participants through the electronic device. Participants were asked to seek out spots of seclusion which no other player had found before, and they could leave short voice messages for each other. Thus, players never actually met but moved through both a virtual and a concrete space with the knowledge of other real people, whom they never met, also there. Blast Theory created a game 'that invited real life to burst into the virtual realm, "contaminating" it with its unexpected, messy and often paradoxical essence' (Chatzichristodoulou 2015: 247). The city formed a backdrop while the participants were actively shaping their own story with a considerable degree of freedom (cf. Chatzichristodoulou

2015: 238). In *Can You See Me Now?* (2001), Blast Theory confused the realms of reality and virtuality even further, placing physical actors (runners) in a real city, who were equipped with handheld computers and chased virtual audience members who participated online and put an avatar of themselves in a virtual map of the real city. Here the audience became active only virtually in front of their computer screen; however, they interacted with a very real environment in a concrete city. Other companies, such as Punchdrunk, put supreme value on sensate experience. They employ strategies that bombard the audience's senses, such as darkness or noise, and give plenty of opportunities for enjoying the environment for its own sake. But they also force the audience to make choices, through disorientation, separation from each other or by dissolution of narratives so that it has to be sought after (cf. White 2009: 219). Felix Barrett, the artistic director of Punchdrunk, states that their shows allow 'the body to become empowered because the audience have to make physical decisions and choices, and in doing that they make some sort of pact with the piece. They're physically involved with the piece and therefore it becomes visceral' (in Machon 2009: 89).

Machon acknowledges that a certain visceral quality – not unlike that of installation art – is also present in traditional stage works and cites the plays of Caryl Churchill or Sarah Kane as examples. However, she also stresses that this is something different from immersive theatre where a spectator can genuinely walk up to or touch something or somebody (cf. 2013: 283). This 'haptic' quality is often central to 'realizing' and comprehending a piece of art.

> Here 'haptic', 'haptically', 'hapticity' [...] is used in relation to the performing, perceiving, sensual body, alongside 'tactile' as the latter tends to connote only the external quality of touch by hand. 'Haptic' emphasises the tactile perceptual experience of the body as a whole (rather than merely the fingers) and also highlights the perceptive faculty of the bodily kinaesthetics (the body's locomotion in space), which involves proprioception (stimulation produced and perceived *within* the body relating to position and movement *of* the body). Haptic perception encompasses the sensate experience of an individual's

moving body, and that individual's perceptual experience of bodies of others. (Machon 2013: 283)

She argues that while a play can make you forget your body because your mind is completely immersed in the action on stage (e.g. the works of Pina Bausch, Robert Lepage or Caryl Churchill), immersive theatre activates your body and you become physically so immersed that you forget everything else (cf. Machon 2013: 57). In other words, where in spectatorial theatre the body is subordinate to the mind, in immersive theatre it is the other way around. This primacy of the body then leads to a different and, she argues, deeper understanding of the performance.

I use 'noetic' (from the Greek derived *noēsis, noētikos, nous*, meaning inner wisdom, subjective intellect or understanding) to denote knowledge that is experienced directly and can incorporate sensations of transcendence. Noetic understanding traverses the ineffable (that which cannot be put into words) in that it can make physically manifest complex emotional or social experiences that defy explanation yet are *felt* and consequently the thing shown *feels understood*. (Machon 2013: 284)

This category of 'noetic' is difficult to grasp, even though it may have an intuitive appeal. It – yet again – makes scholarly analysis difficult because it effectively eliminates any attempt at objective analysis. But it also points to the capacity of immersive theatre to create sensations and an impact that is holistic and much greater than the sum of its parts. Spectators have a multitude of haptic, kinaesthetic proprioceptions and out of these arises the very individual noetic quality of a higher truth. Again, this is a concept that strongly provokes sentiments of authenticity. Something that I intuitively feel to be right, and which is validated by my sensate experience must be authentic, must it not? This suggestion obviously only holds if one acknowledges the role the body and sensual experience have to play in this. Machon finds that the physical presence leads to an experience that is stronger than conventional theatre and will last longer, in the shape of a 'lasting ephemerality' in one's body's memory (cf. Machon 2013: 44). She calls this experience 'praesence', seeking to include all the sensorial impressions, denoting something that is set before being. In other words, she gives a very strong privilege to intuition and sensual experience as opposed to intellectual work in the form of decoding or interpretation. She even argues that 'this style enables practitioners and audience members alike to tap into pre-linguistic communication processes and engages with an awareness of the "primordial" via such sensually stimulated perception' (2013: 76). Her prime example is olfactory impressions which are frequently used in the works of Punchdrunk. The example is certainly well chosen because everyone is aware that olfactory sensations have an extraordinary capacity to evoke memories from long ago or to produce very strong emotional responses almost immediately. Yet, whether the body – or, more specifically sensate perception – should be given such primacy is doubtful. This is specifically true in terms of intersubjectivity. When we talk about bodies, Alan Read points out, whose body are we referring to, the white, young, able-bodied male (cf. Read 2008: 220)? Furthermore, even if all spectators were white, young, able-bodied and male, how could one in any way compare experiences between them if one did not want to return to essentialist notions of perception? Gareth White also doubts whether the physical response in immersive theatre is as strong as Machon wants it to be. He claims that in a book, a framed painting and so on '[w]e do not reach into a work and take something out of it, except in a metaphorical sense. But when we move within the physical space of a work – as we do in immersive theatre – are we doing something that is beyond the metaphorical?' (2012: 227).

In other words, should the body's presence, movement and sensations really be seen as transcending any sensate interaction it has with purely spectatorial artworks? Machon effectively pre-empts this argument by stressing that each immersive experience is extremely individualistic (cf. 2013: 95–97). Consequently, she does not claim that each spectator will have the same experience. An old, disabled, black, female spectator may have a different experience than the young, able-bodied, white male, but nonetheless, it will be a strong (syn)aesthetic response, which is equally valid and can be equally formative for her. Furthermore, in the light of neuroscientific findings, it is not unreasonable to suppose a privileged position for some of the senses. As the research of Diane Ackermann has shown, the connection between our sensory perception and our central cortex is much stronger and also much older in evolutionary terms than the connection between the central cortex and the language centre (cf. Ruthrof 2000: 41–42). Thus, sensory impressions have a far more direct influence on us than any form of language communication could (cf. Schulze 2013: 114). This is also an explanation for, say, the immediacy of olfactory stimulation and its capacity to influence our mood or conjure up old memories.

However, even if it is acknowledged that some senses achieve a more direct and lasting impact than others, one would still have to question Machon's terminology and approach. Is 'noetic', 'kinaesthetic', 'proprioception', 'praesence' or '(syn)aesthetically' really more than just saying, 'I felt that way'? If so, why use this elaborate terminology and not simply state the fact that '(syn)aesthetic appreciation [...] is affective and experiential, semantic sense cannot be dissociated from somatic *sense*' (Machon 2009: 20, italics in the original). More to the point, even if it comes at the cost of a fair bit of scholarly objectivity, would it not be equally as useful and simpler to describe one's feelings without recourse to over-complicated terminology? Furthermore, if this proposition is valid, what keeps us from using the same terminology (i.e. 'I feel') in the analysis of any other performance or play that we see, not just in immersive theatre? Is this terminology a step back on the scale of scholarly objectivity?

While I agree that the approach is problematic and open to attacks in a number of aspects, I would take a different stance on some of the points. By elaborating a new terminology, Machon actually attempts to create vocabulary that helps describe immersive performance in more detail. Simply stating 'I feel' is still much more imprecise than analysing 'proprioception' or 'haptic' sensation in detail. It seeks to operationalize experiences of the senses, grouping them into categories and yet allowing for the intuitive 'noetic' truth. Vague terminology, such as 'noetic', is not indebted to academic neglect on Machon's part;

it is rooted in the performances she investigates. Immersive theatre can only be comprehended and analysed using a holistic approach. She argues convincingly that the multitude of senses activated can create an experience which transcends what is perceptible beyond the surface (cf. Machon 2013: 78–80). Each immersive event is 'frustratingly fleeting, literally "of the moment", utterly experiential in the "you had to be there' sense"' (Machon 2013: 96). Therefore, the terminology in all its vagueness should, most fruitfully, be understood as a point of departure for further development and investigation in this field, which has yet received too little scholarly attention. Finally, the terminology is not apt for describing any other theatrical performance; this is especially true for cases where the performance has a textual basis and can thus be studied differently. Spectatorial theatres often beg close semantic analysis of text and decoding of stage signs. It is in this case that saying 'I felt that way' would be not doing justice to the artwork.

Politics

The noetic feelings, or authenticity, are also indebted to the freedom audiences enjoy in most immersive performances. As Punchdrunk are the example of choice here, I will take a closer look at their politics of performance; however, it must of course be acknowledged that there are a multitude of other performance styles and types which are also successful (e.g. the works of Shunt, drimthinkspeak etc., cf. Machon 2013). In the shows of Punchdrunk, audiences are given no directions, plans or schedule of the performance. Every audience member enters the 'world of the performance' and is consequently free to roam and explore at leisure. This approach more often than not thrills audiences because every new room, level or territory they discover and explore is full of genuinely new sensations and the thrill of discovery (cf. Cavendish 2013). White remarks that this liberty may easily evoke the feeling of being able to come closer to the performance than in any other kind of theatrical setting.

> Speaking to, following or dancing with a performer creates a physical relation, and a sense-sense dynamic which will inform any response or interpretation. But it does not explain another facet of the sensations they generate: the feeling that if we work hard at our role in them, and pursue the action and the performers, we will gain access to the interior of the drama itself. (White 2012: 230)

Each audience member takes on an active role as an individual and an explorer in this performance. The audience becomes both part of the fixture of the performance but also an active, performing body themselves. They are not only decorative elements in a given set but active ingredients in this mixture.

> With Punchdrunk's work, the audience is individually masked for anonymity and invited to enter a sensual world to play within the space and the performance itself. The mask encourages risk taking, a stepping outside of the self. Furthermore, the audience adds to the otherworldliness of the experience; the audience frame the sequences as they watch, often unwittingly, breathtakingly choreographing themselves into beautiful, carnivalesque sculptures. (Machon 2009: 57–58)

White sees in the masks the greatest innovation of Punchdrunk (cf. 2009: 223–224). They disinhibit each audience member and frequently audience members' faces will be no further than a few inches away from a performer's face. Furthermore, as Machon points out, the mask also turns the audience into a collective body. They form picturesque scenes but also act collectively, when for instance following a performer around. This frequently reminds one of a herd of zebras, suddenly turning into one direction. The aspect of following other individuals, intuitively or viscerally realizing that performance can be sought elsewhere, is an important aspect of the performance. Thus spectators are part of a collective but are also always free to choose their own path. Finally, the mask also clearly delineates who is a performer and who is a spectator. Consequently, the performance, while seemingly breaking down (almost) all physical boundaries and separations between audience and performer, still keeps alive a certain separation between the two. The freedom to explore is then only limited by one's personal inclination to risk taking and performers who will push audience members away if they are in the way, and stewards, wearing black masks, who do the same. But still, it must be noted that those stewards are rarely visible and in general very little is off-bounds in Punchdrunk's shows. Each audience member makes her individual journey through the performance. As Felix Barrett of Punchdrunk states, '[a] central feature of the work is the empowerment of the audience. It's a fight against audience apathy and the inertia that sets in when you're stagnating in an auditorium' (in Machon 2009: 89). No two audience members are likely to have the same journey, or even see the same stories, for that matter. In fact, audiences can not only create their personal story but are also able to interfere with the story of the performance (within predetermined parameters) and are able to interact with the performers (within predetermined parameters). This individual, tailor-made journey is both a blessing for audiences in search of authenticity but also places a considerable burden on them, along the lines of: How should I behave? Am I doing this right? Did I get all the stories I was supposed to get (cf. Jones 2013; White 2012)? Barret admits that this is a challenge for the audience but one that Punchdrunk consciously pose.

> You don't need to have an opinion anymore; everyone will have it for you [...] So what we try to do is make experiences that are about the individual having to get out there and stake their claim. We're not going to tell you how to do it, you need to put the work in and uncover the secret yourself. (Barrett in Iezzi 2012)

In other words, the immersive performances of Punchdrunk are consciously designed to activate audiences and let them create their own journeys. This audience empowerment is surely another aspect which fuels the feeling of authentic experience for audience members. Experiencing one's own, personal, unique story is authentic.

Set/frame

The setting in immersive theatre is more than simply the backdrop to the personal journey of each audience member. It forms an important part of the experience and it has even been claimed that in Punchdrunk's shows the set is more important than the performers (cf. Pringle 2013). This is largely due to Punchdrunk's notorious obsession with detail (cf. Remshardt 2008; White 2012). In their shows, every room will fit the period of the piece to the point where one may find aged letters in a drawer or discover a chamber pot that looks used. Obviously, spectators will take this as additional proof of the environment's authenticity. The detailed set and props create a feeling of being in a different world because things look used and real and not like a fake theatrical prop.

> Nothing is cordoned off, little is out of bounds, the stewards, when you can identify them (they are also masked) are satisfyingly obtuse and unobtrusive. It is easy to settle into a space and make it your own, and it is very possible to interfere with the *mise-en-scene* or to help yourself to souvenirs. Although the work's interactivity reflects the zeitgeist, it seems to lack the heavy hands of health-and-safety and customer service. (White 2009: 220)

In other words, if one chooses to explore a certain room in an immersive experience, one will find little proof of its theatricality. On the contrary, one is free to fiddle with objects and soon develops the feeling that this is a real room, inhabited by a real person who uses real objects. Of course, there is also a constraint: if one looks hard enough, one will always find lights, speakers or some other aspect that gives the theatricality away. Nonetheless, I would contend that Punchdrunk come as close to a real experience as is possible in theatre. Maaike Bleeker has argued that theatricality, in traditional theatre, has the capacity to blur the boundaries between fact and fiction. 'Theatricality as a communicative affect emerging from the interaction between spectators and what they see denotes the uncanny moment when the distinction between reality and fiction suddenly ceases to be self-evident' (Bleeker 2007). If this is true for traditional theatre, how much more must the distinction between reality and fiction become dubious in a Punchdrunk show?

David Edgar sees all kinds of site-specific theatre (including immersive theatre) in relation to the 'spatial turn' as a mode of resistance against grand narratives (cf. 2012: 10), and it is true that immersive shows favour the personal over the collective, the individual story and experience over the grand narrative. They also provide a spatial counter world to the real world outside the theatre. Effectively, Punchdrunk shows represent a special form of what Foucault has called a heterotopia of illusion (cf. 1986: 26). Heterotopias are real, tangible spaces, but at the same time, they are obviously not real. For Foucault they are spaces that are closer to utopia or dystopia than to the real world but have nonetheless gained a partial existence in it (cf. 1986: 24). They are a space in between fact and fiction that seeks to stimulate an audience member's mind. The space itself allows for strong emotional responses and for different behaviour than in normal life, because it is a world where different rules apply. Foucault names, among others, brothels or boarding schools as examples of heterotopias (cf. 1986: 26). Heterotopias are 'countersites, a kind of effectively enacted utopia in which the real sites, all the other real sites that can be found within the culture are simultaneously represented, contested and inverted' (Foucault 1986: 24). All these have similar capacities of changing behaviour and specific rules which only apply in their realm.

White has suggested that such spaces can best be understood employing Goffman's frame analysis (cf. 2009: 222). In the case of Punchdrunk, the shows always make use of multiple inner and outer frames that denote the general 'heterotopia' of the performance but also miniature frames for performances within the larger frame. Every theatre is for Foucault a prime example of a heterotopia of illusion because it provides exactly this – the partial realization of fiction in the real world (cf. 1986: 26). By entering into a theatre, one by definition comes in contact with a heterotopia. In immersive theatre, however, this heterotopia is not something to be looked at from the safe distance of a theatre seat, but something to be lived through.

Machon very sensibly proposes that an immersive theatre experience cannot be shrugged off like a bad play after leaving the venue, but the 'experience bleeds into the real world' (Machon 2013: 55). Many companies, including Punchdrunk, take specifically the entrance into the world of the performance as a crucial point. It is understood as a kind of portal, which allows the spectator to leave one's daily business or even one's daily self behind and become lost in the adventure. As Felix Barret states, '[w]e always establish an entrance point to the world we create which is like entering a decompression chamber, to acclimatize to the world before being set free in it' (in Machon 2009: 91). The portal frames the entrance into the heterotopian space, which then allows for sensate and authentic experience. Bodily thinking, being in the moment and visceral sense making, which is intuited and not intellectually or semantically achieved, are made possible (cf. Machon 2013: 104–106). The resulting experience is as ephemeral as both theatre and the concept of heterotopia suggest. Each immersive event is transient and fleeting, but it leaves the participant with more than memories or impressions; as Machon argues convincingly, the participant maintains an 'embodied memory' (Machon 2013: 97) of the performance. She consequently takes the audience and its role to be the pivotal point in immersive theatre. It is about 'direct, actual, physical insertion of an individual audience member within the world of the event' (Machon 2013: 98). The form of authenticity experienced by spectators is best described with Selwyn's concept of 'hot authenticity' (cf. Funk 2015: 20–21). It focuses strictly on subjective criteria, and it is the ascription made by an individual in the moment, not validated by intellectual or external expertise (cold authenticity).

Criticism

Implicitly it has already been acknowledged that immersive theatre as well as the terminology for its description are in many ways open to attack. While it seems that a number of critics and scholars are extremely positive about immersive theatre's possibilities (cf. Cavendish 2013; Machon 2009, 2013; White 2009), or have even heralded it as the possible future of the theatre (cf. Remshardt 2008), others have been more sceptical and have criticized it on various accounts (cf. Jones 2013; White 2012). In the following, I will trace some of the major arguments against immersive theatre while also adding some of my own thoughts.

A cheap thrill

The most obvious criticism is surely that immersive theatre is nothing but a cheap thrill that lacks artistic quality. Certainly there are pieces of immersive theatre which use the (syn)aesthetic approach as an end in itself. Even immersive artists have commented on this phenomenon. Felix Barrett, of Punchdrunk, is one of them. 'The work that has proper rigour, craft and process is excellent. The work that plays with the trickery of taking an audience out of its comfort zone is weaker – it's about quality control' (in Cavendish 2013). It consequently appears crucial to distinguish immersive theatre as an art form from other performative practices, which use similar means but possibly have much less to say. Josephine Machon therefore opts to call 'immersive theatre' only works which provide 'a visceral and participatory audience experience with an all-encompassing, sensual style of production aesthetic' (Machon 2013: 66). She is also quick to remark that the term is often used indiscriminately and for too wide a variety of practices (cf. 2013: 66). For her, these are practices that do not totally immerse a spectator. Among these she counts events which are simply set in a special venue (site-specific) or which have special seating arrangements but are not multisensorial or provide opportunities for the audience to interact. In her line of argument, they should be counted among 'spectatorial theatres' because they adhere to the clear we (watch, passive) and them (perform, active) dichotomy (cf. 2013: 101). She also does not want to count events such as 'murder mystery weekends', 'The Hampton Court Kitchen Tour' (live actors portraying Tudor kitchen staff) or battle re-enactment groups among immersive theatre. She maintains that the intention and framing are different in such events. Whereas Punchdrunk seek to wholly immerse spectators and create a lasting emotional and intellectual impact, the aforementioned events always uphold dividing lines between performance and audience and have a different (e.g. educational) intent (cf. Machon 2013: 69). It seems reasonable that the framing and consequently audiences' expectations and willingness to let themselves go are different in these events. However, it is doubtful whether, say, a re-enactment soldier would not also have (syn)aesthetic perceptions in his battle scene, which are no less strong than the ones an audience member has in an immersive show. After all, the soldier can also smell (smoke), hear (gunfire), taste (sulphur), feel (rain), be part of a collective of moving bodies and so on. Such an actor even wears appropriate period clothing which gives him a one-up on spectators in, say, Punchdrunk's shows, who are dressed in normal street clothes. Consequently, while the framing indeed suggests that such events are different, their practices and experiences resemble immersive theatre to a high degree. They should be counted among immersive experiences then, albeit with a different intention and framing. To not count them would seem like a form of elitism. It is much more useful to regard both immersive theatre and the practices above as springing from the same source, namely a desire for authentic experience. Even more to the point, one can ask if immersive theatre, at least in the style of Punchdrunk, is not even a fair bit abusive towards the audience. Whereas the re-enactment soldier knows exactly what he is in for and what will be expected of him, the theatregoer at a Punchdrunk show is often plunged into the performance without any knowledge about his role or what is to come, which can be confusing and thrilling at best, but also has the potential to be disturbing. This becomes especially evident in the one-on-one sessions which are often incorporated into Punchdrunk shows.

> They [i.e. the actors] report that they are often resisted, and when they succeed in removing it [the mask] they might be met with tears, confessions, and sometimes anger. In these moments they have achieved an intimacy, which is sometimes disturbing to both parties,

and which brings into question that this work is as purely escapist as they believe it is. (White 2009: 228)

The fun of exploration can quickly turn from amusing game to a situation of very real emotional turmoil. There is, as was shown in Chapter 2, a slope of power between performer and spectator in such one-on-ones, in which the performer is always in a stronger position, because he directs the situation and is aware of all the rules of the game. Even more to the point, it is questionable whether theatre can or should involve audiences to such a degree. Alan Read has argued that it is precisely the quality of separation between audience and performance which makes for theatre's appeal. He claims that all experiments from Grotowski to Eisenstein

> to the current penchant for site-specific, relational and digital performance has done little to alter the essential face-to-face encounter of the most perverse relational art, the *theatrical*. 'Looking on' and wondering is the common theatrical mode of spectation irrespective of cultural origin. It is by definition an art of anti-immersion, it is the *gloss on depth* incarnate. This is *not* a problem for theatre! My proposal here, if I have something that specific in this essay, is that it is precisely this repertoire of affects of adjustment, the measurement of resistance to incorporation that makes sitting in the dark watching the traffic of lit stages so interesting. This *is* a problem for performance [.] (Read 2014: 17)

In other words, if it wants to be at its strongest, theatre should strive to uphold the 'immunisatory logic' (as Read calls it) and keep the distance between performance and spectator and rather seek to use 'all its theatricality to unpick its own communitarian stupidity' (Read 2014: 13). Read's point is a very interesting one because he suggests that the very essence of theatre is the separation, and, to a degree, even the passivity, of the audience. However, he also concedes that the wider field of live art (performance) does not employ such boundaries; it has different goals of community and incorporation. By and large, the degree of involvement depends on the taste of the spectators. The huge popularity of immersive performances, however, somewhat refutes

Read's argument, as many spectators are thrilled by the possibility of immersion.

White furthermore questions the concept of intimacy in immersive performances. He follows Nicholas Ridout when he suggests that theatrical intimacy is always flawed in the first place because it is based on a different power economy. The spectator may be uncomfortable and unsure which role to play, while the performer knows this very well. Should I play along? Should I just watch? In the end, theatre follows the economy of paid services, so that the meeting between performer and spectator is never a meeting of equals (cf. White 2009: 227–228). Here, it would seem, the fine line reappears, between the lack of 'the heavy hands of health and safety', or the seeking of thrill and authentic experience, and the risk of things becoming genuinely real or disturbing. Therefore, many immersive experiences provide exit options for spectators and most immersive artists feel that these rules of behaviour and possibilities of getting out were always, if tacitly, acknowledged (cf. Machon 2013: 41). On the one hand, one can argue that the fleeting shadow of the fire curtain is still visible here; on the other hand, one can question what 'tacit' means in such circumstances. In all performances of Punchdrunk, the rules are never explicitly stated. Here the slope of power between the performers who know the rules and spectators who can only guess becomes visible again. It can be argued that this is firmly part of the thrill of immersive theatre and that this play with fire is something that immersive theatre must take as a given. It cannot escape this danger because doing so would mean sacrificing its core ideas. The spectator, while not exactly in danger of dying, is always in danger in an immersive performance and that is part of its appeal.

Promising too much

Such play with fire is certainly strongest for spectators who experience immersive theatre for the first time. It is not unreasonable to assume that the effects will wear off once the spectator has gotten used to the specific format and techniques. In other words, a first-time visitor may easily be overwhelmed by the performance, while a second- or third-time visitor may already have strategies of experiencing the performance. In fact, Punchdrunk's artistic director has stated that their ideal spectator has never been to one of their shows before (cf. Machon 2009: 90). Nonetheless, despite all talk of (syn)aesthetics and noetic experience, it remains questionable, whether all spectators will completely give themselves over to the experience. The theatrical framing raises certain expectations and implies, but also forbids, certain behaviour. Lizzie Clachan, from Shunt, has commented on this.

> With *Amato Saltone* [2006] there was this idea that the audience would come into some kind of key party [i.e. a swingers party] but we know full well the audience know they're in the theatre, know there's not going to be some kind of orgy. We don't want the audience to think that we think they might think that's going to happen. We know that they know so then we can all play together. (Machon 2009: 106)

This suggests a very different experience from what Machon has in mind. Granted, Shunt is also a company that has worked with different mechanisms and a very different style than Punchdrunk. Nonetheless, the complicity between spectator and performance implies a certain distance and insinuates that spectators are – within limits – still aware of the theatrical situation. The question can be asked whether audiences are really lost in the performance at one point and forget the theatrical setting. After all, the immersive and authentic experience is also a show, which is put on every night for a long run. Maxine Doyle, Punchdrunk's choreographer and co-director, has commented on this: 'It's great for us when people say that they feel like they were the only ones having that experience and it felt like the first and only time that event happened in that way, when in actual fact it's happened hundreds of times over the course of a run' (in Machon 2009: 96). Immersive theatre, with all its ambitions of blurring reality and fiction, still remains a theatrical event. Audiences, it can be argued, are conscious of this frame and setting. White therefore concludes that immersive theatre cannot fill the shoes that Machon wants it to wear.

[I]t has no strong claim to creating either fictional or imaginative interiors in a way that is different in kind than in more conventionally structured audience environments. [...] Ontologically speaking, immersive theatre can only achieve what other forms of performance can achieve; a relation in which the event of a work of art occurs between its material being and the person who encounters it. (White 2012: 233)

This argument is hard to defeat; indeed, I am not sure it can be countered with pure means of objective argumentation. Some scholars, such as White or Iezzi, have felt that immersive theatre has gone too far in its promises and cannot fulfil them anymore. Others, such as Machon, Cavendish or White (in an earlier period), have made fervent cases in favour of immersive theatre's potential and felt that they had been given a 'memorable out-of-body experience' (Remshardt 2008: 643). Even more than in 'spectatorial theatre', this battle boils down to personal disposition and taste. While some spectators may become genuinely lost or immersed in the performance, forgetting everything around them, others may keep their guard up and maintain a distance. Immersive theatre, consequently, only works if spectators work with the performance and are ready, open or even eager for such experience. The degree of immersion and the force of the experience are then also individualistic; they strongly depend on the spectator herself. As an expression of authentic experience, immersive theatre relies on the authenticity-seeking spectators.

This, however, is quite a heavy burden on spectators, specifically so if the rules of the game are not made clear. In times, the freedom to explore, to interact and become part of the performance may even hinder any form of authentic experience, as Alice Jones observes:

It's difficult to give yourself over to theatre when your over-riding emotion is anxiety. Anxiety that you're not seeing the crucial key that will unlock the piece; that you're looking too hard at something that means nothing; that you might have to get involved at any moment; or that you're missing out on something more exciting happening in another room. Too many times I have left shows only to discover that the best bit was a secret room I never found or a whispered encounter in a hidden phone box to which I was never privy. (Jones 2013)

Feelings of disappointment ensue easily in this situation. Spectators may even feel frustrated or inferior because they did 'not get' the piece, missed some of the performances or did in some other way not 'behave right'.

There is still, though, a fair amount of aimless wandering, of staring into empty rooms and gingerly opening cupboard doors in the vague hope there might be a performance lurking within. There is still the very real risk of watching an usher for ages in case he turns out to be a Main Character (he didn't). (Jones 2013)

In other words, simply throwing an audience into a world of unknown provenience and rules yet again changes the power economy. It places the burden of enjoyment onto the spectator. If you did not enjoy the piece, you probably did not work hard enough or are not smart enough for this kind of art. Therefore, it is crucial that artists take measures to take away pressure from audiences and help them to ease into their role and the immersive environment. If this is not the case, audiences will more likely be put off another immersive experience.

Politics

The performance in this case can easily acquire the smell of elitism again – a performance that is only enjoyable for spectators with the correct cultural and social capital (habitus) to enjoy it. Effectively, immersive theatre empowers those who are already empowered to enjoy such a performance (cf. Tomlin 2013: 189). On a more practical level, as Patel remarks, with ticket prices well beyond £40, companies like Punchdrunk are already less than inclusive (cf. 2009: 181). Participation in and enjoyment of the performance are, accordingly, accessible to a small selection of the general public, which has both enough economic and enough cultural capital to participate. The immersive experience then becomes symbolic capital, which, according to Tomlin, is commodified as a valuable good for those consumers for whom it becomes a distinctive feature – akin to being a donor to cultural institutions such as opera houses or museums (cf. 2013: 195). Her train of thought is similar to Philip Auslander's observation regarding rock concerts. He claims that attending a live concert becomes social capital and increases one's standing and respect within one's peer group (cf. 2008: 67). Along the same lines, then, immersive theatre is a new kind of artistic thrill for those who have access to enough cultural capital, while a large number of the public might not even go near such an event.[7] If one finds oneself in the unfortunate situation of being unable to enjoy the performance, one is left as part of a masked group, roaming about a strange space, merely becoming scenery.

The masks are crucial in terms of politics. White finds that the masks both lessen people's inhibitions but they also ensure that people are silent (cf. 2009. 225). This silence proves to be a double-edged sword. On the one hand, it ensures that everyone is listening and not disturbing the performance, where without masks one would often have people quietly chatting in the background. In terms of power, however, it also literally silences the spectators. They are no longer subjects who are free to voice their thoughts but they are a silent, scenery-like, exploring mass. Spectators are in this way forced into a passive role where total exploratory freedom is granted, but only within very strict limits, such as silence or masking.

As a part of the masked collective, Machon proffers that spectators form a kind of 'communitas' (cf. 2013: 37–38). However, she remains vague as to what kind of communitas she means and in what way this communitas is established. One would consequently have to ask whether a number of people sharing a space already constitute communitas. If so, what sets them apart from a theatrical audience which is also simply a group of strangers who happen to be in the same space. Bearing in mind Herbert Blau's deconstruction of the 'audience' (cf. 1990), it seems highly doubtful whether an immersive theatre audience can constitute a communitas. The 'herd effect', when for instance moving to a different space, viscerally following the movement of the crowd, does not constitute a community of significance. While notions of collective movement or even collective visceral thinking may play a role, the notion of communitas suggests a stronger bond, which is often characterized by common purpose and belief. It is specifically created within a more or less sacred setting that breaks down personal and formal barriers (cf. Bell 2008: 134–135; Schechner 2006: 70–71). Machon further suggests to see immersive spectators in terms of Rancière's emancipated spectator who shares in the community politics.

> Rancière's call for an emancipated spectator who becomes an active participant in the work of art is modelled in genuinely immersive theatre practice. The creative agency experienced within the artwork of the audience-participant has the potential to lead to a political agency on an individual or collective level. The inherent politics of the work, as brought about by the democratic practice of shared experience, demonstrates the profound potential of this artistic form. (Machon 2013: 120)

It is not easy to say whether Rancière had spectators in mind who are walking about in an immersive space. He explicitly only writes about seated spectators and is in fact more concerned with abolishing the dichotomy of seated/passive and moving/active (cf. 2009: 12). For him, activity is not necessarily a physical problem but an ontological one. Consequently, the better question would be: How active is the spectator in Punchdrunk shows and how much agency does she have? Given the structure of Punchdrunk shows, it has already been alluded that the total freedom of spectators is not as total as might be presumed at first glance. There are some very firm restrictions of what can be done and what cannot be done. The masks and the muting of the audience are but one example of this. The stewards are another. However discretely they may act, they are, invisibly, still always present, surveilling and monitoring the unwitting spectators. Finally, as otherworldly as the shows may seem, they are still shows, meaning that they work according to a precise schedule and with determinacy. Maxine Doyle, of Punchdrunk, has stated that of course there is a plan, and audiences are manipulated to follow that plan up to the crescendo of the show (cf. Machon 2009: 94).

She states that the shows are 'mathematical actually; it's really dense in its organization' (Machon 2009: 96). Such mathematical shows also require mathematically functioning spectators. In practical terms, this means that for the finale of a Punchdrunk show (usually some elaborate choreography) stewards will usher spectators in the desired direction. Indeed, even as I resisted the usher's request at a performance of *The Drowned Man*, she pushed even harder. In other words, I could not have stayed back even if I wanted. This goes to show that freedom is limited in the shows of Punchdrunk and power economies are not dissolved, but have simply become more subtle. Altering the performance and intervening in it, as Machon suggests (cf. 2013: 61–62), is only possible in a very limited way, as she also had to learn when she was ushered out (cf. 2013: 43). The form of agency a spectator has is then certainly much greater than in spectatorial theatre and the freedom to explore and genuinely shape one's own story is unparalleled. However, one must bear in mind the limitations that come with the theatrical form in the guise of safety, practical issues and dramaturgy.

Punchdrunk

Having inspected immersive theatre from a number of angles, and before turning to close readings of two performances, it is time to justify the choice of example and performances under discussion. Punchdrunk was founded in 1999 by Felix Barrett, and has since then created a prolific body of site-specific performance (Remshardt 2008: 640). In total, the company has so far (2014) created over twenty immersive pieces (cf. Iezzi 2012). Their stock-in-trade is taking canonical theatrical and non-theatrical texts, which are then played with and transformed into immersive experiences. Punchdrunk – in a nutshell – are concerned with abolishing the line between reality and fiction (cf. 2012). They seek to create experiences that are as close to a real experience as possible, be it in the form of immersive theatre or even immersive travels. Whether this is still adequately described by the term 'theatre' is questionable because their repertoire and techniques encompass much more than what would traditionally be associated with theatre. Punchdrunk, one could say, are in the business of creating experiences with the help of theatrical and performative techniques.

> I would still call Punchdrunk a theater company, because I suppose everything we do is inherently theatrical, […] [b]ut it doesn't have to read as theater. A lot of what we are excited about is heightening real life – how can you feel as though you're the hero of your own movie. It's tricky, though, because we're most excited about the cross fertilization of disciplines. If you can define it too easily you probably haven't gone far enough. (Barrett in Iezzi 2012)

While it is difficult to pigeonhole Punchdrunk into one performative category, it is safe to claim that they are both a pioneer and also arguably the market leader in the field of immersive theatre.

> Punchdrunk can still be said to be leaders of the 'immersive' pack – which now encompasses companies as diverse as dreamthinkspeak, Look Left, Look Right and You Me Bum Bum Train – a headline-grabbing 2010 project which, like a mad theme-park ride, hurtled solo participants through a maze of surprise scenes they were required to act in. (Cavendish 2013)

Their performances have variously impressed critics and have also become standard points of reference for further investigation in immersive theatre. But Punchdrunk are also a company which has enjoyed large and ever-growing success for almost two decades. This certainly says something about the quality and appeal of their work.

> Even when a new company as visionary and visceral as Shunt came along – occupying railway arches in East London then under London Bridge – elaborately wrought excitements were treated rather as a diverting sideshow. Then the Punchdrunk phenomenon happened. Barrett and his team – primarily hundreds of volunteers – staked a claim to an impossibly grand scale with minimal resources and pulled off their meticulously devised interventions in a style that had everyone, including those in the subsidised sector, gasping. The break-

through shows were 2006's Faust – occupying five floors of a Wapping warehouse – and, a year later, The Masque of the Red Death, which used every nook and cranny of the Battersea Arts Centre in its epic distillation of Edgar Allan Poe. (Cavendish 2013)

Consequently, Punchdrunk can arguably be called 'the game-changing company who've done more to catapult this kind of work into the heart of our culture than any other' (Cavendish 2013). It is for these reasons that they are the subject of this study. However, I want to stress again that there are a number of other immersive companies who create experiences very different from the ones described here. Unfortunately, however, the whole range of immersive practice cannot be described adequately in one chapter, possibly not even in one book. Therefore, Punchdrunk, and specifically two of their most successful shows, have been chosen as an example. *The Masque of the Red Death* 'kicked off the trend for "Choose Your Own Adventure"-style plays' (Jones 2013). Until today it is regarded as a landmark production and is still frequently referenced and discussed (cf. Cavendish 2013; Jones 2013; Machon 2009, 2013: 14; Patel 2009; Remshardt 2008). The second performance, *The Drowned Man: A Hollywood Fable* (2013–14), has been called a show where Punchdrunk outdid themselves in terms of set and detail (cf. Pringle 2013). It is also their most recent large-scale work to date. The shows cover two periods in the oeuvre of Punchdrunk: the first when immersive theatre began to emerge, and the second when they had become a well-established company, receiving regular Arts Council funding, and were produced by the National Theatre (cf. *The Drowned Man*, program book). Arguably, they have become mainstream, and also a company who practises an established form. For all these reasons, the two shows are well suited for the study of Punchdrunk as an example of immersive theatre.

The Masque of the Red Death (2007)

The Masque of the Red Death is certainly one of Punchdrunk's most successful and most frequently referenced shows until today. It was staged at Battersea Arts Centre (BAC), London, in 2007 and 2008. For the show, Punchdrunk took over the entire former town hall and transformed it into an experience of Edgar Allan Poe's mystery stories. With its Victorian atmosphere, marble staircases, grand and small rooms, the building provided an ideal background for the period of the stories. The force the experience exerted on audiences cannot be underestimated. Machon explains that being part of the performance gave spectators 'a palpable *sensation* of having taken laudanum with Poe and (meta)physically entered his *Tales of Mystery and Imagination*' (Machon 2013: 4, italics in the original). The following reading is, as should be evident by now, extremely subjective, given the format of the performance. 'By way of a disclaimer, let me say that there is no way to give an objective review of this production; critical objectivity was the first casualty of this mode of performance for which the description "immersive" is rather paltry' (Remshardt 2008: 640). Consequently, all impressions described in the following are my individual ones, and although it is not unlikely that others had similar experiences, it must be stressed that the performance I experienced is nothing but one textual reading of the piece. Many others are possible, depending on the individual journey. Nonetheless, I shall try to cite and question some concrete manifestations of the strategies of authenticity discussed above. Furthermore, the textual basis of the piece, that is Poe's stories, can also only serve as background information and cannot be fruitfully employed in a close reading here, because although the performance was based on Poe's stories, it did not seek to retell them in any chronological fashion. '[T]he more quickly one dispensed with the expectation that one would watch an enactment of, say, "The Tell-Tale Heart", the more rapidly one could get to the heart of the work, which was not overtly diegetic or even mimetic but experiential' (Remshardt 2008: 641). Nonetheless, the choice of text, that is Poe's *Tales of Mystery and Imagination*, had a profound influence on how spectators could read the performance. Even though the performance did not employ chronologic narration, many of the stories (e.g. 'The Fall of the House of Usher', 'Rue Morgue') are so well known that their characters and fixtures were easily recognizable. This had the effect that spectators had a certain familiarity with the piece and the performances and it was comparatively easy to piece together a story or recognize parts of it.

Frame: Entrance

The experience of *The Masque of the Red Death* began at the entrance of Battersea Arts Centre (BAC), where a large group of spectators was waiting. Everyone had been given a time slot for when to enter the performance. Therefore, the actual performance time varied between two and three hours for each spectator, depending on arrival. The first thing that sets this apart from other performances is of course the mask. White reads the mask with its beak shape as a sign of the carnivalesque. For him, masking is a strategy of licentiousness (cf. White 2012: 221). But the masks were also very much in line with the theme of the plague as their beaks are also reminiscent of plague masks and they consequently set the tone for the night. Felix Barrett finds that the mask changes spectators profoundly. 'I've always felt that the mask was the one thing that removed that sense of trepidation, whatever baggage you're bringing in, it's neutralized by the mask. So you can be a timid person but be crazy in the show world' (Machon 2009: 90). Remshardt had a similar feeling: when he donned the mask, and later on a cloak and a hat, he got 'a pleasant sense of disembodiment, half-presence, a bold childlike curiosity, and a reckless disregard for personal space' (Remshardt 2008: 642). The mask definitely disinhibits spectators. After a little time of adjustment, one becomes very nosey and even obtrusive. While I am not sure whether a timid person will be able to shed their inhibitions completely, the mask certainly helps spectators loosen up and enter a mood of curiosity and exploration. This is crucial because immersive theatre is at its strongest when spectators are ready to give themselves over to the experience. The more one is ready to do so, the stronger the experience will be. Furthermore, the very idea of the mask is easily associated with secrets and mystery. Being in a room with two-dozen masked people makes one feel strange, as if one had by accident wandered into a version of Stanley Kubrick's *Eyes Wide Shut*.

The mask is thus evocative of secrecy, but also danger, as one can never make out another individual person but only ever a mask. Clothes and external appearance also look remarkably similar with the faces missing and seen in a dimly lit space. Therefore, even if one arrives as a group at the performance, very quickly one will be on one's own. The mask thus facilitates that you lose your friends and ensures that you go on an individual journey. In other words, it is the first prerequisite for the authentic, individual experience.

Before entering the world, a front-of-house staff member explained the rules of the performance to all spectators: do not take off your mask, except in the bar, and do not talk. He then gave a diabolical laugh and opened the door for us to enter. The laugh gave the whole moment the feeling of entering a ghost ride at a carnival and left a vaguely eerie feeling hanging in mid-air. The exploration of the space began by walking through a maze of dimly lit corridors and up a staircase. At the top of the staircase I encountered a short, thick-set man in a nineteenth-century suit. He was situated in a wine cellar and began talking to one of the female spectators and even had a short dance with her. The wine cellar was very detailed, including dust on the bottles and even a small bowl of fresh olives on the table. The next room that I entered was evidently a tailor's shop. The tailor himself was present – a very tall man with dark hair. He pointed at me and beckoned me to step forward. He then gave me a black cloak for which I paid with a gold coin that I had been given at the entrance. This is the point where I realized how interactive this performance would be. (It was the first immersive theatre production I had seen.)

Set: Exploration

In terms of set, the tailor shop was perfection to the last degree. There were dozens of black cloaks hanging on the wall and I could smell the fabric and the wax of the burning candles. At this point I began to lose track of theatricalities, such as spotlights or sound emanating from somewhere – everything was a consistent world that was very rich in texture. As Remshardt has it, the attention to detail created 'a simultaneously surreal and hyperreal appearance' (Remshardt 2008: 642). It is Punchdrunk's explicit goal that there should always be more to discover (cf. Barrett in Machon 2009: 15). The whole performance space, with all its objects, rooms, nooks and crannies, is so vast that it is impossible to explore everything in one night. Audiences can realize this very quickly. It is almost sublime to notice that this performance seemingly never ends. It mirrors the real world in that it goes on and on and on; it has no discernible beginning or end. At first, I tried to follow one actor around, but quickly discovered that after some interaction with another actor, he just rummaged through some drawers without doing anything else. I was still looking for narrative and cohesion. As a matter of fact, I would have loved to be told where to go and where the action takes place. The whole performance was so overburdening that I began to feel lost, both physically and in my quest for meaning and narrative because the stories were presented in a non-linear way. I, for instance, encountered young Roderick Usher at one point but was not able to follow him for long. Each room or space seemed more fascinating than the next. The vast marble staircase of BAC appeared even bigger and a very fitting setting. Next I found myself on the ground floor in a room filled with trees – I was in a forest. I also discovered the basement where the Usher girl lay in a coffin. The possibilities for exploration were so vast; it was genuinely confusing. There were 'sitting rooms, dressing rooms, bedrooms, banquet rooms, opium dens, wine cellars, garrets, and laboratories […] secret passageways, such as a fireplace that led to an adjoining room' (Remshardt 2008: 642). Many of the experiences and discoveries were chance encounters. I only spotted the fireplace because someone else was crawling through it. In the adjacent room I found diaries and other papers which all looked like they had been handwritten in the nineteenth century. I assumed they were from the 'Purloined Letter' but am not sure. The detail was extremely striking; everything, from wallpaper to daily objects, looked as if it had sprung straight from Poe's story. Apparently there were a number of microperformances and some one-on-one sessions embedded in the *Masque* (cf. Machon 2013: 4); however, I found none of them.

While one can follow a general outline of narrative and can identify characters, the whole setting with its detail and its vast offerings is both sublime and confusing. However, as the description above indicates, two mechanisms serve to heighten sensual alertness and stimulate feelings of authenticity.

First, the set in its seemingly endless dimensions is subjectively experienced as sublime, thus creating both pleasure and fear. Both sensations are strong emotional states. In a nutshell, the spectators' experience in this is emotional, which arguably is stronger than cerebral or intellectual experience. Second, the extremely detailed set helps to create the illusion of authenticity. The paper that I held looked, felt and smelled like a genuine piece of old parchment. By discovering materials that are genuine and that neither look nor feel like theatrical props, the audience has real sensate experience which can easily spill over into the performance. In other words, the reality and detail of the world also produce the sensation that the acting and action surrounding spectators is more real than in the safe distance of a spectatorial theatre. In Machon's terms it is the tactile quality of props which serves to mark the experience as real. But it is not only the tactile experience, in the sense of being able to touch real objects but the entirety of physical stimulation (brushing up against other spectators, sitting on the floor, crawling through secret passages or climbing stairs) which gives the performance the haptic quality in Machon's sense. When I for instance, at a later point, followed young Usher running down the vast marble staircase into the basement, I had to dodge other spectators and was even a bit out of breath when I arrived in the basement with him. My entire body had been active and was now full of adrenaline and felt the exhaustion of that scene – physically. In other words, spectators have an entire range of physical contacts with the set and space, which gives the experience a very real quality. In consequence, the set encourages audiences to become lost in it and possibly even forget the theatrical frame or at least lose track of time. This is, I believe, what Machon means by absorption. By this point of the performance, I was completely taken in by the characters, the set and the story, and gradually became lost in the pleasure of exploration, forgetting time, and giving myself over to sensate experience.[8]

Politics: A double heterotopia

One of the most interesting spaces in the *Masque* was surely the bar. This is the only place where I was allowed to take off my mask and where drinks could be bought – for real money, not gold coins. This space is interesting for analysis in a number of ways.

> The bar; it is hot; I am sweating; I drink a Desperados. On stage there are vaudeville acts going on. I look around, people chat, and they all seem very emotional. It is peculiar to suddenly see people without the mask again. Now it seems surreal to see their faces without masks. A magic trick comes on stage, a mind reading act of high quality. I am baffled. The actors also interact with the audience. The air is stuffy. The MC on stage has a certain form of danger in his voice and appearance. He is dressed in tailcoats, typical top hat, whitish face and a mustache – like a circus director. He is very charming with the audience but I know that he can be very very nasty. Something about him emanates danger. I leave the bar. The vaudeville is fantastic. (My performance notes)

Having left the bar, I happened to stumble upon the backstage area of the bar where the actors prepared for their vaudeville acts. This was a very peculiar situation. I was in a theatrical performance in which actors portrayed actors preparing for an act, which they then showed on the stage within the performance. Again, I was free to explore and the actors simply ignored me or pushed me to the side when I was in their way. One actress argued with the MC. He seemed very cruel. I was not aware what the conflict was between them but there was definitely tension. I was right: he could be nasty. But what is the role he is playing? Is this his role or the person he portrays to be on stage? Or is it even the role he will play in a later scene, in a different room? This is really a game of double bottom. It is metatheatre in a way, not in *Hamlet*'s sense, but in the sense that the boundary between fact and fiction, and between character and other character or even real life becomes ever more blurry. Here I am not simply watching a play within a play but standing next to actors who pretend to be actors who pretend to do something on stage. The possibility to enter the green room of the show within the show poses questions about the theatricality of the whole event. I can look behind the mechanisms of this show but it does not stop there. What if I looked behind the mechanisms of the framing performance, would it stop there? Furthermore, the roles of performers, vaudeville actors and spectators become much more permeable as I am seemingly able to enter the sacred and usually forbidden space behind the limelight. By allowing spectators into that forbidden space, Punchdrunk not only enable small transgressions but very openly question the limits between theatricality and real life. The vaudeville and the green room both pose these questions and further the feeling of the sublime – this performance never ends, it simply goes on in another green room.

Body and noetics

I continued wandering around the building and decided to explore its limits, and found myself in an attic (?) room at one point. Some doors were locked but this one was open, so I decided to enter. It was dark, safe for a few tea lights. I was alone there. The room was filled with metal shelves, which seemed to be empty. The whole room was completely silent. I was wondering whether I should leave, but then again, why would the room be open if there was nothing to explore here? I stopped and stood. I could not hear a sound save for my own heartbeat. Or was there a sound? I looked to the left, was there movement? I was not sure. This is theatre after all, nothing bad could happen here. Or could it? Was that someone breathing? What if this is the room where you are lured in, in order to be given a jump scare? Or what if some other wayward spectator found one's way here? What if they decide to scare me, or something worse? Was there a sound? My heart was beating fast now. I quickly turned around and left the room. Most likely there was no one in there and possibly this room really did not offer much, but what is of interest here is my reaction. Being absolutely alone in a mostly dark room in a strange building is genuinely scary. The room plays on the *Urangst* of darkness and uses the mind's capacity to conjure up monsters out of thin air in the darkness. This is what Machon means by noetic, or tapping into prelinguistic mechanisms. I was genuinely scared because my instinctive fear of darkness kicked in. Granted, this is a rather cheap way of producing sensation but the important point is that it worked on me. I had a genuine sensation that can be compared to a ghost ride or telling ghost stories as a child. In other words, the room's desolation and darkness were able to instil genuine emotion which sprang from physical experience (seeing, hearing, smelling). The body as a whole works together to build these sensations. They are more and stronger than, say, being scared in the course of a play or a film because one is right there. One is right there with one's own body and has the noetic (irrational) feeling that something could happen; there is seemingly no protective distance. And, what is more, one can choose whether to face the fear and explore or run. It is the spectator's choice. The experience of fear is thus another very real sensation a spectator can get, despite knowing (or does one still know?) that one is in a theatrical performance. The mechanisms of noetic experience and of body and the play on instinct and *Urangst* are strong forces in immersive theatre.

Politics: Power and climax

After some more exploration I entered the great hall again only to discover that the finale was close at hand.

> I am back in the basement, suddenly there is smoke everywhere and loud noise, stewards and actors are ushering us around, shouting. We are being forced into the great hall, which had been closed so far. They force us to go. An orgiastic dance by the entire ensemble begins. I am surprised how big the room is – a ballroom. The actors are in a frantic dance while we stand around them on all sides of the hall. Suddenly they all collapse and from the end of the ballroom a towering figure, larger than life in a hooded cloak enters the room. This is the Red Death, the prince at the other end is scared, but he cannot and will not escape as Death slowly but unstoppably makes his way towards him. When he gets him the prince collapses. Then somebody pulls the

cloak away from the Red Death and there is no one underneath – the actor has vanished. There is nothing underneath it, no structure that would support the costume, no actor, nothing, just thin air. In this very moment, the lights on a stage at that end of the hall come up and we discover a band that we had not seen previously, they start playing. Suddenly, the ballroom transforms, the actors get up again, behind us bars are being manned and opened. This is a party now. (My performance notes)

In the final scene of the performance, the power economy becomes evident again. By means of smoke, shouting actors and ushers who quite directly nudged us in one direction, we were forced to follow to the finale of the show. The finale has a strong theatrical climax, and it did not fail to exert the intended effect of having me stand with my mouth wide open. However, it also laid bare the theatricality of the whole event. One is no longer free to explore but has to function in the theatrical machinery both as a backdrop to the dance and as a good spectator to watch the finale. At the time, however, I was not conscious of that. The whole experience was overwhelming to such a degree that I could not reflect on these dimensions. I genuinely felt immersed, and played along or followed the actors' instructions. Of course I knew deep down that this was all a performance, but that did not matter in the moment. I had bought into that evening to such a degree that I was willing and eager to enjoy the sensations of the alarm, the smoke, the being herded along with other spectators and the uncertainty of what was to come. This is certainly a form of suspension of disbelief, but it is far more intense than in conventional theatre. The mask and the entrance rooms had begun to prepare me and helped to ease me into this state of mind (transportation). Vast and detailed spaces had inspired confusion and a sublime admiration, giving me the feeling of being lost in this world which seemed so complete and endless (absorption). The double heterotopia of the bar and the stage further blurred the boundaries between what is fiction, what is acting, what is real life (praesence). These effects all left me physically and mentally exhausted. The bar and dancing in the end were very necessary as a 'decompression chamber'. They helped you to slowly ease back into the real world.

In conclusion, I must admit that all these effects are strong, but they also found fertile ground with me. Other spectators who refused to let themselves go and did not seek immersion probably did not have such strong experiences. Some of the tricks – specifically those that make use of instinctual behaviour or *Urangst* (such as darkness) – certainly work on everybody to a greater or lesser degree; but if one refuses to give up the mental defences, the state of immersion (praesence) that I experienced will not be attained. In a nutshell: immersion is a phenomenon that requires the spectator to play along. The more one is willing to participate, the hotter the experience will be. This is also where the structural similarity to authenticity lies. Many of the experiences in the performance are of course authentic through physical presence, (syn)aesthetics and so on. But authenticity is also a quality that is sought out by spectators themselves. The feeling of total immersion is nothing but the experience of strong noetic, (syn)aesthetic, haptic experiences. These are validated as authentic because they are produced by sense and body, which is the very source of (perceived) authentic experience. However, to obtain them, one has to want to find them. The performance provided a number of strong stimuli for authentic experience, but the marking has to be done by the individual. You need to want authenticity, then you will find it. What is even more important is certainly the number of immersive performances a spectator has attended. Whereas in the *Masque of the Red Death* I had been a first-time immersive spectator, in the *Drowned Man* I had already seen a number of immersive shows and I had a different approach then.

The Drowned Man (2013)

The Drowned Man: A Hollywood Fable was produced by Punchdrunk in collaboration with the National Theatre in 2013–14 (cf. program book). It was staged at a former Royal Mail sorting facility next to Paddington station that offered enormous open spaces over four floors. Felix

Barrett's ideal spectator may be a first-time visitor who is genuinely blown off his feet. But if one knows the proceedings and mechanisms of this kind of theatre, it can become harder to be genuinely dazzled by the experience. However, *The Drowned Man* showed considerable effort to even delight long-time fans.

> Felix Barrett and his vast design team have excelled themselves in this, a show that offers a level of design audacity and complexity that throws even *Masque* into the shadows. Their mastery of such a range of scales is the production's most powerful achievement – the experience of walking through a forest filled with caravans nudges up against that of walking into one of those caravans, opening a drawer, and spending ten minutes reading a desperate love letter by candlelight. If you find a script on a shelf, every page will be filled with detail, if you find a jewellery box it will almost certainly contain a treasure or a secret. (Pringle 2013)

The amount of detail in this show was indeed extreme to the point where every drawer, wardrobe or cupboard would contain just the objects one would expect to find there. And they would look as if they were in constant use. The experience in this show began in a more professionalized manner than in the *Masque*. One entered through a little, well-organized maze of barriers, checking cloaks and other large objects and then, again, had to wait the turn to be admitted. The way first led to corridors dabbed in red light, passing a large wall painting showing the logo of the 'Temple Studios'. We finished in a dead end where a silent steward gave us the masks. The usher from the *Masque* had been replaced with a pre-recorded voice that gave us instructions. We are about to enter the Temple Studios, we do so at our own risk, tonight is a wrap party but they are still filming and the voice (male) warns us not to leave the studios or walk around in the badlands. Here the performance already lays the first seed for its scare tactics and for inducing a state of heightened attention and also curiosity. Are we really doing this at our own risk? What about the badlands? Is this one of the rules or boundaries of the performance or is it part of it? The announcement sets a tone of mystery and danger for the night, because it is ambiguous about its own status. Furthermore, the possibility of attending a film set and seeing the past glamour of 1950s Hollywood studio smells of excitement.

A freight elevator opens and a movie actress in a glittery dress appears. She explains the connections and stories surrounding the characters with the help of photos on the walls of the elevator. This is our only clue about the stories. It is something about love (actor–actress) and another love story of a couple who never made it in the industry. She asks us to say good-bye to our friends. The elevator stops, and she opens the door halfway and encourages us to leave; when half the people have left, she suddenly slams the door shut and takes us to another level where we all leave. I exit and there are cardboard boxes stacked on and on. I wander through this little maze and arrive at a market square, complete with fountain and shops surrounding it.

Set

I explore the shops and slowly begin to agree with Pringle, who believes that in this show the actors 'largely play second fiddle to the set' (Pringle 2013). All products are genuine products from the 1960s, or at least from what I am able to tell, they look like it. The tins are heavy and still sealed, filled with tomato soup, peas or corn. All the shelves and the daily objects look like they have recently been used. An inspection of the cashbook reveals that it has also recently been used. It is up to scratch, recording all purchases made in the last days. I am again free to touch and inspect everything at leisure, although it seems that elsewhere more interesting things might be happening. One can easily buy into the illusion if one chooses to. I am more sceptical this time and try to seek out the theatrics of it. Obviously, the floor, which is all black and smooth, gives the game away a little bit. I later on find the first forest (the badlands). And again, everything is realistic, except if one looks up to the ceiling. It is dark and stretches far but still it cannot look like a real forest canopy. But the floor has changed, too. I am now walking on mulch. I can smell the wood and I am obviously forced to walk differently than on the smooth surface. The space forces you to take different physical attitudes (hapticity). Everything is gloomy, you cannot move as fast as you could normally because your vision is limited by the mask and the floor is uneven. The forest with the trailers provides a sensation of nature, but not in a good way. I encounter actors who seem desperate; one girl throws up in front of a trailer, and someone else assaults her. I move on and find a small church in the forest. It is made out of corrugated iron sheets and looks dilapidated. I enter the church and discover a small congregation of straw effigies in there. In an adjacent room, there is an altar with numerous burning candles and a statue of St Mary. In the next room there is just darkness and water on the floor. Again, Punchdrunk play with the *Urangst* of darkness. But the setting is also well chosen. The church, traditionally heralding salvation and a joyful message, is perverted here, as in so many horror stories, probably beginning with Dracula's Carfax Abbey. The straw effigies beg associations of voodoo practices or heathen burning rituals. This church emanates a perversion of religion and at the same time employs some of the classical *topoi* of horror films (church, voodoo, darkness). Only this time, the whole thing is not on the screen but I am in the middle of it. You cannot shake the feeling that someone or something might be lurking just around the next corner. It is well possible that I am simply conditioned by films to expect something to happen, for example someone to suddenly appear behind me. Maybe films have taught me their scare conventions for so long that I am now also willing to apply them when I find myself in such a situation. But the scary thing is that sometimes actors do suddenly appear and scare unwitting spectators. Or even just another masked spectator, inspecting a space, may be genuinely frightening when encountered unexpectedly. It is for good reason then that I am always alert to new sensations and very consciously inspecting my surroundings. Punchdrunk's method of letting the audience choose their own path effects that one is always expecting to find something, one is always in a heightened state of attention. One encounters an anticlimax (empty rooms) just as often as sudden action (actors appearing). You can therefore never be sure, quite literally, what lurks around the next corner. The feeling that develops is one of uncertainty, and that anything could happen anytime. In this way, the performance imitates the structure of life where there is no set dramaturgy but simply the possibility of (random) things happening, of chance encounters, excitement or boredom.

The church confirms the impression of the trailer park and the half-finished love letters and poems I had found in one of the trailers: there is nothing good in this world. Anything which could give hope is not present here. Some time later I find my way to the bar.

> Again drinks (at reasonable prices) and live shows, singing. I see the elevator actress again. She announces the two stars from the film will be performing a magic trick. A woman is put in a card board box and the man puts long, pointed wooden sticks through the box – at least two dozens of them. The box is on a tiny table, which is very slim. I do not see where the woman could be hiding. She reappears undamaged. Brilliant magic. (My performance notes)

High-class stage magic is one signature of Punchdrunk. In this show, it has a similar function as the double heterotopia in the *Masque*. Stage magic is designed to make the audience wonder: How did they do it? Or shout in enjoyment: that's impossible! All stage magic has that effect. It produces a feeling of satisfaction that is derived from being fooled and fascinated by the seeming impossibility. But it also opens the ever-so-slight possibility that it might be actual magic. I would argue that this is part of its appeal: confusion to such a degree as to enable the possibility – or maybe even the wish – that it might just be true. Stage magic is a performance of the numinous, the wondrous or even the supernatural. The magic in Punchdrunk must then be read as a conscious tool in the wider frame of the performance. It gives spectators the feeling that in this whole performance something magic might just be happening. It opens the ever-so-slight possibility of bewilderment and supernatural events. It lays the ground for a thick experience and is at the same time part of it.

Body

This thick experience is fuelled further by appealing to a number of senses, not just sight and sound. Smell, for instance, plays a crucial role in this. As was remarked above, smell – of all senses – has the most immediate impact on our central cortex and is thus able to produce very strong positive or negative reactions and associations. The smell of mulch in the forest and the strong scent of apricot candles and powder give very different sensate qualities to the spaces. They help to establish them as genuine places, not theatrical spaces. Whereas a conventional theatrical space will always more or less have the same smell about it, no matter if on stage a love scene is played out or a war is going on, in Punchdrunk productions the smells vary. The space becomes more real because it smells as it should smell. A make-up room will smell of powder and make-up, while a living room may smell of apricot candles or an executive office will smell of stale whisky and cigars. The scents thus underline the quality of the real within the rooms. Smell is one powerful part of the thick, (syn)aesthetic experience. But furthermore, it also serves as strong emotional counterpoint or to underline a scene. In one room, whose floor was covered in dirt and sand, I encountered an actor, a sweating, shirtless young man. He hectically rummaged through a box, desperately looking for something. He was crying and seemed desperate. At the same time I noticed a strong smell of cinnamon in the room. At this point, the visual sensation (desperation, crying) did not at all match the olfactory sensation (Christmas, tea, comfort). The smell served as a counterpoint and gave the scene a grotesque quality. As a consequence of that heightened sensation I was much more drawn into that scene and it left me with strong emotional confusion. The whole scene consequently provided yet another forceful emotional reaction, which was produced by the symbiosis and mismatch of smell and sight. Another good example of sensate experience is the one-on-one session I was fortunate enough to experience during the show.

> Suddenly a dark lady walks towards me. She is veiled and wearing a black dress. She takes me by the hand and leads me to a secret door which she unlocks. I follow her inside. She shuts the door behind me and leads me to another room. The room is well lit. Two lamps that look almost surgical are directed towards a metal table about two metres in length that is made of large iron bars or tubes. She beckons

me silently to sit down (or lay down?). I sit down. She tells me a story about a girl who always lived in the dark. She could not see the sun and prayed to the moon that he would give her happiness. I cannot follow the whole story. At one point she begins to slowly take off her veil. Her face is pale as hell and full of black marks that look like soot. Her hands also show dark, sooty patches. She looks me in the eye for a while and then very slowly removes my mask. She again tells me something about darkness and then produces a piece of cloth, bringing it close to my eyes, hesitating a moment, presumably to see if I would resist (I don't), and she blindfolds me. She then takes me by the hand and leads me to a door, where she keeps talking to me again about the girl in the darkness and how to see in the darkness. She moves my arms. She takes me to another room. I am now again walking on sand. She leads me around the room by the hand. Bit by bit she lets go until our hands hardly touch. I follow her but with our hands touching only ever so lightly. Suddenly she vanishes. I stand alone in the darkness. No sounds. Then she suddenly reappears next to my ear and whispers something. I wince. My senses are alert; my heart is pounding. She keeps on leading me, ever faster and at one point, pushing me from behind. I resist strongly. She stops. She takes my hand, pours sand on it. I feel the grains dropping and they stay underneath my cuff and my jewellery. She tells me something about the light and about how the moon was treacherous to her prayers. Suddenly a very bright light comes up. I can sense it through the blindfold. Again, a big surprise and very disturbing after all the darkness. The light goes off again. She whispers something in my ear. I can smell her breath. She gently hugs me and I hug her back. She pulls me further towards her and we breathe together, feeling each other's chest move, for twenty seconds or so. It is very intense. I feel the warmth of her body and feel her rib cage moving. She lets go of me and then vanishes again (to get my mask), comes back, takes the blindfold off. I see nothing, just darkness and she gives me back my mask and quickly ushers me out. I am back where I started. (My performance notes)

The whole event is a game of trust, power and sensate experience. Being alone with the performer of course has a whiff of exclusivity to it because, evidently, she is performing just for me at this moment.

The first encounter between her and me had a slightly uncanny feeling to it. I was absolutely unsure what would happen and the room had all the associations of a dilapidated operating theatre, which again evoked memories of horror films. The moment of staring into each other's eyes is also very intense. It is an experience of a form of intimacy because I can really look a person in the eyes. I am not far away but very close to her. Furthermore, just staring into a stranger's eyes without saying any words for more than a few seconds is a powerful theatrical tool. It creates a new relation between the two persons involved because such an encounter usually does not happen in daily life. It is a quite unique and new experience and is also able to produce strong emotional responses. A good example of this is Marina Abramović's performance *The Artist Is Present* (2010) at the MoMA, in which she sat on a chair and looked strangers into the eyes who sat across from her. This performance had a powerful impact on visitors who frequently cried or felt that they had found an emotional connection to the artist (cf. Biesenbach 2010). The same mechanism is at work in the one-on-one performance of *The Drowned Man*. A moment of human connection and intimacy is created, albeit accompanied by a feeling of uncanniness because of the soot and the surroundings.

The blindfolding then essentially starts a game of sensate experience. By taking away the power to see, other senses become much sharper and one relies much more on haptic and audio sensations. Indeed, I could concentrate much more on them. The game forces willing participants to focus on their other senses, thus sensually highlighting the whole experience. A number of individual senses are stimulated in their own way and separately in this performance: first the staring, then the feeling of touch, the walking on sand and the hearing of the lady's whisperings. As a form of counterpoint these individual perceptions highlight the other ones and also make you appreciate your full sensory function once you can use all your senses again. In short, by selectively activating the senses, the impressions leave a stronger mark in the person's memory, which will in the end help facilitate the feeling of a thick experience ((syn)aesthetics).

Furthermore, one has to advance considerable trust towards the performer. Being led by someone else is always a matter of trust. Here, trust must be advanced towards a stranger, which serves as some form of bonding. In the beginning, I completely gave into the game, until the hands of the performer and mine barely touched. I intuitively followed her movements with our hands only touching ever so slightly. This trust was consciously violated at the moment when she started to push me from behind. Earlier I became more and more relaxed and assured of our mutual trust and our movements were almost like a dance together, following each other, whereas now the event turned almost aggressive. I resisted her pushing. I was aware at that moment that she would not push me into or against something dangerous but still, my body resisted her. I could tell myself a hundred times that it was okay but there seems to be some (very sensible) ur-instinct that urges us not to let someone else push us somewhere if we cannot see. In other words, my resistance was a visceral reaction that I could not evade in this moment. Such an instinctive reaction is easily marked as authentic, because it is genuine and involuntary.

Other sensations are not just as but nearly as visceral as this one. For instance, the moment when one is suddenly alone is genuinely uncanny. Again, I could tell myself that nothing bad could happen, but there is still this *Urangst* that somebody might jump at me or attack me because I am unable to see or defend myself. Furthermore, the dripping of the sand on my palm was unexpected but a pleasant sensation. It helped me to focus even more on my tactile experience while I was blindfolded. Again, this sensation is genuine. Sand is really running on my hand. This has nothing to do with make-believe, but it is a genuine physical sensation. One is forced to concentrate on a sensation that one does not regularly have and with an intensity (due to lack of sight) that is much greater. The fine grains of sand also stayed with me for the rest of the performance. They remained underneath my rings and my bracelet, chafing my skin and every now and then reminding me of the experience. I took away, physically, parts of the experience, as it were. Finally, the embrace and the breathing together in the end also provided a very strong sensation. I was embracing another living human being, who was really breathing. I could smell her breath and feel her ribcage move, and in the same way, I suppose, she could feel me breathing. This situation establishes a moment where something very basic and again visceral is shared: the contact of two living bodies. In conclusion, one can say that the one-on-one experience maintained a strict power hierarchy – the lady was in control all the time. But if one submitted oneself to this power, the performance provided a number of powerful sensual stimuli, which are easily perceived as authentic.

Politics

In terms of politics, *The Drowned Man* comes with similar strings attached as the *Masque*. Every spectator is free to explore, but *The Drowned Man* also had an interesting voyeurial dimension that touched upon the politics of watching. When I entered the cinema, off the central market square, a cartoon was playing there in an endless loop. But this suddenly changed and I was fortunate to witness this.

> The cinema in the small town suddenly reveals itself to be a see-through screen, the film which is playing (a cartoon) stops and we see the Woyzek (?) guy standing on the other side, Vitruv's Man is projected on his body, his shirt is off, a doctor (?) is examining him and other masks are watching. I can see them but they cannot see me. This is also a game of voyeurs. (My performance notes)

The politics of watching here announce unequal terms. I can see the other spectators watching, but they are not aware of my presence behind the screen because the projection comes from their side. I am thus invisible. This establishes an economy of voyeuristic watching, which is based on the pleasure of seeing while not being seen. This economy also implies that what one watches is real because others have no reason to behave as actors. I encountered a similar configuration at one of the houses where the large mirror, overlooking the bedroom-cum-living room, turned out to be see-through from the other side. At one point I stumbled upon it in a hidden room and could then watch actors and other spectators from the other side. There is a certain delight and naughty pleasure in the voyeuristic gaze and it establishes the idea of the real as implied by this economy.

The exploration of the space, in terms of politics, is free, but the stewards are present just like in the *Masque*. They are very discrete, wearing black masks and clothes and usually blend into the background. They only appear when a spectator offends the rules (which often are unknown to them). These rules are frequently based on practical considerations. For instance, I was sitting on a chair at a clearing in the forest and two other spectators sat down on the couch next to me. Immediately a steward appeared out of nowhere and beckoned them away, while I was allowed to stay. The reason became obvious, when half a minute later an actress had a scene on that couch. Policing is thus very discrete and it is well possible that one's experience of the space is never disturbed by stewards. However, the feeling that one is permanently under surveillance is not far-fetched, or, in other words, if I can have that voyeuristic gaze at other spectators, who might be watching me? Am I really that alone and free all the time? Even in the rooms which seem completely deserted, might there be a camera, recording if I were to steal something? If one disconnects a little bit from the immersive experience, these questions will surface quite quickly and one will notice that the set must also be controlled by someone. As Doyle put it, the show is almost mathematical (cf. Machon 2009: 96). Quite frequently, the light changes in order to illuminate a piece of action or to highlight some movement. Also the sound, which is generally always present, will vary in volume. Who controls all this? Is there a big brother who is watching every corner of the performance, making sure it goes to plan? It is obvious that a cast of more than thirty actors, performing on four vast levels, including sound and complex light changes, need to be mathematically controlled by someone. So if one chooses to blank out the immersive experience, one quickly finds that one is possibly not as free in this performance and as unpoliced as initially suspected. However, such considerations will only surface if one chooses to detach from the immersion. The entire performance does its best to provide opportunities for not doing so. The entire piece was much less clear to me than the *Masque* because the story was only very vaguely recognizable. I tried in the beginning to work out a strategy that would provide me with the most narrative, but again failed. Once I had (again) let go of the desire to be told a story, the piece was much more fruitful, I was able to relax and immerse myself. In other words, as long as one tries to seek out stories or follow a master plan of exploration, one will fail at the core of the performance. One will simply walk past what the performance has to offer.

With the reduction of narrative, this piece offered more room for immersion and exploration, but, as is evident, this depended to a large degree on the willingness of the spectator. The performance only provides the infrastructure for authentic experience, and the spectator chooses how immersive their event will be. Some of the effects employed are direct, immediate and cannot be ignored (e.g. darkness, sand, breathing). They will influence every spectator to a greater or lesser degree. Other effects need more work by the spectator (e.g. detailed sets). The degree of immersion thus again depends on audiences' willingness to give themselves over to the experience. The huge popularity of Punchdrunk, however, shows that a considerable number of people are willing to do so and are thrilled by immersive experiences. In conclusion, immersive theatre is not a cause for authenticity; it is a symptom of a culture that seeks this kind of experience out. Immersive theatre, through its means of bodily experience, set and politics, provides the space where immersive experiences can be found and made, depending on how far one is willing to go. Immersive theatre must thus be regarded as one expression of the culture of authenticity and this authenticity is both sought out and marked by the individual.

4

Documentary Theatre

Exposition: the workings of the actual *past + the* virtual *past may be illustrated by an event well known to collective history such as the sinking of the* Titanic. *The disaster as it actually occurred descends into obscurity as its eyewitnesses die off, documents perish + the wreck of the ship dissolves in its Atlantic grave. Yet a* virtual *sinking of the* Titanic, *created from reworked memories, papers, hearsay, fiction – in short, belief – grows ever more 'truer'. The actual past is brittle, ever-dimming + ever more problematic to access + reconstruct: in contrast, the virtual past is malleable, ever-brightening + ever more difficult to circumvent/expose as fraudulent.*

–Cloud Atlas (Mitchell 2004: 408, italics in the original)

One of the most obvious cases of authenticity in contemporary theatre is a hugely popular and prolific strand of performances: documentary theatre. Documentary theatre (DT), in the various guises of tribunal plays, verbatim theatre or documentary drama, has been called the UK's 'market leader' of new theatrical productions in the first decade of the new millennium (cf. Sierz 2011: 58).

The enormous popularity of verbatim theatre, documentary drama and a number of hybrid forms in the first decade of the noughties has been widely acknowledged by scholars (cf. Lane 2010: 59; Reinelt 2006: 70; Sierz 2011: 58). '[S]ome theatre companies such as the Tricycle, Recorded Delivery or Hope Theatre Company have devoted themselves entirely to documentary drama' (Canton 2008: 319). The 'remarkable mobilisation and proliferation of documentary forms across Western theatre cultures in the past two decades' (Forsyth & Megson 2009: 1) is, however, by no means limited to the UK. Similar tendencies have been made out in Russia (cf. Beumers 2010), Germany (cf. Irmer 2006) and other countries. The first part of the chapter will take a closer look at some of the aesthetic means and strategies of authenticity that can be found in 'documentary drama'. After a brief historic discussion of the term, it will elaborate those strategies by situating DT in its contemporary cultural context. In the second part of the chapter, three documentary plays will be examined in the light of authenticity, before turning towards criticism of the genre. The chapter finishes with a discussion of three examples of documentary drama that do not adhere to classical strategies of authenticity and the real but rather seek to complicate such notions and to critique their own ontological status.

Origins and definitions

DT comes into existence in the first quarter of the twentieth century as a means of political communication. Companies like the US-American Living Newspaper of the 1930s are cited as a prime example (cf. Lane 2010: 59). Aesthetically, however, there are a number of forerunners, which have remained influential until today. Paget claims that Meyerhold, Brecht and Piscator must be seen as the godfathers of the genre (cf. Paget 1990: 42). Meyerhold's experimentations with the audience, Brecht's agit-prop estrangement techniques and Piscator's overt use of montage and of documentary source material are early beginnings of the genre from the 1930s onwards (cf. Paget 1990: 37). Nonetheless, what is today understood by DT only came into being in the politically and ideologically charged decade of the 1960s, where theatre moved away from the Absurdist strand of the 1950s and became overtly interested in, and a medium of, politics (cf. Irmer 2006: 16). History plays in this time offered 'a dramaturgy that replaced fictional narrative or parable with "real" situations and characters' (Irmer 2006: 17). Frequently, Peter Weiss' *The Investigation* (1965) is cited as the first 'pure' example of DT (cf. Irmer 2006: 16; Lane 2010: 59). Unsurprisingly, it is also Peter Weiss' definition of DT that has gained wide currency and is still used and discussed today.

> The documentary theatre is a theatre of factual reports. Minutes of proceedings, files, letters, statistical tables, stock-exchange communiqués, presentations of balance sheets of banks and industrial undertakings, official commentaries, speeches, interviews, statements by well-known personalities, press, radio, photo or film reportings of events and all the other media bear witness to the present and form the basis of the production. The documentary theatre shuns all inventions. It makes use of authentic documentary material, which it diffuses from the stage, without altering the contents, but in structuring the form. (in Irmer 2006: 18)

The core values of the genre are already evident here and have been succinctly summarized by David Lane, who remarks that the unifying element between all forms of DT is that the words in their script 'have already been written or spoken by others' (Lane 2010: 66). Today, as will be discussed at length later, academia and theatre practitioners alike have become suspicious of the pure value of documents as unadulterated facts. Documents of all forms and shapes have been manipulated, constructed and discredited in a number of ways with regard to their truth-value. However, in order to engage with DT at all, one has to find a way of acknowledging the documents and also grant them a certain status in reference to reality. Janelle Reinelt has suggested – along the lines of David Hare's notorious 'what happened happened' statement – to adopt a realist epistemology for such cases 'where knowledge is available through sense perception and cognition linked to objects/ documents' (Reinelt 2009: 9). She is quick to point out the obvious theoretical flaws of this assumption but believes that it is this attitude that helps spectators to make sense of events: 'The indexical value of documents is the corroboration that something happened, that events took place' (2009: 10). In other words, DT has a status different from fictional plays because there is a link to events that did happen (fact) as opposed to events that could happen (fiction). In the 1960s, DT was still seen as a medium where real characters treated real events with a link to the real world (cf. Irmer 2006: 17). Today, this status, unsurprisingly, is much more ambiguous. Nonetheless, DT still has a very specific claim to being more true than fictional theatre and possibly more authentic. Annika Esch-van Kan sees DT (in accordance with Dawson and Paget) as 'a literary, or theatrical genre [...] that uses pre-existing documentary material (such as newspapers, interviews, official transcripts of trials, or government reports) and claims to offer access to a hidden truth' (2011: 414). The truth claim of DT varies between the various genres, and a differentiated terminology has evolved to accommodate for that fact. Reinelt (2009: 13–14) and Paget (2009: 233–234) both see tribunal plays as having the strongest claim to authenticity, because they seek to alter their source material as little as possible and also seek to create the most naturalistic staging of a courtroom hearing. Verbatim theatre, however, frequently takes more liberties with the use of its source material in terms of adding, cutting and editing. For the purpose of this study, 'DT' will be used as an umbrella term for all plays and performances that stake a claim to using documentary material in Esch-van Kan's and Weiss' sense. The specificities of each strand (verbatim or tribunal) will be discussed accordingly.

The lure of the real: Modes of documentary and aesthetic strategies

The most curious property of DT in the early twenty-first century is surely its proliferation and success. In a time fiercely critical of the value of documents and truth claims, a format which asserts just that seems strangely out of place. Indeed, both Reinelt (2009: 8) and Paget point out that DT is epistemologically strongly rooted in a faith in empiricism and positivist notions of reality.

> [T]he very concept of 'documentary' was forged in the last century, and documentary became a key mode of expression in theatre, film and

literature. It was part of a 'faith in facts', a belief that the world could be made better through information, and a widespread excitement about the new possibilities in technology. (Paget 2009: 227)

Why then, it must be asked, has DT seen such a renewed success and popularity in the first decade of the millennium? It has been pointed out that DT, with its claim to facticity, is theatre's answer to reality TV (cf. Lane 2010; Reinelt 2006; Sierz 2011) and that contemporary culture has a special appetite for experiences of 'the real'. 'Our culture is saturated in serving our desire for the "real" experience, reaffirming that conditions for verbatim theatre are perhaps better than ever' (Lane 2010: 64). Some DT productions are very imitative in their staging of reality TV formats such as *Big Brother* (2000) or *Pop Idol* (2001), or scripted reality shows such as *Wife Swap* (2003) or *The Apprentice* (2005) (Lane 2010: 64). This is indicative of a trend in cultural production that seeks 'the real' or even just representations of the real or simulacra of reality. Furthermore, in the political climate of the first decade of the millennium, it seems that spectators and audiences felt they were not being told the truth by public institutions. Theatre, for some, effectively took over the role of journalism, purporting to show the real truth behind the official story.

> Verbatim theatre grew in popularity across the millennium thanks to the public's distrust of politicians, journalism and respected organisations such as the BBC and the Metropolitan Police Force, and the rise of celebrity 'real-life' drama via reality TV programmes and talent competitions. Theatre's reputation as a politicised and critical medium for exposing the truth fed a public desire for the 'real' answers to political scandal, providing an alleged clarity that other mediums could not provide. (Lane 2010: 77–78)

Again, the wish for true stories, for closure and a reality behind official narratives is a phenomenon which is by no means confined to the theatrical realm or the realm of television. It rather permeates a number of fields of contemporary cultural production.

> Today, given the anxieties created by the digital age's affront to old and
> established views of reality, and to the ongoing global uncertainties
> unleashed by the War on Terror, the British public's desire for reality is
> more intense than ever – and this is manifested not only in a seemingly
> insatiable appetite for reality TV, but also in a need to be assured that
> the best theatre is somehow 'real', explanation enough perhaps for the
> current vogue for verbatim theatre. (Sierz 2008: 102)

As Sierz makes plain, there are a number of factors, ranging from
politics and history to contemporary use of media, which contribute to
the success of DT.

In order to begin an investigation of DT in the first decade of the
2000s, it makes sense to take a closer look at the cultural climate of
authenticity, as described in the previous chapters. Many of the points
already made there also apply to DT practices. The popularity of reality
TV is certainly indicative of a 'documentary culture'. 'British audiences',
as Reinelt remarks, 'have been as enthralled with reality TV as their
American counterparts' (2006: 71). Consequently, DT has been seen as
a symptom of 'a hunger in audiences for factual truth, theatre's answer
to reality TV, when what you see is not fiction at all' (Sierz 2011: 58).
However, both, reality TV and DT, must be viewed in their cultural
context. They are a symptom of a great unease and distrust in public
institutions and mainstream narrative on large parts of the audience.
In this time after postmodernity, media-generated reality is perceived
as un-authentic, or not fully true, because facts are frequently spun and
changed. In other words, reality and along with it the facts have become
a performance.

> The hypertheatricalization of contemporary culture can itself lead
> toward a valoraization and desire for 'facts', for the materiality of
> events, for a brute display of evidence as a reaction against the fear
> of total fiction when all else fails. [...] Living in a world of simulation
> where everything is understood to be only a copy of a copy of a copy
> and nothing is for sure, public rehearsal of the facts becomes one way
> of holding on to the very notion of facts and of building a meaningful
> narrative around them. (Reinelt 2006: 81–82)

Reinelt's remarks should be kept in mind as a sort of background noise for understanding the following considerations regarding DT and authenticity. They are an expression of a culture that is in search of a reality that is not mediated, direct and tangible in a factual sense. Audiences seek to hold on to or even rescue the notion of truth, which seemingly is lost in contemporary society. This unease with medial representation finds outlets in a number of channels.

> Documentary forms throughout the representational media – in art, photography, theatre, film and television – in the present have risen to prominence partly because the participant in a live event and the witness of events have special claims to being something to be trusted. […] The urgency of all this has been ratched up by growing disaffection with political process and an associated lack of trust in agencies formerly supposed to honour social duties of care (health service, the police, the law) and be trusted accordingly. (Paget 2009: 234–235)

DT modes are then, fundamentally, a way of re-establishing trust and truth, where these values have been found lacking in institutions and media that had formerly been endowed with them. The quality of authenticity, in DT as well as in other forms of cultural production, is – it is important to note – ascribed by the perceiving individual. It is useful to recall the three propositions, made by Funk et al. about authenticity, namely, that it is fragmented (not a unified, inherent quality, while it may still claim essential truths), it is contested (academically and individually), and, last but not least, authenticity is performative, that means, the authentic discourse effects its own validation as authentic.

> As an aesthetic construct, authenticity is deeply implicated in the process of communication that is realized in the interplay between production, aesthetic object, context and reception. Authenticity, in this regard, becomes a matter of form and style in which the authentic is realized as a performative *effect*. (Funk et al. 2012: 13, italics in the original)

In other words, similar to intimate theatre and immersive theatre, audiences endow DT performances with the attribute of authenticity.

Often the focal point of such an ascription is the witness who gives testimony of events. The persona of the witness is endowed with the unique ability of producing effects of authenticity. The witness has a special claim to having been there and to having first-hand experience, which can be shared with the spectators. The statements of such a 'primary source' will 'automatically gain the badge of authenticity' (Lachman 2007: 308). The witness must be understood in a broad sense here either as an actual person or as a document, relating facts. The factuality of the witness is the quality which seems to escape representation and lying; it is true, by virtue of its ontological status (fact) and therefore trustworthy.

New politicization

Trust and the loss of trust are one crucial feature of structures of feeling in the early 2000s. It is not only Jacobi (cf. 2014: 30–31, also Funk 2015: 2, Hughes 2011: 124–136; Tomlin 2013: 117–118) who claims that the millennium and subsequently the attacks of 9/11 marked a shift both in politics and also in structure of feeling on a global scale. Lane claims likewise:

> It was not only the perceived failure of new British writers to engage with the political that made way for verbatim theatre. The failures of the media to faithfully report events without manipulating evidence, and the repeated failures of hallowed institutions – the police, the army and the government – to conduct themselves with integrity were a significant contributory factor. Whilst the events of 9/11 in isolation were responsible for creating a renewed climate of political interest, the reactions of those guiding us through the aftermath – Bush's administration, Blair's Labour government, the BBC, the Metropolitan Police Force – were the real target of criticism. Britain joined the US in invading Iraq on the basis that Saddam Hussein could launch weapons of mass destruction in forty-five minutes; the BBC alleged that these facts had been 'sexed-up' and that they had a witness to prove it. (Lane 2010: 61–62)

European as well as US culture gained a new politicization and an interest in facts. Facts were what it was all about regarding the war in Iraq and Afghanistan. Did Iraq indeed have weapons of mass destruction? Could the images shown by Colin Powell in the UN Security Council be trusted? In this period, a renewed interest in the debate of political issues and most importantly in truth arose because of a prevailing feeling that the public had frequently been lied to. David Edgar maintains that the post-9/11 period was characterized by fact-based theatre or theatre as journalism (e.g. Hare's *The Permanent Way*, 2003) because conventional journalism, in the people's perception, failed to do its job (cf. 2012: 8). Not shy of metaphors, he remarks that '[t]he war on terror brought politics back on to the world stage, and it's no surprise that politics returned to theatrical stages as well' (in Forsyth & Megson 2009: 1). Theatre in his view becomes a function of the political process or an extension where the other channels of public discourse fail. In this line of argument, Carol Martin has elaborated six functions of DT in contemporary culture:

1. To reopen trials to critique justice
2. To create additional historical accounts
3. To reconstruct an event
4. To intermingle autobiography and history
5. To critique both the operations of documentary and fiction
6. To elaborate the oral culture of theatre (cf. Martin 2006: 12–13).

It is no coincidence that the first three functions are all concerned with creating versions of the truth, which have been withheld from or neglected by mainstream narratives. DT seeks to establish different narratives and give voice to minority discourses but also to present truths that had been hidden before. Nicholas Kent, former artistic director of the Tricycle Theatre, famous for its tribunal plays since the mid-1990s (cf. Esch-van Kan 2011: 421), has expressed that theatre could fulfil such a political function. He repeatedly 'emphasized that the initial impulse to set up tribunal plays has been triggered by the deficiency that public hearings were not being televised [...]. Theatre appears as a substitute for journalism entrusted with the task of mending journalism's failures' (Esch-van Kan 2011: 416). This political function becomes most obvious in tribunal plays, which have been the Tricycle's signature performances for a long time. '[T]ribunal theatre consists of the meticulous re-enactment of edited transcripts of state-sanctioned inquiries that address perceived miscarriages of justice and flaws in the operations and accountability of public institutions' (Megson 2009: 195). In other words, tribunal plays seek to symbolically mend the flaws of judicial proceedings. The terminology 'perceived miscarriages of justice' already hints at the fact that with tribunal plays there is usually a clear opinion towards one side of the story. Such restaged public hearings are frequently not a neutral place for finding truth, as a courtroom is supposed to be, but are biased with an opinion. Tribunal theatre is selective and frequently agit-prop in its choice of issues. Public politics here becomes the subject of theatre's own politics of subversion. DT, by subverting official narratives, creates its own version of truth and narratives, which it hopes will be trusted more by the public. Prominent examples of such plays are certainly Nicolas Kent's *The Coulour of Justice* (1999), which treated the racially motivated murder of a young black man; Richard Norton-Taylor's *Bloody Sunday: Scenes from the Savile Inquiry* (2005), which re-opened the investigation of the military's behaviour in Northern Ireland in 1972; and Richard Norton-Taylor's *Called to Account: The Indictment of Anthony Charles Lynton Blair for the Crime of Aggression Against Iraq – A Hearing* (2007). The list could easily be extended, but it already becomes evident that the interest of DT is in perceived miscarriages of justice and to, at least theatrically, right a perceived wrong.

The authority of verbatim theatre is derived from the presentation of verbatim testimony, documents, minutiae and so on (cf. Megson 2009: 195–196), in short, witnesses in a broad sense. In tribunal plays, the testimony of witnesses in a narrow sense is used to lend authority to the performance. The act of testifying (i.e. speaking 'the truth and nothing but the truth') implies that one has access to one unadulterated, single Truth. In other words, tribunal and witness plays are epistemologically rooted in the positivist idea of a single truth that has shaped our judicial system. This very idea must be seen as the opposite of lying, deception, misleading and spinning the facts, which is perceived to take place in politics every day. If David Edgar is right and 9/11 and its repercussions brought politics back to the stage, then DT brought the notion of truth in politics back to the stage.

Subject matter: The real

The truth claim is closely linked to DT's subject matter, that is, stories that have some ties to the real world – events that did happen as opposed to events that could happen. This connection with the real world is partly also responsible for DT's success. DT can be understood to offer a confrontation with the real in a double sense. First, because of its use of archival material, documentary theatre has a claim to being closer to factuality than fiction – to being close to 'being there' and to showing 'the real thing' (Martin 2006: 10). Steven Bottoms has argued that in the politically charged climate of the first decade of the millennium, fiction was apparently not good enough for questions of world politics.

> Mere dramatic fiction has apparently been seen as an inadequate response to the current global situation. It is less clear why no similar trend has been apparent in the U.S. [...] Perhaps one reason is that British dramatists seem to have retained a basic faith in their ready apprehension of 'the real': most Britons still believe (somewhat gullibly?) in the underlying truth/reality of the news as mediated by the BBC and by newspapers such as *The Guardian*. (Bottoms 2006: 57)

DT answered the audience's call for dramatic work which treated not events somewhere in the realm of fiction but which took on the events surrounding them in the real world. DT is a symptom of the need to deal with and confront oneself with the surroundings of the real world. In other words, it is likely that the events happening in the world of global politics exerted such strength that audiences, even in the theatre, were not willing to escape to fiction-land but rather sought confrontation with the real world.

This confrontation then establishes the second sense of the word 'real' in this context. As has been noted, DT performances typically deal with topics which are violent and disturbing, such as war, terrorism or murder. Robin Soans, in *Talking to Terrorists* (2005) – for instance – has a former member of the Kurdish Workers Party describe his imprisonment and torture: 'For the first hundred days of interrogation we were naked. The women were raped, most of the men had batons shoved up their arses or were forced to sit on beer bottles 'til they disappeared up' (2005: 44). It is evident that the description here can only give a fleeting glimpse of the horrors suffered by the inmates, which can in all likelihood never be understood by someone who has not been in the same situation.[1] These traumatic events can best be conceptualized as an expression of 'the real' in Lacan's sense (cf. Lacan 1998). The real is a form of experience that is strong and painful and stands outside the symbolic and representative function of language.

> The Lacanian Real, then, is that which is excluded from language and representation [...], the Real cannot be articulated or brought forth in representation, but its very absence in our construction of a coherent reality is always already marked by symptoms of its inaccessible presence. (Tomlin 2013: 164)

Tomlin hints at the paradox situation that the real, that is, exactly the thing which cannot be represented, is used in DT and represented on stage. The 'real' events are still present in their absence and demand treatment – they loom over victims and spectators alike, as it were. Tomlin consequently argues that through an individual's confrontation with the absent material and the real events, an engagement with the real is possible (cf. Tomlin 2013: 166–168). In other words, attempting to comprehend the incomprehensible is the only way to engage with such issues at all.[2]

These issues consequently stand outside the symbolic order. They cannot be represented adequately – neither by language nor by non-verbal signs. DT can be an ideal frame for treating such traumatic events (cf. Favorini 2009): while it cannot represent the event adequately, it can bring the individual that has experienced the trauma to the stage.

The person of the witness becomes the focal point for an audience's contemplation of traumatic events.

> [T]here is both a legalistic and a spiritual component in Western notions of witness, and it is these components that powerfully charge the theatrical experience of tribunal and verbatim theatres. The witness is cursed (or blessed) with first order experience. [...] The theatrical team and audience are seekers, it seems to me, who derive a second order expression and experience in workshop, rehearsal and performance. [...]. Theatre's ancient connection with religion, its occasionally profound moment of *encounter* once again adds charge (or can add a charge) to performance. (Paget 2009: 236, italics in the original)

In DT, audiences and performers both encounter the real, by proxy, as it were. An actor who performs the verbatim material of the witness is as close as one can get to the actual experience. The enactment of the witness provides audiences with a fleeting glimpse at that, which cannot be represented and which yet is 'real' in the double meaning of the word.

Set: Mixing world and stage

The staging of the witness, of her testimony and persona, plays a crucial role in this confrontation. DT must strive for verisimilitude in order to achieve the effect of authenticity. The tribunal plays at the Tricycle, and many other verbatim plays for that matter, follow a very austere staging, lending them an idea of realism and non-theatricality (cf. Botham 2008: 315; cf. Canton 2008: 321–322). The aim is to minimize the distance between stage and world as far as possible. Therefore, DT often uses evidence and testimony like in a court of law (cf. Martin 2006: 11). While evidence is all that is factual, such as official documents or statements, it is crucial to note that testimony is always narrative, in the sense that it is told – even by a first-hand witness – according to learned conventions of storytelling and structured according to principles of narration.

DT's 'practitioners use the archive as evidence to create a performance of testimony; audiences understand what they see and hear as nonfiction;

the actors ostensibly perform "verbatim"' (Martin 2006: 11). Of course what an audience sees is verbatim, but even if the original witness came directly to the stage, it is important to remember that her testimony has already been tainted with imprecision and shaped by narrative convention. Anyone trying to recall a story from when they were eight years old – as does, for instance, the witness in Soans' *Terrorists* (cf. 2005: 36) – even if it is a traumatic event, will have to admit that their memory may not be perfect, that they may have perceived things incorrectly or that they may have added details in retrospect, especially if the event was a traumatic one. A witness' memory then has, at best, a claim to subjective truth, not to any form of objective, neutral truth. In DT, this truth claim ontologically becomes more obscure because effectively an actress portrays a witness, whose testimony is already tainted with narrative cohesion and mnemonic imprecision.

However, despite all these *caveats*, DT's scenography and methods of staging still encourage audiences to endow the performance with authenticity. The truth claim is strongest in tribunal plays. Tribunal plays poetically, structurally and phenomenologically mirror the courtroom and blur the lines between art and life (cf. Esch-van Kan 2011: 421).

> [S]taging devices that turned into conventions for tribunal productions: the stage set replicates the hearing room, there is no stage action, the lighting remains unchanged, and the house lights are up throughout the performance, the audience is surrounded by plasma screens that project documents in question […], actors speak in an accelerated naturalistic TV-like fashion […], voices are amplified with microphones, and the actors do not return on stage to take their applause […], yet in fact all the above-listed devices are obviously used for effect and attune to create the illusion of authenticity. (Esch-van Kan 2011: 422)

Such mechanisms help the audience read the performance more like a real event than a theatrical production. Where tribunal plays take their credibility from the mechanisms and mannerisms of the courtroom, other DTs will frequently use techniques from other areas of factual discourse, such as news programmes. The poetics of documentary are strongly connected to the discourse of factuality, which verifies DT's truth claim.

> The function of this discourse is almost always imported from non-dramatic modes of signification – like the news broadcast, the current affairs programme, and the documentary proper [i.e. film documentaries]. It normally comprises such rhetorical strategies as voice-over captions, charts and statistics, and direct ('talking head') address of the camera/audience. All these things have been so naturalised in our culture that they are perceived as the mediation of 'straight facts'. (Paget 1990: 5)

In other words, an austere set, which may display such things as monitors or projections of documents or even statistics, is something that is borrowed from factual media such as the news programmes. When an audience perceives these signs, they go into their default mode of 'factuality'. Having created this atmosphere of factuality, DT can then proceed to create its own truth or to pass off as factual its own version of events and stories. As long as the message is credible within the frame and limitations of the performance, and – one must probably concede – confirms to audience's expectations about that character, it may well be taken as factual. What was really said and what is part of the archive is mingled with fiction through this staging that uses strategies of factual presentation. This continues in the use of media, which in DT 'are deeply connected to notions of the real whether material or immaterial' (Martin 2009: 75). By employing devices such as monitors and projections, DT further authenticates its own narrative, because it moves away from illusionary, classical actors' theatre towards technology-based, factual news studios. Documents that can be shown are real and, therefore, everything pertaining to that discourse on stage must be real. For instance, the play *Three Posters* (2006), a play centred around a last tape by a Lebanese suicide bomber, deliberately confuses reality and fiction by using media recordings and live performances on screen, which are not marked as such (cf. Martin 2009: 79–81). Recorded video messages are shown alongside other ones, which are, unbeknownst to the audience, performed live. Which tape is authentic or real, part of the archive or made up, thus becomes dubious. Finally, the austere staging also affects the method of acting used in DT. In extreme cases, actors will become pure mouthpieces with almost no creative input of their own. As Alecky Blythe, the director of London-based company Recorded Delivery (e.g. *London Road*, 2006), notes:

> Rather than learning a text, the actors copy the speech patterns and physicality of the interviewee. The show is rehearsed and performed with the actors wearing earphones through which they hear the edited interview playing, and they copy exactly what they hear, including every cough, stutter and hesitation. (Blythe in Soans 2005: 96)

The actor is less concerned with any notions of method-acting or character work but rather with imitation. While only Recorded Delivery works with the technique of earphones for the actors, they always become a mouthpiece for someone else's words. Actors become an empty vessel to be filled with the voice of the real witness coming in from a place somewhere off stage, indeed possibly from the site of the real itself. In Recorded Delivery's case, the earpieces and the technique are visible to the audience and so it is evident that the actors simply voice what is real without adding or editing. The actors become mere 'talking heads' like in a television documentary.

While not all DT makes use of headphones, all of them employ similar techniques and try to make actors sound and appear as true a representation of the actual person as possible. Derek Paget, discussing modes of authenticity in television documentaries, claims that we have become so used to the combination of image plus reporter/reporting voice in the twentieth century that we need it to feel the situation is real, so that it touches us and becomes part of our reality (cf. 1990: 32–33). Audiences over the past, say, fifty years have learned the conventions of realism and authenticity, mostly through television, but also on stage. Even today, in a time when the very idea of unadulterated facts is rightly disputed, these mechanisms are still employed and, surprisingly, still seem to work.

Although factuality itself is in crisis (and the regular controversies over TV documentary dramas are part evidence of this), the 'phantom objectivity' of camera/microphone technology even yet haunts cinema, TV, and even theatrical representations of reality to the extent that the imaginary is still often accepted very readily as the real *provided it conforms to the conventions of realism*. (Paget 1990: 114, italics in the original)

In short, for DT as much as for documentary television, what matters is not authenticity but adhering to the conventions of authenticity in terms of staging. Authenticity (again) is performative, not essential. DT heavily borrows its techniques from television and employs the conventions of factuality, reliability and authenticity that have been shaped in the second half of the twentieth century. Key in this endeavour is the elimination of most of the theatricality.

Object authenticity

'Documentary theatre tends to base its claim to authenticity on the assumption, explicit or implicit, that the source documents are themselves incontestably "true", or at least self-evidently "real"' (Upton 2009: 179). Upton here takes a stance similar to Reinelt, stating that something did happen and the document is a direct reference to that event. DT gains its force through the promise of portraying real events, of which audiences can be sure that all the gore and terror on stage really happened and are not simply derived from the fantasy of a writer.

Audiences crave facts, especially if they are portrayed in a dramatic fashion. Paget even claims that facts have become a 'fetish' for us (cf. 1990: 3). A number of DT performances, especially tribunal plays, present timelines, official documents or even maps in their appendix (cf. e.g. *The Colour of Justice* (Norton-Taylor 2014c: 292–300)). On stage, these documents are frequently displayed on screens (e.g. Gillian Slovo's *The Riots*, 2012) (cf. 2014: 857). Practically all tribunal plays reference and foreground their source material as genuine in the preface (cf. Brittain et al. 2014: *passim*). The facts are so fascinating for the audience precisely because of their connection to something outside the symbolic order.

The special quality of the document is that it is real; its reality forms the basis for the authority of the narrative. Only because the document is fact and not fiction can DT performances develop such a force and immediacy. In terms of authenticity, the document is, in contrast to immersive theatre, not endowed with 'hot authenticity' but rather with what Susanne Knaller has called 'object authenticity' (cf. Funk 2015: 18). The document is not validated by personal experience but by an outside authority. Minutiae or protocols may carry official stamps or signatures; photos or films may bear logos or seals. The document is validated as genuine much like an art expert would authenticate a painting by, for instance, Picasso. It is thus a form of 'cool authenticity' (Selwyn, cf. Funk 2015: 20–21) that lies at the heart of DT. Subsequently, the authenticated document can be used in order to produce more emotionally charged effects in confrontation with the real. That the document is genuine, that is derived from the real world, is, however, not to say that the document is capable of showing the Truth. While the document itself may carry a certain truth-value, it is clear that it cannot claim to be telling an exhaustive account of the truth. Lane and others have pointed out that, even with the authentic document in hand, DT always tells us one version of the truth which it constructs (cf. Lane 2010: 66).

> The most fundamental point to make is that whenever television programme makers, film-makers, or screen/tele/stage playwrights tell True Stories, they try to persuade us to consume their product with a very particular promise – the Promise of Fact. Prior assurance of 'truth', prior 'authentication' provides a cultural passport to credibility in the True Story. (Paget 1990: 3, italics in the original)

Consequently, it is clear that object authenticity is a prerequisite for contemporary DT. The witness in a broad sense is validated by some outside authority. This can happen in the guise of office stamps or seals or it could also be the use of dialect or sociolect for a witness in the narrow sense.

Offering closure

The construction of narrative, dramatic cohesion and climax in DT, based on the documents, often follows a political or activist agenda of its own. 'Those who make documentary theatre interrogate specific events, systems of belief, and political affiliations precisely through their own version of events' (Martin 2006: 9). The practitioners bring the documents into an order, edit and cut them and finally arrive at a version that is much more coherent and conclusive than the real world is, where documents and facts more often than not stand next to each other unlinked.

> [I]t is not only a conception of theatre as the unreal or merely artificial that is useful for understanding contemporary public life, but on the contrary, theatre's capacity for creating a new real, making manifest the real, embodying the real within the realm of images and sensations as well as the realm of discursivity. (Reinelt 2006: 71)

Where public discourse about a certain political issue may well be confusing, full of contradictory opinions or contradictory facts, DT is able to offer closure by means of theatrical dramaturgy, while the real world remains confusing. This is frequently the case with tribunal plays – it is inherent in the concept. A tribunal ends with a verdict, and even if the play itself does not openly take sides – many tribunal plays seek to make a balanced argument – the audience is put in the position of a judge and can then 'close the case' for themselves. Some tribunal plays, however, quite openly declare their stance on the subject they treat. *The Colour of Justice* (1999), for instance, suggests that the murder of Steven Lawrence had been racially motivated and not properly investigated by a police force marked by institutional racism (cf. Norton-Taylor 2014c: 292–293, *passim*). 'At least the theatrical public' can 'experience a certain catharsis from the performance, if not from the actual workings of justice' (Reinelt 2006: 80). In other words, where public discourse may well never end at all, DT can offer satisfying, in times simple, answers. It thus caters for audiences' demand for closure and completion.

[T]he appeal of the old-fashioned documentary may be that it meets a deep collective urge for the link between knowledge and truth [...]. In this case [*The Colour of Justice*], audiences know that documents, facts and evidence are always mediated when they are received; they know there is no raw truth apart from interpretation, but still, they want to experience the assertion of materiality of events, of the indisputable character of the facts [...]. (Reinelt 2006: 82)

Whether all audiences are endowed with such critical distance regarding discourse and document as Reinelt suggests is a matter of debate; however, the high regard for facts and the longing for cohesion and closure are not. This trend, some would argue, is an inherently human desire (cf. Funk 2015: 4) and it has become evident in many areas, not just theatre. Bruzzi has proffered that docusoaps on television provide audiences with closure and entertainment of everyday events. They tell small, coherent narratives out of authentic stories of the everyday and they focus on crisis and character rather than issue (cf. Bruzzi 2000: 85). In other words, everyday events are dramatized by cutting and editing and made into an interesting story, which, nonetheless, has a whiff of authenticity about it because it was taken from real life and the protagonists are not (professional) actors.[3] Both, the longing for closure and reconstruction and the hunger for authenticity, for something less represented and more genuine, can and should be read as one expression of a contemporary structure of feeling that seeks to reunify fractured discourses.

Authentic documentaries

In the following, I will survey three documentary plays which adhere to the 'classical mode' of DT. They will help to exemplarily illuminate the aesthetic strategies and political consequences of authenticity, before turning to plays and performances that seek to challenge these notions.

Talking to Terrorists (2005)

Robin Soan's play *Talking to Terrorists* premiered in April 2005 at the Theatre Royal in Bury St Edmunds and subsequently went on an extensive and hugely successful tour of the UK (cf. Soans 2005). The play's topic is terrorism, or, more precisely, the actual people who commit and support acts of terrorism. It is based on interviews with 'people from around the world who have been involved in terrorism' with the aim of knowing 'what makes ordinary people do extreme things' (Soans 2005: back cover). These ordinary people include 'peacemakers, warriors, journalists, hostages and psychologists. Their stories take us from Uganda, Israel, Turkey Iraq and Ireland – to the heart of the British establishment' (2005). In short, the play treats a very politically charged and brutal subject with a global focus.

Right from the beginning, the play stakes its claim to facticity. '*A number of names have been withheld or changed at the request of the interviewees*' (Soans 2005: 22, original emphasis). This sentence carries two implications. First of all, it communicates that the names and persons involved in the play and their stories, which the audience is about to see, are not fictional but based on real-life events and real people. Second, the names of some of the interviewees have been withheld. The withholding of names of witnesses is a common feature in TV documentaries and the 'quote-off-the-record' is found daily in the newspapers. Withholding the names in a play about terrorism signifies that the real persons evidently feel that there is some kind of danger involved in speaking publicly about their experience of or connection with terrorism. They might stand the danger of losing their job or even their lives if their statements and names were connected. Thus, the preface of the play makes readers and audiences (as always with the Royal Court, the complete script was available as a programme book) aware that the subject of the play is as real as it gets. It implies that audiences will be shown unadulterated statements and facts collected from witnesses who have a claim to having been there, to having first-hand experience. Their first-hand experience is even so strong that they are still in danger today. This is the first and most basic truth claim that the play makes. Subsequently, the play continues to blur the line between fact and fiction, when it states that it is based on interviews with 'individuals whose voices became the play's characters. Their stories were collected, in the rehearsal room and elsewhere, by a team of actor-researchers' (Soans 2005: preface). The turn of phrase 'voices who become characters' has a very strange ring to it. Are they voices or characters? Are they manifest in the world or ephemeral, as voices should be? In other words, where do these voices come from and how do they translate into becoming a character on a stage? The phrase implies that the original voice of the witness is transformed into a character on stage, which would then render it fiction again. So if read closely, the sentence acknowledges that the play does not display the unadulterated witness and her statement but it positions itself in the liminal space between fact and fiction.

Moreover, what – one may ask – are 'actor-researchers'? Actors usually try to find things like emotional truth; when they get into a character they treat their subject instinctively, creatively and physically. 'Researchers', on the other hand, carry strong connotations of science, neutrality and factuality. In this line of thought, the term 'actor-researchers' sounds like an oxymoron. This oxymoron, however, is placed deliberately because it validates the play's truth claim. It brings together the roles of fiction and science, thus endowing fiction with the association of neutrality and facticity. The play again positions itself in liminal space and privileges the notion of subjective truth found by the 'actor-researchers', which may very well stray from facticity but still seeks to find the authentic core of someone's statement.

Having staked its claim to truth and factuality, the play itself also uses metareference to further authenticate its content. For instance, in a scene in which the ex-ambassador of the UK to Uzbekistan talks to his superior about confessions which have likely been obtained through torture, a woman tells him, 'this question of torture is very difficult; and he wants you to know that both Jack and he lose sleep over it' (Soans 2005: 71). For an audience in the UK in 2005, it would have been immediately evident who is meant by Jack. The play here clearly references Jack Straw, Britain's foreign secretary at the time. This is a form of metareference because it brings the real world from outside the theatre into the intradiegetic world of the play. In other words, even if this dialogue never took place, it sounds realistic and it references a real-life politician and therefore could at least have taken place like this. What is more is that the ex-ambassador is also not just anybody or a made-up character. Again, audiences at the time were likely to have heard the name of Craig Murray, an ex-ambassador of the UK to Uzbekistan who quit his job after his complaints about the use of confessions obtained through torture by British intelligence services had remained unheard (cf. Murray 2006). The play here intermingles the extradiegetic real world and the world of the play to form a unity of truth, and of authentic voices. The message the audience understands is clear: this is an authentic conversation, even if it is off the record – this is what really happened.

Apart from these truth claims and the intermingling of fact and fiction, which are both fairly standard devices for DT, *Talking to Terrorists* possesses another quality which will help the audience to ascribe authenticity to the performance: the quality of the real. The real, as was elaborated above, is here used in the double sense of referencing real world events and also of provoking a Lacanian confrontation with the real. The former quality is fulfilled by the play taking as its source material the violent conflicts of, say, Northern Ireland, Uganda or Palestine – conflicts well known to audiences. The latter quality is given treatment through detailed descriptions of acts of atrocity. A good example is the account of a former Ugandan child soldier who talks about killing captured enemies:

> Back in our camp the prisoners were made to dig their own graves. One of our officers told me, 'Go spit them in the eye'. He told them, 'No bullets will be wasted on you. After you have dug your grave, I will call my best men. They will hit you on the head with an akakumbi'. That was a short, heavy hoe. They stood two at a time, and our strongest men smashed their foreheads and the backs of their heads until they dropped in the grave and died. (Soans 2005: 55)

The *topos* of a line of people standing, waiting to be executed with brutality, is well known to twentieth-century audiences, familiar with historic documentaries, the news, feature films or the internet. These acts can be described verbally; the horror, however, escapes verbalization. This is made plain after the monologue by a relief worker that '[i]t's hard to understand the impact on most children because they switch to survival mode' (Soans 2005: 55).

The child soldier's inability to process the atrocities he had to witness induces the audience to seek to comprehend the events, at which they must also fail. This is all the more so because they have heard the truth claims before and know that this is not fiction but that it really happened. There is no simple way out for the audience along the lines of 'this-is-only-fiction'. The mechanism at work here is to confront audiences with traumatic and painful events. Such events of brutality and torture usually escape communication to a large degree. Elaine Scarry has convincingly argued that all forms of pain and torture escape the symbolic order of communication (cf. Scarry 1985: 3–5). In other words, pain stands outside the symbolic order but the play confronts audiences with the events that are in themselves incomprehensible. The play is full of acts of utmost brutality, ranging from children who are raped and have their knees nailed together to stop them from running away (Soans 2005: 26), to a person's fingernails being pulled out who is afterwards boiled alive (67), over to torture trough electroshocks to the testicles (44). The detailed description of brutality and pain, which in itself is indescribable, encourages a confrontation with one's own non-verbal, mental reception of deeds of atrocity. The narration brings the audience into contact with the Lacanian real in the shape of trauma. This is not to say that an audience will understand the events afterwards, but the very drastic nature of them lends the performance a special force and produces visceral reactions precisely because the subject is so drastic.

This confrontation with the real as well as the play's truth claims become a very effective unity in performance. Michael Billington, reviewing the Oxford performance, gave it five stars and notes as follows:

the eternal question raised by factual theatre like this is whether it does anything fictional theatre can't. Watching Max Stafford-Clark's calculatedly low-key production, I would say it does. It sheds light on a dark subject. It forces us to think about what actually constitutes 'terrorism'. It shows that people acquire a strange eloquence when talking about subjects close to their hearts. (Billington 2005)

The 'strange eloquence' which he refers to is exactly the uneasiness, or possibly visceral reaction, that comes from the confrontation with the real. The play seeks to communicate and at the same time cannot communicate. The audience, however, is forced to ponder. Furthermore, Bilington's review also shows how the immediacy of theatre is best apt to confront audiences with such abject subjects as death, torture or mutilation. Liveness is not an unimportant factor which lends the performance its force and helps audiences attribute authenticity.

Stuff Happens (2004) and *Black Watch* (2007)

Very similar mechanisms are employed by two plays that have become well-known treatments of the war in Iraq and Afghanistan, namely David Hare's *Stuff Happens* (2004) and Gregory Burke's *Black Watch* (2007). They are expressions of a renewed interest in global politics, its repercussions and a craving for narratives and counter-narratives, when it was widely felt the truth had been compromised by politicians. The two plays prove especially fruitful when analysing truth claims, authenticity and the notion of one single truth. The very question of truth and lying is at the heart of *Stuff Happens* because it has as its subject the war in Iraq, the reasoning for which has been a highly contentious topic until today. It was directed by Nicholas Hytner at the National Theatre and it attracted considerable media attention. Criticism ranged from it being a dull retelling of well-known facts to praise for also citing pro-war arguments (cf. Sierz 2011: 74 f.). Some felt that it made utterly plain that it did not claim to be historically accurate (cf. Billington 2004; Esch-van Kan 2011); others felt that the play did indeed offer facts (cf. Spencer 2004) or were critical of its dubious status (cf. Weidle 2011).

To begin with, the set of *Stuff Happens* was the classical, austere DT set, with very little furniture, props or set, apart from some screens and chairs. *Stuff Happens* was staged very much like a TV documentary 'presenting static, usually seated actors delivering their heavily edited interview transcripts directly to the audience, much the way that "talking heads" might speak to a camera' (Bottoms 2006: 59). The cast, in classical documentary mode, is already on stage, assembling while the audience arrive (cf. Hare 2006: 3). None of the individual cast members can be singled out in terms of clothes or other properties to be portraying one specific person; they are interchangeable and frequently change roles. An audience can read this as a conscious rejection of theatricality and make-believe. Instead, the actors indeed seem like mouthpieces who simply transport the true words a public figure has said. In this respect, Hare uses the 'collective of actor figures to create the illusion of factual theatre' (Weidle 2011: 71). Regarding the play itself, it also contains a truth claim, albeit one that is more ambiguous than the one in *Talking to Terrorists*. Hare claims in *Stuff Happens* that it is not a documentary drama but that it combines archival and verbatim material with fiction. He claims to make a clear distinction but such a distinction is problematic as the audience will take things for real (cf. Weidle 2011: 67). Hare's author's note, to which Weidle is referring, reads as follows:

> *Stuff Happens* is a history play, which happens to centre on very recent history. The events within it have been authenticated from multiple sources, both private and public. What happened happened. Nothing in the narrative is knowingly untrue. Scenes of direct address quote people verbatim. When the doors close on the world's leaders and on their entourages, then I have used my imagination. This is surely a play, not a documentary, and driven, I hope, by its themes as much as by its characters. (Hare 2006: author's note)

This author's note is problematic for a number of reasons. First, for an audience which goes and sees the play, the author's note is not present and so they must take things at face value. As all statements are presented in the same manner and no special emphasis is put on verbatim parts, everything may seem a genuine piece of verbatim speech. Second, if one takes a closer look at the note, it becomes evident that even for readers the distinction between fact and fiction is not unanimously clear. Hare claims that the events have been 'authenticated' and surely everyone will know about the war in Iraq; but what about the meeting between Bush and Blair, which Hare later on narrates (cf. 35–45)? Or what about the conversation between Colin Powell and George Bush (cf. 47–52)? Did they really happen, and if so, did they happen in just that way or are they a product of Hare's imagination? Each of the first three sentences of the author's note contains a truth claim: 'history play, authenticated, what happened happened, nothing untrue, verbatim'. In other words, Hare authenticates his material very strongly before he concedes that he also used his imagination and that he wrote a drama, not a documentary. This, however, stands in contrast to the austere documentary set which the audience sees and to the strong truth claims made beforehand. In other words, Hare deliberately authenticates his fiction and obfuscates the pedigree of the individual scenes and speeches. Here, the line between fact and fiction is blurred once more.

The intent to obfuscate and establish everything as factual becomes even more obvious with the first line of the play: 'An Actor: These are the actors, these are the men and women who will play parts in the opening drama of the new century' (Hare 2006: 8). This sentence again seems to be plain and straightforward at first sight, but it is, as a matter of fact, much more difficult. Who are the people on stage? Are they men and women who take part in world politics or are they actors? The word 'actors' also has the double meaning of performing in a play or executing an action, as a politician does. The people the audience sees on stage are evidently both, actors (theatre) and actors (politicians); at least that is what the sentence communicates. It mixes fact and fiction. Furthermore, these individuals will 'play parts in a drama'. So are world politics simply drama? But is the war in Iraq not very real with soldiers dying? Are we still trapped in the Shakespearean concept of world as stage? This statement uses metaphor to establish a link between the world of stage and drama and the real events that happen in Iraq and elsewhere. The real-life 'drama' becomes the drama on stage and vice versa. By employing metaphor and double-edged language, the play manages, if not to authenticate its very status but at least to destabilize the boundary, between fact and fiction. It opens audiences up for the possibility that what they see is authentic and offers real and true insight into the events that took place. Audiences have no author's note at hand: this is all they see and they have to take it at face value (cf. Schulze 2012). Over the course of the play, Hare frequently uses the trust built in the beginning and mixes fact and fiction. Some excerpts of well-known speeches are reproduced alongside statements which are made up. Thus the metareference to real-world speeches, which may be known to the audience, can authenticate other speeches which might be made up, following the logic: 'I knew the speech before, so this one may be true as well, I just do not know it.' Hare constantly constructs narrative and dramatization without marking it as such; for instance when Colin Powell and Dominique de Villepin are alone in conversation but Powell is '*icy*', there is a '*chilly silence*' or the stage directions demand that Powell is mistrusting de Villepin (70–71, italics in the original). Some critics have claimed that audiences should not be underestimated and that they are in most instances able to distinguish between fictional and factual parts, such as the Bush–Blair encounter (cf. Billington 2004). Similarly, Annika Esch-van Kan has argued that the frequent comments by actors, such as the one in the beginning, serve as a distancing device and that the play openly shows that it is taking sides (cf. 2011: 419). She finds that the paratext does not support a reading as facts:

> To the contrary, it can well be argued that *Stuff Happens* accepts the inaccessibility of the 'events' themselves and is enmeshed in the web of stories that make those events intelligible. Following this reading, one could find the play to explore the blurring of reality and fiction and destabilize the suppositions of an allocateable historical truth and the attribution of any truth-value to documents. (Esch-van Kan 2011: 419)

Others, however, such as the *Daily Telegraph*, found the play a 'masterly piece of political theatre, offering a fascinating insight into the processes of high power in our ominous post-9/11 world [...], the must-see drama of the year' (Spencer 2004). In other words, the reviewer felt that genuine insight about historical facts and the inner workings of power could be gleaned from it. Of a similar but more critical opinion is Steven Bottoms, who finds that Hare is fabricating and authenticating his own version of events and truth (cf. Bottoms 2006). In conclusion, the play can be read in both ways, as claiming a specific anti-war truth, or as destabilizing the notion of one unified, single truth, and exposing that there are diverse truths (cf. Bilington 2004). Esch-van Kan claims that *SH* disturbs master narratives (cf. 2001: 420); however, she does not specify which one she sees as the master narrative: pro-war or anti-war? Depending on personal point of view, one can certainly argue for both that they are the master narrative. In the whole debate, two factions become apparent: the ones who find that Hare makes a strong claim to truth and authenticity and the ones who see it as more balanced. While the argument cannot be decided, it is evident that the sheer amount of debate and its necessity point out that the mechanisms of authentication in the play are strong and have fulfilled what they were designed to do.

The other play treating the War on Terror to be discussed here is Gregory Burke's *Black Watch*. Commissioned by the National Theatre of Scotland in 2007, it revolves around a group of Highland regiment soldiers who have returned from their various tours of duty in Iraq and Afghanistan. The play draws on interviews that Burke led with them but it also uses fictional material. John Tiffany, the director, has pointed out that the play is comprised of both interviews and fictional scenes.

> I asked Greg [Burke] not to write a fictional drama set in Iraq but that instead we should try and tell the 'real' stories of the soldiers in their own words. This led to Greg interviewing a group of Black Watch lads in a Fife pub over a couple of months [...]. Luckily, Greg had been secretly writing some fictional scenes set in Dogwood, and these made a powerful contrast with the pub interviews. (Burke 2010: x–xi)

So the aim, according to the director, is to tell 'real stories'. However, he finds that they can be brilliantly combined with Burke's fictional scenes. This means nothing but that the verbatim part needed to be enriched with fictional material and dramatized accordingly. Surely the dramatic journey created thus is very effective, as David Smith has pointed out.

> Gregory Burke's magnificent Black Watch rips us out of our domestic comfort zone. His masterstroke is that he does not attempt to write a war drama. Instead, drawing on interviews with soldiers who fought in Iraq, he lets them speak in their own words. The result is a raw, rough, thrilling piece of reportage which takes us inside that incommunicable fire in the role of embedded audience. (2008)

Smith is a journalist for *The Observer* who reviewed the play, and apparently to him the distinction between fact and fiction was not as clear. He feels that Burke is not writing a fictional drama but rather lets the soldiers speak in their own words; in short, he takes the fictional play for factual. This is emphasized by his choice of words when he claims that the play takes the audience into the 'incommunicable fire' and embeds them as if they were there. The play to him feels like he is having first-hand experience, too. It offers the chance to come close to something which is not communicable, something that stands outside the text and the symbolic order. It is no coincidence that he specifically takes the soldiers' voices as the reference point for authenticity. Surely one of the strongest mechanisms of authenticity in the play is the soldiers' voices: all the soldiers speak in a very strong Scottish dialect, and indeed even the play script is written in Scottish dialect. The authenticity produced by lads speaking in their seemingly natural voices authenticates the whole performance so that 'not once in two hours do you remember you're watching actors' (*Sunday Times* review in Burke 2010). 'The authentic voices ring through Black Watch in all their Highland colloquial, profanity-peppered, matter-of-fact glory' (Smith 2008). This effect is further intensified by strobe lighting, sound effects of grenades exploding and machine guns firing. Together with the authentic voices, the effect produced is that the audience may feel closer to having been there, to knowing what war was really like for the soldiers: in short, to having access to the truth of war.

Last but not least, *Black Watch* also uses the tool of metareference. Its very subject is of course events and issues drawn from the real world, which are well known to every audience member. Nonetheless, the play still has real politicians such as Alex Salmond or Geoff Hoon appear on stage (cf. Burke 2010: 8), which obviously helps to authenticate the action, as described above. But more interestingly, the play also employs a self-referential type of metareference. The author himself is present as a character in the play and the process of creating the play is discussed (cf. Burke 2010: 5;, he is shown in conversation with the squaddies in a pub and they quiz him about the play he is going to write.

Cammy   What day you want tay know?
Writer   What it was like in Iraq.
Cammy   What it was fucking like?
Stewarty Go to fucking Baghdad if you want to ken what it's like.
Writer   No. I'm sorry.
Beat.
What I mean is … I want to know about your experience, what it was like for you. For the soldiers. On the ground.
Cammy   It wasnay like I thought it was gonnay be. I don't know what the fuck I thought it was gonnay be like, but it wasnay like what it was.
(Burke 2010: 7)

The speech of the characters marks them as authentic expressions of Scottish soldiers, in terms of the dialect, the swear words and even the aggression. In this respect, the play uses verisimilitude, while the set is classically austere. The characters' speech, uniforms and behaviour, however, strive for classical verisimilitude. The entire conversation is structured as if it had happened in a pub – and possibly it has. Because the writer appears in the scene, the audience gets the impression of being part of his research process. It seems like the playwright has simply typed up all the taped material into a play. The material itself is superbly evanescent in its meaning. The soldier Cammy is unable to describe his experience of war in a meaningful way: he does not know what he thought it would be like, neither what it was really like, but he is sure that the real experience he had was not like what he imagined war would be. His authentic Highland colloquiality fails him when he tries to communicate the authentic experience of war. The language deconstructs itself – becomes contradictory – because the issue cannot be put into the symbolic order of language: 'It wasnay like what it was.' The poetics as well as the semantics of this short statement mark the speaking subject as authentic in two ways: first, because it displays the subject's helplessness in his failing attempt to communicate the experience of war. Second, this form of communication is a well-established tool in documentary films of all kind: a witness who is short for words to describe terrible events. For an audience then, the speech and the character can be marked as authentic because the mode of a witness lost for words is so well known and rings true.

For the audience, this lays bare the theatrical machinery and thus strips away another layer of theatricality. The play becomes more like a documentary proper where one may see the journalist interviewing somebody. The observation one takes away from this is simple: this play is about something real, and it is about people speaking in authentic voices and not about something that is made up, because the figure of the writer undermines the suspension of disbelief in this context. This becomes evident in the reviews, which felt that the play was very authentic and realistic (cf. Marks 2011; Smith 2008 (US production)). Even more than *Stuff Happens*, *Black Watch* becomes a play which manages to be perceived as authentic and true on several levels.

Criticism

As is evident by now, DT is contentious and open to attack in a number of ways. In the following, I want to retrace some of the more relevant arguments and also rebut them, before turning towards DTs that seek to critique their own mode of action.

Archive and selection

The very choice of subject matter opens any DT production up for criticism: Why was this topic chosen and not another? Or, similarly: how can the choice of documents pertaining to that topic be justified? That choice is, almost by definition, eclectic. Furthermore, as Carol Martin has pointed out, even if a DT practitioner seeks to be as neutral as possible, any attempt at inclusivity and neutrality about a certain issue is always flawed because of the very nature of archival material and documentation.

> Most contemporary documentary theatre makes the claim that everything presented is part of the archive. But equally important is the fact that not everything in the archive is part of the documentary. [...] The process of selection, editing, organization, and presentation is where the creative work of documentary theatre gets done. (Martin 2006: 9)

In other words, it is not only conscious choices made by directors and writers that bias a production but the very nature of the archive. Some issues, which could equally be treated by DT, have never been documented; a whole number of accounts and counter-discourses are always absent from any archival issue. In short, the nature of the production of documents and witnesses in a broad sense is already inconclusive and shaped by powerful forces, which can be found again in the material. The archive itself is a manifestation of power and discourse; it is *a priori* selective. Consequently, even with the very best intentions of neutrality, '[d]ocumentary theatre creates its own aesthetic imaginaries while claiming a special factual legitimacy' (Martin 2006: 10). It legitimizes its claim at factual neutrality through the nature of the document (object authenticity), and effectively blanks out doubts about the nature of the archive, which – through inclusion and exclusion – is always a means of power (cf. Tomlin 2013: 136).

Furthermore, the archive as an institution has become doubtful as well. Today, with platforms such as YouTube and Facebook, the archive grows at an unprecedented rate, becoming ever more inclusive, soaking up all information, whether crucial or banal. The very value of the archive can thus be questioned because the archive is now also a place that can change within minutes. It is no longer a place of conclusion, where documents are put to rest, but it has also become a place of live events and simultaneity.

> The way in which the West has traditionally conceived of a document as a material artefact, such as an item of writing, photograph, video, etc., that can be placed in an archive is undone by the implosion of the real, the live, the simulated and the mediatised. (Martin 2009: 82)

The document itself loses it status in terms of being real because digital documentation is more prone to manipulation. Furthermore, the document loses its tangibility and is thus removed from the empirical world; it is not manifest anymore. Martin observes that the discourse surrounding DT is more about the way 'in which we sanction and privilege certain forms of information over others' (Martin 2009: 89). Therefore, she claims, DT should rather be seen as a process than as a product. The archive is still rooted in the older, analogue world and so is the audience's faith in facts. DT is then in the position to negotiate the translation of the archive into the twenty-first century. The opportunity DT has in this respect is to negotiate the shortcomings of the old archive as described above. In the worst case, it will simply literally translate the old archive into a world that has no use for it anymore.

Invisible politics

Along similar lines, it is easy to accuse DT of having its own agenda and invisible politics. That is to say, it not only selects the issues and documents it wants to treat but also brings them into an order of discourse with very particular aims. It certainly takes part actively in the formation of public opinion and shapes the discourses which are its subject. 'In practice, much of contemporary documentary theatre is written contemporaneously with the events that are its subject [e.g. the Tricycle's riot plays of 2011]. It directly intervenes in the creation of history by unsettling the present' (Martin 2006: 9). DT in this case is far from being a neutral observer but is an active agent, with goals and politics of its own, that can influence current events and debates. An extreme example is Richard Norton-Taylor's play *Justifying War: Scenes from the Hutton Inquiry* (2003), which had as its subject Tony Blair's reasons for joining the invasion of Iraq. The play was staged before the inquiry had come to a conclusion, which eventually exonerated Tony Blair of guilt for going to war in Iraq (cf. Sierz 2005: 58–59). It was centred around the death of weapons expert David Kelly, the whistle-blower who made it public that the threat of Iraqi ABC weapons being ready for use in forty-five minutes was made up (cf. Norton-Taylor 2014a: 428). The play in its entirety has a bias towards the notion of an unjustified war and a government that spins the facts and pressures individuals in order to legitimize their course of action. It thus tried to shape the discourse according to its own judgement, or, more positively phrased, offered a counter-discourse, springing from the same facts as the actual inquiry. To put it bluntly, any agent participating in a discourse shapes that very discourse and cannot claim to be anything like a neutral observer anymore.

> So even if viewers of documentary performances know, along with Hayden White, that 'all discourse constitutes the objects which it pretends only to describe realistically and to analyze objectively', the appeal of the documentary trace is still not rejected, and the link to the truth claim still functions as at least partially persuasive in performances that evoke the documentary discourse – persuasive of the link to facticity through the trace, if not the total truth of the account. (Reinelt 2006: 83)

Derek Paget, citing Foucault and White as well, is also of the opinion that narrative is a function which creates non-existent objective truths (cf. Paget 1990: 164–165). In other words, DT creates and shapes the histories it claims only to uncover. Furthermore, theatre obviously also has an agenda of its own. Every DT production has to make artistic and narrative choices, which will shape the material and the outcome of the production. Thus, even if everything that is said is taken verbatim from someone else, the omissions and sequence of speeches may still crucially shape the overall message of the performance. David Edgar, commenting on his Watergate documentary *I Know What I Meant* (1974), states as follows:

> I edited the White House tape transcripts into a 45-minute television play, in which every word spoken on screen had been actually spoken in reality, and we had the transcripts to prove it. But, in fact, of course, the play was bristling with impurities: the whole process of making it had consisted of value judgments. (in Megson 2009: 197)

It is necessary to bear both these flaws, the fundamental one of poststructuralist objections to history-telling, as well as DT's own political agenda in mind in order to remain conscious that it cannot be a neutral format.

However, if one, as Derek Paget suggests, sheds the modernist notion of a faith in facts (cf. 1990: 8), one can also read DT as a modus that 'is expressive of a profound political scepticism which disputes the notion that "facts = truth"' (1990: 17). So, while some DT plays seek to authenticate the witness and adhere to the concept of one truth (cf. Bottoms 2006: 57), the format can also destabilize such notions. In other words, DT can complicate and debate the very status of its factual subjects. This can happen through a number of techniques, such as, for instance, Brechtian estrangement effects. In this case, '[d]ocumentary Theatre does not necessarily portray the real *realistically*' (Paget 1990: 83, italics in the original). Through the use of montage and estrangement, DT can address the issue of neutrality and factuality, while still operating with a factual subject matter. In short, if DT sheds the notion of realism, and some productions have done so, it can still treat factual subjects but not claim authenticity.

Moreover, it is not necessarily negative for DT to have its own political agenda. It can very well serve as a counter discourse to mainstream narratives. Its politics can be a mode of resistance to power and dominant discourse. DT can seek to tell its audience not one single truth but rather give versions of different truths which had not been heard before. 'Governments "spin" the facts in order to tell stories. Theatre spins them right back in order to tell different stories.

[...] Depending on who you are, what your politics are and so on, documentary theatre will seem to be "getting at the truth" or "telling another set of lies"' (Martin 2006: 14). Reinelt sees DT even as a place of public forum/debate in the Habermasian sense, but also points out the limitations of the very narrow, theatre going sample of the population (cf. 2009: 12). Nonetheless, if DT actively embraces its own limitations in terms of truth and factuality and lays open its own political agenda, it can fulfil a useful and important role in the shaping of public discourse.

> [T]he widespread appeal to the truth of 'factuality' is ultimately one further manifestation of the crisis of understanding into which capitalist societies in the twentieth century have plunged. The dominant order's truth-claims can and must be challenged by, and on behalf of, those whose own truth is persistently occluded, deleted and consigned to the margins [...] (Paget 1990: 172)

DT becomes a corrective to dominant ideologies and discourses. It can offer a voice and stage to those who had no part in the discourse before, it can be used as a forum for public debate, as ideology or as serving the hegemony, and it *always* has a political dimension.

General truth

When discussing DT's politics and its claims to truth, it is important to shed light on the concept of truth itself in DT. By claiming facticity, it validates concepts of apodictic, unified and essential truth. In other words, it often carries the implicit presumption that there is one and only one truth. DT, as has been shown, goes to great scenographic lengths in order to establish that what it shows is true and factual. 'The most advanced means of replication and simulation are used to capture and reproduce "what really happened" for presentation in the live space of the theatre' (Martin 2006: 9). *Guardian* journalist Richard Norton-Taylor, one of the leading practitioners of tribunal plays, has staked a very direct claim to truth for DT: 'The role of the theatre in exposing the truth and reality, unvarnished, is making a welcome comeback' (in Esch-van Kan 2011: 416). The practitioner evidently feels that he can command something like 'truth unvarnished' and is conscious of his active role in spreading that truth. Similar remarks have been made by David Hare (cf. Hare 2006 and Hare in Soans 2005). This claim to one solidified, exclusive truth which does not permit alternative versions is highly problematic (cf. Martin 2006: 10–11). Lane remarks that DT 'often carries a promise to present the unmediated truth, "not merely *a* version but *the* version of what occurred"' (Lane 2010: 66, italics in the original). It has, however, been claimed that audiences are well aware of the complexity of DT's truth claim and understand that the version of events which they see is a construct (cf. Bruzzi 2000: 4–7). This view is seconded by Paola Botham, who also feels that audiences are aware of the editing process (cf. 2008: 315). On the other hand, Ursula Canton, who interviewed students after a performance of *Vincent in Brixton* (2003), a play which treated Vincent van Gogh's time in London, found that a large number of them genuinely believed to have learned something factual about the painter, despite the play being fictitious in large parts (cf. Canton 2008: 322). In all likelihood, the awareness of the audience regarding editing and truth claims depends on the individual piece of DT and the individual audience. However, as the arguments above show, the truth claim of DT is a contentious field. This is not only so regarding DT's relationship with the audience but more so on the fundamental level of truth itself. In postmodernity and also today, truth as an essentialist concept has come under suspicion. Steven Bottoms has taken up this point and claims that many DT productions actually reintroduce the author as a godlike *hors de texte* figure (cf. Bottoms 2006. He claims that such texts adhere to Derrida's idea of a theological text, where the author is hovering about as an authoritative, validating figure, 'providing a constructed authorial perspective on the real' (Bottoms 2006: 59). DT in his view validates its truth claim by bringing that authority figure onto the stage and into the play. Of course, the truth claim is even more problematic in areas where a solidified truth, a hegemonic version of history, is not present, such as – for instance – in Northern Ireland (e.g. *Bloody Sunday*, Tricycle 2005) or Palestine (e.g. *My Name Is*

Rachel Corrie, Royal Court 2005). Here, history remains a battleground and is comprised of parallel, contradictory truths (cf. Upton 2009 179–180). Consequently, any DT performance that claims such truths is bound to fail one way or another.

As this study takes as its fundamental premise practices of reconstruction, which manifest themselves in a metamodern structure of feeling, some words on the deconstruction of essentialist notions of 'truth' with regard to DT seem in order. Ursula Canton has suggested a functional approach to truth that does not allow for absolutist notions but seeks 'different degrees of reality or factuality', depending on the situation because 'neither the return to theoretically outdated concepts nor the radical relativism of postmodernism can offer satisfactory interpretations of documentary and biographical theatre' (2008: 318). In her view, truth in documentary theatre should be understood as a gradual and situational concept, which arises in the interplay between audience and performance. In practical terms this leads to the study of the effects and consequences that truth claims have, rather than the study of their validity (cf. 2008: 319). Concretely, she holds that the radical relativism of postmodernity is not useful and a framework needs to be established for conceptualizing the real world: 'But how could this be achieved without re-establishing the absolute ontological categories that have been successfully and convincingly deconstructed?' (2008: 325). Her answer, drawn from the work of sociologists Thomas Lucker and Peter Berger, is a functional analysis: 'Any considerations about the "ultimate validity or invalidity (by whatever criteria) of such knowledge" are deliberately discarded as irrelevant, since they are not necessary to explain how a society's concepts of knowledge structures its members' experience of reality' (Canton 2008: 325). In other words, reality may be nothing but a function between audience and performance, not an absolute thing, but the repercussions of that truth, its effects on the audience, are very real and can be observed. This approach is not unlike Funk's concept of *black box authenticity* or Vermeulen and van den Akker's metamodern structure of feeling: ontological discussions of the status of truth and facticity are deliberately discarded in favour of a pragmatic approach, which focuses on the *effects* of these concepts. 'Although the relativity of the concepts of "fact" and "fiction" is maintained, the acknowledgment of binding rules for their use in specific discourses overcomes the idea of an all-encompassing relativity that is often advocated in postmodern argument' (Canton 2008: 325–326). By studying the effects of authenticity, one quickly arrives at the conclusion that the specific discourses surrounding its use are highly similar and not arbitrary at all. Radical relativism is consequently not only unproductive but also not employed in everyday life. Audience members ascribe truth individually, using reality or its discursive construction, only as a point of departure. Along the same lines, authenticity arises as an ascription that is attached to the truth-value of the performance.

Pushing this point even further, Paola Botham argues that it is necessary for DT to make an unconditional truth claim. She holds that DT functions as a Habermasian forum of public debate (public sphere). Verbatim theatre 'can [...] be interpreted as a serious effort to reclaim the public sphere, in the sense of making available private testimonies with political significance to a wider audience' (2008: 312). She contends that in order to create a functional and effective discourse at all, it is necessary to make unconditional statements and to leave radical scepticism and relativism behind. One of her main arguments is Thomas McCarthy's rebuttal of deconstruction with regard to discourse.

> We can and typically do make contextually conditioned and fallible claims to unconditional truth (as I have just done). It is this moment of unconditionality that opens us up to criticism from other points of view. [...] It is precisely this context-transcendent [...] surplus of meaning in our notion of truth that keeps us from being locked into what we happen to agree on at any particular time and place, that opens us up to the alternative possibilities lodged in otherness and difference that have been so effectively invoked by postmodernist thinkers. (McCarthy in Botham 2008: 317)

To put it briefly, if one never dares to make statements of unconditionality or dares to make a truth claim, any debate of an issue will never move forward or may not even develop, because one would drown in conditionalities and *caveats*. A Habermasian public sphere cannot develop in a climate of radical relativism.[4] In Botham's view, DT becomes a forum of public debate, which may give rise to various voices. Truth constitutes itself within that discourse by situative agreement. She draws heavily on Habermas' notion of intersubjectivity when she claims that fact and fiction have to be seen as discursive practices which make it 'possible to critique a representational version of truth without surrendering the idea of truth itself' (Botham 2008: 316). For her, then, the strength of DT 'lies precisely in its power to exceed postmodernism's infinite itch for deconstruction' (Botham 2008: 316). By and large, this is also an advocation of a realist epistemological position. Validity claims along the dimensions of truth, rightness and expressiveness are 'built into everyday communicative practice and are inescapable even for the most trenchant sceptic' (Botham 2008: 317), so why then should they not be applied to DT as well? In summary, DT's truth claims can be viewed as a necessary tool for enabling a discourse that does not seek closure and completion but rather favours contradictory truths from which audiences form their own opinions (cf. Highberg 2009: 173, cf. also Tomlin 2013: 142). It becomes a genuine form of public debate and its truth claims instigate further participation in the debate.

Antitheatricality

If taken seriously, however, the concept of the public sphere and the forum of debate would also mean that DT is – at least theoretically – open to any outcome. This has been cited as a strong disadvantage of DT:

> [Y]ou could argue that the deliberate anti-theatricality of the Tricycle tribunals, and the self-conscious minimalism of the interview-based play, allows their makers off the hook. The point about writing fiction [...] is that you can present a thesis unencumbered by factual specifics. One advantage of verbatim theatre is that you can present factual specifics unencumbered by a thesis. (Edgar 2012: 9)

Similarly, Aleks Sierz has castigated DT for its lack of a thesis, but more importantly for its lack of aesthetic means and imagination. For him DTs are just 'powerful public forums, but they can't be said to stretch drama's aesthetic boundaries, or even suggest ways of changing the world. Like Reality TV, they simply tell us what we already know' (Sierz 2005: 59, cf. also Sierz 2008). Proponents and practitioners of DT claim that it is precisely this political function of DT which is very necessary for an art and theatre sphere that has lost touch with the real world and has become too self-referential.

> All revolutions in art, said someone, are a return to realism. Given that most artforms, in the hands of metropolitan elites, tend to drift away from reality, what could be more bracing or healthy than occasionally to offer authentic news of overlooked thought and feeling? [...] What a welcome corrective to the cosy art-for-art's sake racket which theatre all too easily becomes? [...] Why can't we just admit that theatre using real people has become a fabulously rich and varied strand, which for many years, has been pumping red cells into the dramatic bloodstream? (Hare in Soans 2005: 107–108)

While I do not intend to take part in the debate whether DT is good or bad theatre, – because in all likelihood this is a question of personal taste – the aesthetic means (or lack thereof) seem worth a short debate. If Sierz is right and DT is hugely antitheatrical and Hare is also right in that DT offers treatment of real problems and the real world, the question arises: Why theatre at all? Why not read a factual book on the matter? In other words, why do practitioners go to great lengths to hide traces of theatricality in order to present facts in a medium that was designed and is recognized for fiction?

If this thought is taken to the end of the line, DT works at its abolition: *in extremis* it only presents facts with no theatrical alterations whatsoever. Why practitioners choose exactly theatre as the medium for the debate of factual issues needs explaining. What makes the theatrical form so special and apt for this kind of presentation? 'Why? Perhaps because this material though imitative of TV, also capitalizes on a mythology specific to theatre – that of presence' (Bottoms 2006:

59). There is evidently something special about theatre that makes it useful even for such more or less dry debates. Bearing in mind Botham's statement, the answer indeed lies in theatre's capacity to produce affective responses. 'Theatre, after all, combines the emotional weight of storytelling with truth-telling and a sense of experiencing something happening right in front of our eyes' (Martin 2006: 14). The purely neutral non-fiction book can never claim theatre's immediacy. The concept of 'immediacy', in various terminological guises, has haunted theatre scholars and is frequently cited to mark a situation as somehow special. It is a very fishy term and therefore some elaboration is in order. I believe that the choice of the medium theatre can be very precisely explained if the concept of theatricality is analysed in terms of 'immediacy', or rather 'liveness'.

Philip Auslander has written a widely received book in which he debates the concept of 'liveness' and its ascriptions, such as 'immediacy', 'magic of the stage', 'community' and so on. He asks if there really are clear-cut lines of distinction between live and mediatized (or recorded) performances, when one becomes ever more like the other (e.g. instant repeats in a football stadium and use of video in performance) (cf. 2008: 7). He thoroughly destabilizes the dichotomy live/recorded (cf. 48–55), arriving at the conclusion that ontologically there is no fundamental difference between the two. Auslander's book has a brilliant intellectual scope and the argument he proffers is extremely fruitful. Nonetheless, he errs when he claims that there is no ontological difference between the live and the recorded. This is so for two reasons. First of all, he fails to recognize that the experience of a live event is very different from the experience of a recorded event. If one accepts, along Josephine Machon's argument of (syn)aesthetics, that the multitude of sensory impressions when attending a live performance (sight, hearing, taste, smell, touch) is much greater and consequently forms a greater unity of meaning than the consumption of a recorded performance, which only stimulates two senses (hearing, sight), then one must concede that Auslander is wrong. The experience of the live event is a thicker event than the consumption of the recorded one and therefore leaves a stronger impression in the spectator's memory. Second, and more importantly, one should consider and expand on Matthew Goulish's notion of failure (cf. Goulish 2004). Doing so, one can find another very fundamental ontological difference: every live performance can fail. 'Regardless of its emphatic presence and authenticity, then, live performance (re)produces its own fundamental, provisional and often spectacular ineptitude. It makes failure occur just as failure enables its occurrence' (Bailes 2011: 7).[5] This means that any actor, singer, dancer or any other performer in a live performance may always make a mistake, trip, forget their lines or fail in a thousand other ways. Live performance is always endowed with the potential of failure. A recorded performance can never fail (the technical systems of rendition might, but the performance cannot). In other words, any audience member at any live event is conscious of the possibility of failure: this is one central aspect of what has imprecisely been called the 'magic of the stage'. This becomes, for example, blatantly evident in the circus where a dangerous tight-rope act might result in injury or death. While audience members know that the act has been rehearsed hundreds of times and will in all likelihood not fail, there is still the possibility of failure, injury and even death. This is precisely the reason why audiences hold their breath and are emotionally drawn into a performance. A similar situation appears in a theatre performance where actors may forget their lines, stumble or just forget to bring a prop on stage. Consequently, and contrary to Auslander, the live event is of a different status to the recorded event and one need not recourse to ephemeral phrases like 'the magic of stage', as Auslander claims. On the contrary, one can very concretely investigate the force of liveness with Machon's (syn)aesthetic approach and the concept of failure. Auslander defines liveness, following Baudrillard, as '*that which can be recorded*' (Auslander 2008: 56, italics in the original). Considering the argument above, I would like to define live as any performance which can fail. Sarah-Jane Bailes has pointed towards the potential of failure and also the inherent link with authenticity.

> Those broken moments, where things are glimpsed on stage that seem
> to be going badly, foreground a radical potential inherent within the
> labor of all live performance: that is, theatre's facility as 'live' action to

de-compose and reauthenticate before us. Instances where stuttering, verbal confusion, accidents, physical awkwardness, and exhaustion evidence the breakdown of technique or the intrusion of some other reality upon the fictive world, remind us that theatre's liveness – its still-auratic power which arguably sets it apart from other technically reproducible art forms – is intrinsically unreliable: a live event can never guarantee its outcome [...]. Dogging the heels of all live performance is the ontological impossibility of preventing accident or error in the execution of an act. (Bailes 2011: 99)

Coming back to the original question, why specifically theatre is chosen in order to debate non-fictional events, the consequences of this argument are evident: the live event is ontologically different from the recorded event; it exerts a much greater force than a non-fiction book on the subject or any other non-performative factual treatment could. For practitioners this means that by employing theatre they can achieve a much greater effect than with other means. Therefore, while DT may aesthetically work to minimize theatricality, it will never abolish it because it would lose a substantial part of its power and effectively become a non-fiction book.

Complicating documentary

It is apparent that, for instance, *Stuff Happens* and *Black Watch* use techniques of authentication and treat their source material with a strong idea of truth in mind. This strand of DT can be regarded as more or less 'classic', because it takes as its premise the goal to reach some sort of hidden truth. However, as will be discussed and shown in the following, not all documentary plays operate on this presumption. They emphasize their 'own discursive limitations, with interrogating the reification of material evidence in performance' (Forsyth & Megson 2009: 3).

DT can, in this view, be more than a display of facts which seeks to validate one course of history by authenticating its source material.

Along these lines, scholars have detected a certain bifurcation in contemporary DT:

> one strain of recent documentary plays bonds with naturalism and strives for the uncovering of a hidden truth, the other strain emphasises the experimental aesthetics of documentary theatre and self-reflexively explores the relationship between representation and reality. (Esch-van Kan 2011: 416)

In practical terms, this means that a number of contemporary documentary plays are conscious of their own status and form, and, thereby become more alert to the dangers of apodicticity. They do not seek one single true discourse but willingly offer several and are doubtful regarding their presentation. Steven Bottoms claims that creators of such DT understand their work not as reality but fathom their text as process (cf. 2006: 67). He names Moises Kaufmann's plays *Gross Indecency* (1997) and *The Laramie Project* (2000) as successful examples (cf. 2006). Forsyth and Megson have phrased DT's ambition if it seeks to complicate and question notions of truth very succinctly: 'instead of reaching for a wholly objective representation of "truth", much documentary theatre has functioned to complicate notions of authenticity with a more nuanced and challenging evocation of the "real"' (Forsyth & Megson 2009: 2). While it is evident that a number of scholars feel it is necessary to depart from essentialist notions of truth and narrative in DT, it is interesting how the words 'truth', 'authenticity' and 'the real' are interchangeably used by Forsyth and Megson here. This indicates that the connection between essentialist notions and the discourse of DT cannot be as easily dissociated as one might wish. Even in this scholarly approach, truth, authenticity and the real still figure in close proximity because they are evidently linked. A number of practitioners have, however, successfully challenged these paradigms.

Enron (2009)

Lucy Prebble's 2009 play *Enron* is certainly one example of DT which does not want to spin a master narrative and validate its own truth claim.

This becomes clear directly in the beginning. The author's note runs as follows: '[t]hough this play is inspired by the real events leading up to the Enron collapse,[6] it should not be seen as an exact representation of events. It is the author's fiction, as changes have been made for dramatic effect' (Prebble 2009: author's note). In the following, Prebble directs readers towards journalistic explorations of the real Enron collapse and towards non-fiction books. This premise is very different from the one seen in Burke's or Hare's plays, where strong truth claims are presented. However, one may argue that again this author's note is only available to the reader, not to the audience on the night. While this is correct, it will quickly become evident that the staging also makes it very plain that the play takes real events as its source but does not claim to be narrating the Truth. The prologue features the more or less well-known song from Enron's commercials, which could be seen as a way of metareference. However, the melody does not sound natural; it rather has an '*eerie, mechanical sound*' (Prebble 2009: 3). This quality of the singing strongly suggests estrangement and this suspicion is confirmed when '*Three suited individuals enter, finding their way with white sticks. They have the heads of mice*' (2009: 3). At this point, it must be evident to the audience that what they are about to see may have as its source of inspiration real events but will not portray them in a realist manner. Even the voice-over from the real Enron president Jeffrey Skilling must be regarded not as a strategy of metareference because directly after that the actor portraying Jeffrey Skilling comes on stage, which makes the difference between real person and actor all the more apparent. The play thus distances itself from realism and thereby from claims to authenticity and absolute truth. After this beginning, the figure of a lawyer comes on stage and, in typical DT fashion, addresses the audience directly.

> Lawyer: [...] So when we tell you his story [i.e. Jeffrey Skilling], you should know it could never be *exactly* what happened. But we're going to put it together and sell it to you as the truth. And when you look at what happened here, and everything that came afterward, that seems about right. (Prebble 2009: 3, original emphasis)

Again, the claim to facticity made by the lawyer is a very different one than in the plays discussed before. He explicitly points out the fictional status of the play and directly teases the audience with regard to its hunger for unmediated truth. The audience, according to him, will be content with the truth they are being sold. With this turn of phrase he obviously encourages the audience, albeit in a subtle way, to reflect on their desire for truth, what they hold to be true and what they 'buy' as truth. Even more so, being sold the truth implies that truth is a commodity, something that can be marketed, exchanged and bought, but not something essential or eternal. The entire play that follows then does not seek realism in staging; nor does it adhere to the austerity usually found in DT. On the contrary, the play uses elaborate sets with lights, sounds, dancing and singing (cf. 20, 21), lavish parties on stage (cf. 53) and even an employee riding onto the stage on a Harley Davidson (cf. 57). The staging, while elaborate, is, however, by no means realist; it is rather over the top. It distances itself from both realism and the austerity of DT. The ensuing mixture could best be described as epic in the best Brechtian sense. For instance, the stock price of Enron – the focal point of its success and collapse – is constantly displayed on stage (cf. 21) and Jeffrey Skilling even seeks to manipulate it through his thoughts (cf. 92). The display of the stock price here is a reference to the real world, but not in the sense of verisimilitude. It rather makes plain that the events treated in the play have a basis in the real world – the very real collapse of Enron – but it does not seek to imitate them. The stock price is an epic device in Brecht's sense because it is at the same time something familiar and something which is caricatured and estranged. The value of the company can increase and decrease substantially within minutes, depending on whether traders dance and sing in harmony or discord in a dance and musical act (cf. 21–22). The epic moment is further underlined when the bad companies that Enron creates for its debt are represented as hungry Raptors on stage (cf. 43) or when the bankers of Lehman Brothers become Siamese twins. Michael Billington, who gave the production five stars, finds this very stimulating: 'It could all be dry as dust. But the pulse and vigour of play and production stem from their ability to make complex financial ideas manifest. Everything is made visually apprehensible' (2009). *Enron* is not so much a DT play but a piece of Brechtian epic theatre. Authenticity in this case becomes secondary because the play claims it nowhere. Apart from the metareferences to real persons and real events, it does not seek to link itself to the authentic. By exposing its own status, it can instigate a debate of the issues and misdemeanours surrounding the Enron case, which are, after all, very real.

Taking Care of Baby (2007)

A case of much deeper interrogation of DT and its own status was created by Dennis Kelly. His play *Taking Care of Baby* premiered in 2007 and has since then toured successfully in Europe and the United States (cf. Brantley 2013). David Edgar has chastised verbatim plays, such as David Hare's *The Power of Yes* (2009) and Gregory Burke's *Black Watch* for the author appearing on stage. In his opinion, theatre becomes too meta-textual and strays too far from its subject matter if the author appears as a character (cf. Edgar 2012: 9). Dennis Kelly's play is certainly more than meta-textual. It is even meta-theatrical because it questions what we hold true and what we accept as truth in theatre and other forms of representational media, such as newspapers. It 'fooled audiences into thinking that a fictional play about a woman accused of murdering her baby was a real documentary drama' (Edgar 2012: 9). It is understandable that audiences have felt that they were watching DT because the play begins with a classical truth claim: '[t]he following has been taken word for word from interviews and correspondence. Nothing has been added and everything is in the subjects' own words, though some editing has taken place. Names have not been changed' (Kelly 2013: 5).

As staged with deliberately muddling transparency, Erica Schmidt's production begins, as so much documentary theater does, with a group of performers filing onto the stage to take their seats in a row of chairs. The lines they subsequently deliver, we are told by a

> disembodied voice, 'have been taken word for word from interviews
> and correspondence'. [...] The implicit promise is that evidence will
> be laid out for us impartially, so we can piece together a satisfying
> solution ourselves. (Brantley 2013)

It takes quite a while for the audience to realize that the play is 'actually
a satirical fiction' (Sierz 2008: 105) and not a real-life story. The play
deliberately misleads the audience. It claims to present a discourse of
factuality and authenticity, while in truth (no pun intended) it should
claim a discourse of fictionality. It lies to the audience, deliberately, with
the intention of critiquing its own status and audiences' expectations
of truth and authenticity. One can even say that it, unbeknownst to the
first-time audience, playfully takes on the conventions of truth claims
and authenticity. This becomes manifest for the first time when the
character of Dr Millard speaks about truth and lying.

> DR MILLARD: Generally speaking. Lying doesn't really work. When
> you think about it. Whether you're lying to yourself or to another
> human being, we sort of know the truth. Somewhere. Generally,
> generally somewhere we know the truth. Not always, but... (15)

On the most basic level, the figure of a doctor, preferably in a white lab
coat, is a signifier for science, neutrality and trustworthiness. The white
coat and the title emanate an aura of factuality, of indisputable facts. The
doctor in Kelly's play holds a course on lying and its impossibility. Later
on, the audience will learn that the doctor himself is a liar who possibly
made up an illness and was not thorough in his research. The play is
almost cheeky in its use of lying right in the beginning. It is as if the
play shouts at the unwitting audience: 'Look, I am going to lie to you
and I am telling you about lying right now, but you will not hear it
because you will believe my white coat and the explanation I give you!'
Consequently, the doctor gives an explanation of brain size and lying,
involving primates, which sounds credible and scientific. The doctor
even comes back later on, discussing the prevalence of untruthfulness
in society (cf. 20). Here again, the play seems to scream its mendacity
at the audience, which in turn fails to recognize it (cf. Brantley 2013).

In a similarly playful and at the same time meta-textual way, the author also appears as a character on stage, or, in fact, he does not. There are a number of instances where the author is referenced (cf. 21, 59–60) or where people in a taped conversation refer to 'us', instead of 'I' (cf. 62), implying that the author is with them. In other words, here absence also creates presence. The author remains elusive and is never present on stage, but always implied when characters refer to 'Mr Kelly' or when he is heard as a voice offstage on tape recordings (cf. 21, 60 f., *passim*). The author here is indeed the godlike *hors-texte* figure, because he is never physically present but always hovers about, externally validating the discourse. This becomes apparent when the author speaks about truth, which, again implicitly, he does on a number of occasions. It is the author's outspoken aim to 'get at the truth' (66, cf. also 18–19, 21, 65–66). This is exactly the author who believes he can present the one correct and single truth. In his presence-absence, the play subverts this thought and ridicules the practice. This finds obvious expression in the second part, where the truth claim is displayed again but this time it is full of mistakes: 'The following has been word from taken word for interviews and correspondence. Everything is in the subjects' own words and place, nothing has been added though some has taken editing. All names have been changed' (31). Here, the audience can for the first time become suspicious of the truth claim. On the other hand, the mistakes could also be attributed to technical difficulties or could simply be overlooked. There are, after all, still a whole number of truth claims involved. As a matter of fact, the entire play seems to revolve around the single word 'truth'. Characters bring it up and discuss the concept so often (cf. 21, 27, 45, 46, 4, 65–66, 77) that it is hard to miss the isotopic field. So possibly, audiences will understand that this is 'about truth' (23), only not in the sense that they had thought in the beginning. Over the course of the play, it becomes clear that all characters are lying or not telling the truth to a degree. For instance, the MP's story about rescuing her daughter from a highly dangerous drug den is later on narrated again by the daughter's boyfriend. He tells his side of the drug story, in which there are no gangsters or danger at all, but just a college party and the presence of a very overprotective mother (cf. Kelly 2013: 86). This intradiegetic example shows the audience how the same facts, seen through different eyes and narrated differently, become two completely different stories. Another example is the doctor's fictitious Leeman-Keatley syndrome (cf. 20–21), which is also entirely made up, including the experiments by Leeman and Keatley, which he describes. Still, the terminology he uses and his position of authority, set against the backdrop of a truth claim, make it more than easy for an audience to buy into the story, especially as stories of child murder and psychological disorders (often named after the scientists who discover them) have not been unheard of. There were four prominent cases of infanticide in the UK, which most likely served as inspiration for the play. All four were initially found guilty but subsequently exonerated because 'the expert evidence of Professor Sir Roy Meadow, crucial in convicting them, was found to be flawed' (Young 2009: 81). The US reviewer even felt he had to make clear to his readers that the play was all fiction because the story would sound so credible and familiar: '[j] ust to make things clear – because your program will not – there is no real Donna McAuliffe, although you may swear you remember reading about her case' (Brantley 2013). In the last part of the play, the whole structure of truth collapses and the truth claim reveals that nothing is in order: 'Te foling has beenlown takhen wormed for wspoord frondrm intews and cughorrevieence. Nothything has been odded and evering is in the subjts' awn wongrds, tho sam editing hoes keplan tace. All nas havece been chaed' (87). The scrambled structure of word and sentence is the clear sign that a sentence, a word, spoken on stage or written on a page is itself not to be trusted. It can be changed, it can be nonsense and it has no intrinsic truth-value. In this line of argument, the play rejects closure. All stories in it are countered by other stories, and audiences are given good reason to be suspicious of the truth of any of them, but none is validated in the end. The play leaves the audience with numerous possibilities but no answers at all.

Kelly's play does not just put truth on trial, it puts media and political spin, family lies and even verbatim theatre itself in the dock. I have never seen so many people buy the script at the interval, a sign of just how slippery and unsettling this play is. (Gardner 2007)

Very much in line with what Derek Paget demands of good DT, *Taking Care of Baby* does not offer truth but rather seeks to interrogate the status of DT and its truth claims (cf. Paget 1990: 172). The play completely ignores any facts, because it has no basis in real life, but it rather asks how willingly audiences buy into the promise of the documentary, of a true story and of authentic voices. It exposes our craving for truth, closure and authenticity.

Walid Raad and The Atlas Group

In the work of Lebanese-American conceptual and performance artist Walid Raad, truth and authenticity are carried to the extremes. He

> subverts ordinary documentary theatre by complicating and interrogating archival truth. The result is a genre that can invite contemplation of the ways in which stories are told – a form of Brechtian distancing that asks spectators to simultaneously understand the theatrical, the real, and the simulated, each as its own form of truth. (Martin 2006: 12)

Raad's work, however, does not in its entirety qualify as theatrical. While one can surely argue that all of his works have a performative quality, it is important to make a distinction between his gallery works and the performances. In terms of gallery pieces, he has 'created a striking body of conceptual work in which the crucial issues of authenticity and authorship [...] are broached in such an irritating and incisive manner' (Nakas & Schmitz 2007: 38). His performance work, which revolves around the same issues, is no less striking and successful; it has been shown widely in the United States and Europe (cf. Lepecki 2006: 93). Both in his visual art and his performance work, the centrepiece is The Atlas Group Foundation, which Raad describes as follows:

> The Atlas Group [TAG] is a project and a foundation established in
> Beirut in 1977 to research and document the contemporary history
> of Lebanon. The Atlas Group locates, acquires, preserves, displays,
> produces and studies audio, visual, literary and other documents that
> shed light on this history. The documents are preserved in The Atlas
> Group Archive in Beirut and New York. The archive is organized in
> three file categories: Type A (attributed to an identified individual);
> type FD (found documents); Type AGP (attributed to The Atlas
> Group). (TAG, Raad 2005: 9)

The description of TAG sounds fairly neutral, similar to that of hundreds
of other historical foundations around the world. This truth claim is
further supported by a neat little organizational diagram on the inside
cover of the book (cf. TAG/Raad 2005). What many readers will fail to
take in is that TAG not only finds and researches documents but also
'produces' them. In this context, the verb 'produce' has an ambiguous
status: it can either signify the putting together of facts into a new unity,
say, combine a few photographs into an album, or describe the process
of manufacturing facts. As will be seen, with TAG often the latter is
the case.

Visual art

In his visual artworks, Walid Raad and TAG have often exhibited photos
of Lebanese history. In *My Neck Is Thinner Than a Hair* (2000–3), TAG/
Raad investigate car bombs used in the Lebanese civil war. Allegedly,
only the engine survives the detonation of a car bomb and is frequently
catapulted through the air and found in a different place in the city.

> With this project, The Atlas Group examines the multiple dimensions
> of the wars and investigates the public and private events, discourses,
> objects and experiences surrounding the 3641 car bombs that were
> detonated during this period [1975–1991]. (TAG, Raad 2005: 9)

The photos on the gallery wall then show damaged engines lying on
streets somewhere, with bystanders around them. Whether these
documents are real and whether they actually show an engine after a
car bomb detonation remains questionable. 'Despite "legends" in the

form of statistics, summaries and notes purportedly illuminating their background, the true authors of all these images remain shadowy, and along with them the authenticity of the photos per se' (Nakas 2007: 49). Raad takes factual events, the war in Lebanon and the car bombs, and displays evidence of their occurrence. Whether this evidence is genuine is not important because the surrounding discourse of the gallery and the historical knowledge of the war validate the photos in the minds of visitors as genuine. A similar strategy is used in a project in which Raad/TAG display the notebooks of the fictitious historian Dr Fadl Fakhouri (cf. Schmitz 2007: 42). Fakhouri, so the story goes, met with his colleagues, other distinguished scholars, every Sunday at the horse track in order to bet on the horses. They did, however, not bet on the winning horse but on how many fractures of a second the photographer would miss the moment when the winning horse finished the race. The notebook contains the photos of the horse at the finishing line, the names of betting historians and some remarks and statistics – all neatly explained in scholarly manner with arrows and references, when on display in a gallery. The photo is the centrepiece of this display and it is also part of its credibility claim. Despite technological advances and the manipulability of photos, photography still has a connotation of witnessing, of being something like a neutral observer to events, or, in short, incontestably true (cf. Schmitz 2007: 43).

TAG/Raad use the document to question the validity of documents. The photos may show a horse, milliseconds before winning a race. But even if this is an unmanipulated photo of a horse winning a race, is this a photo from Lebanon? Is this a photo from the right time (e.g. civil war)? Did the historians actually bet? The discourse surrounding the document is as fluid and open to manipulation as the document itself is. Truth and fiction are brought in very close proximity by Raad and often the borderline between the two vanishes entirely.

He opts for the profoundly fictive and manipulable in the allegedly factual, so as to overstate the querying of historical contexts and their construction. In historical writing there is always a clear line separating truth from falsehood. In fiction, though, everything is at once untrue and yet truer than truth itself. (Schmitz 2007: 42)

Lecture performances

The difficult relationship between truth, fiction and their representation becomes even more interesting and obvious in Raad's 'lecture performances', which have been shown widely in the United States and in Europe (cf. Schmitz 2007: 41).

> In these lectures – where Raad invariably appears in a dark suit, always speaking in a low, authoritative, yet polite voice, with a slightly stressed Middle-Eastern accent, and in scholarly paced cadence – the [...] artist presents in a Power Point display the same photographic prints, videos and 8mm short films as so many 'files' archived by The Atlas Group. (Lepecki 2007: 61)

The topic of authenticity, truth and historical narrative is broached in the lectures with much more force than in the gallery exhibitions. Deception is the central tool in this performative game, where Raad is not shy to both mislead and lie to the audience.

> In Raad's performances what is constantly being challenged by the poetics of the text as it meets the image through the means of the voice is precisely our capacity for remembering. Even to remember something as simple as the terms under which Raad introduces The Atlas Group. Raad's prefacing words in his lectures – that The Atlas Group is an 'imaginary foundation' or a 'fictional project' whose task is, among others, 'to produce documents' – subtly but invariably become a lost file to his audience. Raad induces with his play of images, words and memory, with his fluid weaving of facts and fictions, and with the authoritative voicing of someone performing both the role of 'native informant' and 'scholar', a misfiling of crucial information. (Lepecki 2007: 63)

Raad himself has a very playful approach to TAG, his own status and that of the performance. He frequently gives different dates for the founding of TAG (among them his birth year, 1976), changes its place of operation or calls TAG a fictional project whose purpose is to archive documents about events that have not yet happened (cf. Lepecki 2006: 90). Despite such playfulness and contradictions, the deceptive strategies work surprisingly well. The Hebbel Am Ufer theatre in Berlin, for instance, never announced on its homepage that Raad's lecture, which took place in their house in 2006, was theatre and fiction (cf. Hebbel am Ufer 2006). Bert Rebhandl, reviewing the performance, also completely failed to take in its fictitious nature (cf. Rebhandl 2007). This is understandable because the 'documents [...] are nevertheless presented to an audience during quite serious lectures' (Lepecki 2007: 62). Raad is frequently criticized for this during post-show discussion (cf. Lepecki 2007: 61), and he has stated that audiences regularly fail to take in the initial statement that TAG is imaginary and documents are being produced (cf. Lepecki 2007: 63). This says a lot about an audience's short-term memory, and thus further interrogates the concept of remembering and the archive. However, it is not only the audience's memory which fails them. More importantly, it is the desire for facts and authenticity which lays the ground for believing in the performance's veracity. The narratives that Raad creates are always metareferencing some well-known reality or historical moment and are consequently already quite believable. Furthermore, people go to see a serious lecture and are in 'factual mode', as it were; they are willing to buy into the concepts of facts, documents and truth. This is what Raad interrogates.

Similar to other DT performances, the set plays a crucial role. As has been shown, DT often relies on austerity in order to validate the factuality of its discourse. Raad employs a similar strategy – the scholarly lecture:

> a successful, scholarly 'lecture' (the austere desk, the glass of water, the stack of paper, the Powerbook computer, the little lamp, the wire-rimmed glasses, the dis- creet suit – all necessary accessories for the respectable lecturer); and by consciously staging in high-profile institutions (such as the Whitney in NYC, or the Haus der Kulturen der Welt in Berlin) the unexplored and undertheorized theatrics of knowledge always embedded in scholarly presentations, displayed clearly how historiography is the primary discursive tool behind any desire to ideologically control current political discourses and actions [...]. (Lepecki 2006: 94)

The setting (renowned institution) and the set (academic lecture) lend the performance credibility. This is, just like in other DT pieces, a matter of setting the tone for the audience. Because of the austere staging, an audience will expect an austere, factual lecture. Furthermore, the use of media, as Carol Martin has suggested for DT in general (cf. Martin 2009), is of great importance. The use of Power Point helps to establish scholarly objectivity, but more importantly, it displays something which is not actually there. The projections of images, which are essentially just some flickers of light on the wall, represent some manifest, tangible reality outside the lecture theatre, but they are only a representation, and they reference a real world that remains absent. Like the present/ absent author figure in other DTs, the image on the screen serves as an *hors-text* and metareference to the outside world. But the document, while represented, remains crucially absent: none of the documents have any physical existence in the performance. They are virtual objects, which claim to have a corresponding reality, but no one is able to prove this. In the lectures, 'we find no tangible documents that could be held and passed around for us to see, touch and verify their actuality. [...] Rather all documents exist just as light and shadows, as pixels, as optical beings' (Lepecki 2007: 64). It is telling that Lepecki references tangible documents as a counter example to Raad's projections. The physical, tangible document still has a very strong claim to truth and authenticity simply because it is physically manifest and cannot be discussed away. In order to make up for this absence, Raad constitutes himself as the trustworthy, tangible focal point in this game of smoke and mirrors. He becomes the persona of the witness who has claim to first-hand experience, to having been there, to having spoken with witnesses, to having met the people who took the photos. The physical presence of Raad is indispensable, because without him and his performance, there would be no validating authority present, and audiences could in turn not mark the documents and stories as authentic. Performance in this case is very much performative – it produces very real effects.

The success of this strategy is to a large degree dependent on Raad's acting, in which he draws on both classical stereotypes of the witness and the scholar. For instance, Raad, although normally an almost accent-free speaker of English, always uses a slightly exaggerated Middle-Eastern accent in his lecture performances.

> Raad's accent operates both *geographically* – *conferring* on the expert's voice the phonetics of an 'authentic' Middle Eastern man; and *performatively* – *his* accent emphasizing the central role of the scholar's vocal apparatus as an instrument for claiming and securing authorship and authority. (Lepecki 2006: 90, emphases in original)

The mechanism is similar to the strong Scottish accent in *Black Watch*. To put it bluntly, the deviation from Standard English in most cases makes a voice sound authentic. In Raad's case, the accent marks him geographically but also as an authentic witness, someone who has first-hand experience of the topics he speaks about. Furthermore, academic pace, set and use of media serve as validation because they are taken from the factual sphere of academic discourse, where – at least in theory – truth should be spoken. Authentication then comes with both an affective (accent) and an intellectual (lecture) component in the performances.

Aesthetic facts

Raad's work with TAG arguably has stretched what DT can be in contemporary culture and has also made an immense contribution to the theoretical understanding of performance and DT. As should be evident, his work interrogates questions of closure, narrative authority or single truth claims. The work is even unsure of its own status because it is situated on the borderline between performance art, theatre and visual art.

> This work goes alongside yet also beyond performance and visual arts while strategically using both, along with literature, film, photography, and video art. I see its theoretical success on three main levels: (1) it proposes and enacts a critical theory of history's relationship to performativity [...]; (2) it unmasks the role of the historian as an author (moreover, as an authoritative author); and (3) it reveals

the fundamental role of the audience as a crucial accomplice in the production of the historian's authority – the audience as a partner in the historian's many forgeries, reveries, conscious or unconscious manipulations, political desires, ambitious poetics, and feverish archival drive. (Lepecki 2006: 94)

Lepecki is right in stressing the fundamental role of the audience, because it is – as in other theatrical areas – they who ultimately mark a performance or play as authentic or not. Authenticity, as has been argued before, is a function of the audience and it is individual. In the case of Raad/TAG it is created through an affective and an intellectual process. What Raad's work exposes is audiences' willingness to buy into discourses of truth and authenticity, and how they become complicit in creating historic narratives of Truth.

In his performance *I Feel a Great Desire to Meet the Masses Once Again*, which I attended in Paris on 13 October 2007, Raad treats issues of homeland security, illegal abductions and secret prisons. He mixes personal anecdotes, for instance when he was stopped and questioned at airports, with detailed reports about the flight numbers of the CIA planes which abducted people to secret prison camps. This lecture is accompanied by a Power Point presentation which tracks and maps the flights and shows photos of the aircrafts. Here, the document produced is the map, again seemingly a source of neutrality and objectivity. The whole performance almost borders on a large-scale conspiracy theory, but it is presented in such an earnest manner, with the strategies described above, that I was certainly not the only one in the audience who initially bought into the story. Up until today I am not sure if all the details about the planes and abductions were made up or if some of them were possibly true. In the Q&A following the lecture, I asked him what role truth played for him. He stated that truth was central for him, but that we needed new concepts for truths. He suggested that all of the documents he presented were facts – some of them historical facts, others aesthetic facts. The notion of aesthetic facts is an interesting one. If aesthetics is understood as the theory of the consequences of an encounter with art (subjective), then 'the fact' is not to be found in the document itself but only in the subjective perception of the onlooker. The fact becomes a subjective feeling of truth and authenticity, while the document on its own is devalued. This is the most radical repositioning and questioning of historical documents. It foregrounds the radical potential to rewrite history through context and discourse. The only truth to be found about the civil war in Lebanon, about car bombs or secret CIA planes is found as an aesthetic relation between me, the spectator and the performer who conjures up images made of pixels of light on the wall. This is the absolute primacy of subjective perception and interpretation, which then becomes personal narrative of fact. Is this a comprehensive view of history? Who decides which images to create and which story to tell? Certainly, this use of document and archive does not seek the ultimate concept of truth, but it can serve to sensitize audiences towards these concepts and it helps sharpen their conception of truth. It encourages the spectator to envision truth as personal and situative. When ultimate truth is demolished, the archive becomes a doubtful place, but by becoming conscious of its limitations, and by allowing fictionality to enter the factual discourse, there is possibly a chance to find hidden, individual, truths, deep in the vaults of the seemingly endless archive of The Atlas Group.

An Ending

#128: 'Don't waste your time; get to the real thing.
Sure, what's "real"? Still, try to get to it.'

–*Reality Hunger* (Shields 2010: 53)

A time of authenticity: A zeitgeist diagnosis

This study is as much a diagnosis of the zeitgeist as it is a study of theatre. We are living in a culture which seeks authenticity. In its various guises it permeates all areas of cultural production. While it is of course not the only current cultural practice, it is clearly discernible. Liz Tomlin, who by and large sees authenticity, the real and similar phenomena as an expression of simple sentimentality or postmodern fragmentation, concedes that we live in 'a society that appears insatiable in its demands for the authenticity of true stories based on interpersonal, rather than social or political relationships' (2013: 192). This leads to a fundamental foregrounding of individuality and individual micro narratives (110), which, according to Tomlin, are firmly embedded in neo-liberal capitalism (193).

I have been trying to suggest that the culture of authenticity can not only be read in terms of postmodern nostalgia and parody but should be seen as an expression of a new structure of feeling. It seems that essentialist concepts such as the real, authenticity or truth have returned. Even Tomlin can – just like Baudrillard – never do without these categories, although she constantly puts them in inverted commas (cf. 2013: 137–138, 112). My suggestion is to do away with the inverted commas. The real, truth and the authentic are prevalent categories and whether they are taken for real or as discursively constructed only makes a difference in an ontological approach; for audiences it frequently does not make a difference. If authenticity is such a major force for audiences, it is a magnitude to be calculated with. Authenticity is performative and therefore enacts its own paradoxical reality. While Tomlin's examples seem at times dated, in the sense that they could easily be – or indeed are – from the 1990s and do not fit contemporary structures of feeling (cf. 103–105), I by and large agree with her analysis. However, I argue that not only deconstruction but also reconstruction leads to individual narrative.

As Hassan and Jameson suggest, Postmodernism is – among other things – a way of reading contemporary culture. In this study, I have given evidence that another reading is possible and that it is more apt for describing contemporary preoccupations and anxieties: it describes structures of feeling after Postmodernism from a point of view of individual reception. We may have arrived at another crucial point in time at which the relation between reality and representation is renegotiated, and poststructuralist radical doubt can neither explain the artistic strategies of such works well nor explain the demand for them.

Audiences are interpreting works differently today than they did in the 1990s and they also go for different kinds of works, which offer possibilities of truth, intimacy, hapticity and so on – in short, authentic experience. This is not to say that the central practices of Postmodernism, such as irony, detachment, pastiche, fragmentation and deconstruction, have vanished or been devaluated. Quite the contrary, they are still there and, specifically, the theoretical underpinnings are as valid as before; but they simply are less employed, particularly in popular culture. Instead, new practices of reconstruction have emerged, seeking to fit together the disparate parts of experience and to mend the flaws of Postmodernism. These practices can be characterized with Funk as reconstruction, or as metamodern in the shape of a corporeal, (syn)aesthetic approach, an aesthetic of trust in the form of intimacy, or confrontations with the real. Fundamentally, audiences appear to be in search of first-hand experience, which they find lacking in their everyday life. The phenomenon of authenticity must be conceived of as a paradox that is both marked and unmarked and, through this mechanism, gains its efficacy. It embodies both the fake and the original and thus voids these dichotomies. It is – precisely because of its position in an ontological limbo – the only entity that can sew together the fragments of deconstruction.

It may be said that the examples I chose of theatres of authenticity are eclectic or even rhizomatic. They exemplarily display features of authenticity, and their success indicates that these mechanisms speak to a wide audience. However, they are only a few expressions of this culture of authenticity. More examples can be found in the field of theatre and performance as well as in television, visual art, clothing or food. The sheer amount of cultural production and recent academic publications, which treat subjects such as 'the real' or 'authenticity', shows that the culture of authenticity is a growing field, which deserves further academic attention.

In theatre, authenticity can take many shapes. Emancipation as an ontological process of spectators is one of them. This phenomenon, however, is always an individual one and, as specifically the one-on-one performances have shown, impossible to produce for a mass market. Furthermore, authenticity is a transitory phenomenon; it has no lasting quality but is marked in the moment. Intimate theatre offers glimpses of the real because the genuinely real escapes representation. Nonetheless, audiences seem to be more than willing to go on an individual quest for transitory, authentic experience.

More often than not, this transitory state is achieved by addressing the senses. This is specifically evident in immersive theatre, which is a counter movement both against a culture of virtuality and theatre's process of sanitization. Where the 'théâtre serieux' has vanished and theatres have become more and more sanitized, immersive theatre offers a sense of tangibility and even danger by the shape of first-hand sensoric experience, as opposed to images and narratives pre-fabricated and consumed through media. Immersive theatre is not a cause for authenticity, but it is rather another symptom of the culture of authenticity. It delivers the infrastructure by which authentic experiences can be generated. As I have shown, however, these mechanisms can only unfold their full force if the spectator plays along and is willing to give herself over to this experience.

The live event, which is multisensorially experienced by the spectator, is the locus of all authentic theatres. Rebutting Philip Auslander's claim that there be no fundamental difference between a live event and a recorded one, I argue that failure is the litmus test for a live event. Specifically DT needs the force of the live event in order to generate authentic experience. Consequently, I define a live event as any performance that can fail. This is precisely the reason why practitioners make use of DT and do not simply write a non-fiction book about the issues they seek to treat. Live events create stronger (and authentic) experiences; their impact on audiences is greater.

In Tyrannos: Speculation

I realize that a number of my arguments regarding the death of Postmodernism or the emergence of a new structure of feeling will not sit well with many scholars. Some of my statements are broad and lay themselves very open to criticism. This is good. Along with Thomas McCarthy, I believe that discourses are only ever advanced if one makes statements of truth and unconditionality, which expose one's opinion and make one vulnerable to criticism (cf. Botham 2008: 317). Therefore, I intend to push my points a little further in the following.

Authenticity is not a primal phenomenon itself, but it springs from a culture that is felt to lack depth and first-hand experience. Audiences want to reinstate concepts such as truth, authenticity and the real in a world that is increasingly perceived as mediated, fake or mendacious. As Tomlin has remarked, today the problem is not a belief in reality but too much belief in the simulacrum; that is, some people do not believe that 9/11 is real but would rather consider that the US government had staged it (cf. 2013: 145–146). In such times of ontological uncertainty, we have again arrived at a point where the relation between image and reality is renegotiated and poststructuralism cannot give adequate answers. While Tomlin concedes that a certain return of the real in performances that have an experiential quality is discernible (cf. 144), and also acknowledges that there has to be a distinction between different orders of the real (cf. 144), she – just like a number of other scholars – still reads some of the performances discussed in this study as postmodern and fragmented, supporting a deconstructivist approach. I claim that deconstruction and poststructuralist doubt have become the new orthodoxy. This may not be a problem for academia – it is a problem in everyday life.

The theatre's and audiences' hunger for authenticity are but one expression of a culture that is almost desperately in search of essentialist concepts, of which authenticity is only one. The current upsurge of religion as a firm ontological system speaks volumes about a longing for safety and the original. The return of nationalist parties to the European stage possibly heralds a new age of nationalism that elevates the nation to a similarly sacrosanct status. Also, the current penchant for conservative lifestyles is indicative of a profound move away from doubt, irony and situationality. In a nutshell, the same ontological unease that produces authenticity as a cultural practice, in my view, also produces a number of practices and phenomena that are essentially dangerous to a free, democratic, metamodern state.

In all likelihood, issues of mediatization, of second-hand experience, virtualization and ontological doubt are going to accelerate in the decades to come. At the same time, we are humans. We live in our bodies of flesh and blood that have sensate experiences and a mind that seeks closure, truth and the real. We live in a tangible world. Hence, we will have to continue to negotiate our concrete existence, our concrete world, a fast information economy, cultures of virtuality and an ever-more diverse and interconnected world. It is more than understandable that people will longingly gaze for something essential to hold on to.

If, however, we allow essentialist concepts such as authenticity or *telos* to enter our culture uncritically, we are facing the very real danger of a neo-essentialist backlash in many areas of life, not only in theatre. There is good reason why poststructuralist practices sought to defuse the poisonous arrow of essentialism. Today, with poststructuralist theory in mind, it may have become safe to play with it again. However, this undertaking is as dangerous as the metaphor implies. In the best case, such concepts can invigorate contemporary culture and give crucial new, even activist, impulses after decades in which irony and detachment had become the norm. The hunger for essentialist concepts can be used to bring into harmony poststructuralist doubt and the experience of a life, which is by and large still essentialist. However, essentialism in its many guises can also very easily lead to intolerance or even fanaticism. If we begin to perceive the proliferation of such concepts outside the narrow field of theatre and the arts, it becomes evident that authenticity and its entourage might also lead us back to darker times.

Notes

Chapter 1

1   The term 'structure of feeling' is used throughout in Raymond Williams' sense (cf. 1961: 65 f.).

2   He, for instance, claims that the response 'fine' to the question, 'How are you?' constitutes a lie, which is highly debatable (cf. Keyes 2004: 7).

3   Interestingly, in the same week Germany's largest weekly quality newspaper *Die Zeit* battled with similar concepts when it stated on the front page that authenticity was more in demand than ever, but asked what that concept was and how one could find it (cf. Schnabel 2014).

4   For other (more extensive) treatments of the subject, see Trilling (1972), Kalisch (2000), Guignon (2004), Straub (2012), Dietschi (2012) and Funk (2015).

5   Incidentally, this is one of the main concerns of Plato: the blurring of fact and fiction by poets which, according to him, leads to a gradual erosion of exactly the sense of having one's place in the world. Poetry opens up the possibility of playing out multiple personalities. The divine, orderly system is destabilized through this form of 'inauthenticity' (cf. Plato 2000: 600e, 603b).

6   Freud has called Copernicus' findings the first great blow to mankind's self-love, when mankind discovered that their planet was not in fact the centre of the universe (cf. 1963: 285).

7   For a more detailed discussion of subjectivity and its development in the Renaissance, see Marshall (2002).

8   For a good discussion of this issue in literature, see Behler (2000) and Röttgers (2001).

9   I am aware that a number of issues with regard to Derrida's notion of logocentrism could be debated here. However, the scope of this study forbids it and I must refer the reader to Derrida (1976: 354–376) and Zarrilli et al. (2009, chapter 2) for some initial ideas.

10 I am aware that there are several theories more on acting, such as Meyerhold's biomechanical approach or corporeal mime. However,

for the purpose of this study, the two most frequently used strands of acting will be sufficient.

Chapter 2

1   I am aware that the notion of one solid unit called 'audience' has been very convincingly and fruitfully deconstructed, first and foremost by Herbert Blau (cf. 1990). In fact, it seems likely that a number of FE's works are indebted to his work. The term 'audience' is then, in the course of this study, only used as a shorthand to denote the entirety of persons present at a theatrical event.

2   The term 'distribution of the sensible' refers to the politics of performing and spectating. In his *Politics of Aesthetics*, Rancière states,

> I call the distribution of the sensible the system of self-evident facts of sense perception that simultaneously discloses the existence of something in common and the delimitations that define the respective parts and positions within it. [...] The distribution of the sensible reveals who can have a share in what is common to the community based on what they do and on the time and space in which this activity is performed.' (2011: 12)

In other words, a 'distribution of the sensible' refers to the rules that govern who can have part in the discourse, at what times and through which means.

3   It should be noted that the text of *Speak Bitterness* is constantly changed and expanded, which often makes it seem very current.

4   The catalogue is in essence Platonic in the sense of order with each thing and person having their proper place. This line of thought is evident throughout the *Republic* and specifically in Plato's discussion of the organization of the state (cf. 2000: 370a), and the craftsmen and their proper duties (2000: 598c–d). Each thing has its unique place and properties given to it by god, and each person has his or her faculties according to talent and formation (e.g. king, guardian, worker). Accordingly, each thing and each activity is categorized and given a proper place that cannot be changed.

Chapter 3

1 Considering Umberto Eco, one could also talk about a present without depth that gives rise to the absolute fake (1998: 31). This is at the core of immersive theatre, and it is a conscious simulacrum that displays a reality that is not present anymore but very much wished for.

2 I am aware that the analogy with 'deep play' can only go so far. Geertz explicitly points out that for deep play to happen, not only must participants be completely absorbed within the play but the stakes must also be significantly higher than the reward (cf. 1972: 15–16), which is obviously not the case with immersive theatre.

3 For a more detailed discussion of Benjamin's two concepts and their implications for immersive theatre, see section 'Body'.

4 A similar point is made by Susan Bennet, who even traces a trajectory of increasing passivity from Ancient Greece all the way to the nineteenth century (cf. 1990: 2–4).

5 Eco makes plain already in the early 1970s that the absolute fake is an offspring from a present without depth and that something being fake is the precondition of pleasure precisely because it is not real (cf. 1998: 52). His prime example is also Disneyland, which for him becomes more real than the real, a 'total theatre' (1998: 45).

6 As White has shown (cf. 2012: 31), if anything, spectators may become more self-conscious and less absorbed in a one-on-one situation. One-on-ones are simply an expression of authenticity and intimate theatre. The one-on-one performances that are part of a larger-scale immersive production, however, must be taken into consideration as a part of the whole. As was shown in Chapter 2, they are a very strong means of creating authenticity and thus, while not being immersive themselves, contribute to the overall effect of authenticity and immersion.

7 Of course, this reproach could be made against theatre in general whose selection of the public is often a very narrow one, with the possible exception of long-running West End shows and musicals. On the other hand, it has been claimed that it is precisely the unorthodox, video-game- quality of immersive theatre, which has attracted audiences that would traditionally not attend theatrical performances (cf. Machon 2013: 22).

8   Her concept of 'absorption' is not unlike Csikszentmihalyi's 'flow', which
     he sees as a pleasurable state of 'losing oneself in the action' (Schechner
     2006: 97), which usually happens in play and game. This highlights again
     the game-like quality of immersive theatre.

Chapter 4

1   Very similar mechanisms are at work in other plays that have violence
     and suffering as their subject, such as – for instance – Nicolas Kent's
     Srebrenica (1996), which revolved around the Serbian massacre in
     the Balkan war (cf. Kent 2014: 200–290), or Richard Norton-Taylor's
     Nuremberg (1995), which treated the Nazi war crimes trials (cf. Norton-
     Taylor 2014b: 113–194).

2   One could in this context probably also fruitfully apply Kristeva's concept
     of 'the abject' (cf. Kristeva 1984) to analyse DT's confrontation with
     'the real'.

3   Whether actors in docusoaps are conscious of their role or are acting at
     all cannot be discussed here at length. For a good discussion and further
     research, see Bruzzi (2000), specifically pp. 1–22 and 76–85.

4   It may be objected that Habermas' theory of the public sphere is first and
     foremost a sociological and political one and therefore not applicable to
     theatre. I would object, however, that as all DT is always political (see
     above): it is precisely a political theory of discourse, which needs to be
     applied here.

5   While Bailes investigates 'performances of *failure*', rather than
     performances *that fail*' (2011: 62, italics in the original), such as the
     works of Forced Entertainment, I focus on actual failure, which is
     ontologically inscribed in every live performance.

6   Enron was an energy company and one of the largest corporations in
     the United States. After a comet-like rise in market capitalization, the
     news broke in 2001 that the company's success had largely been due
     to large-scale accounting fraud. The ensuing scandal had far-reaching
     consequences for accounting regulations (Sarbanes-Oxley-Act) and
     the new economy, and it sparked huge public debate about corporate
     behaviour and regulations. For a detailed account, see Fox (2003).

Works Cited

Agamben, Giorgio. *The Man without Content*. 1999. Trans. Albert, Georgia. Crossing Aesthetics. Eds Hamacher, Werner and David E. Wellerby. Stanford: Stanford University Press, 2008. Print.

Alexander, Jeffrey. 'Cultural Pragmatics: Social Performance between Ritual and Strategy'. *Sociological Theory* 22.4 (2004): 527–573. Print.

Anon. 'Strategies of the Metamodern (Editorial August 2010)'. *Notes on Metamodernism* (2010a). 28 March 2013. http://www.metamodernism.com/2010/08/01/strategies-of-the-metamodern/.

Anon. 'What Meta Does and Does Not Mean (Editorial October 2010)'. *Notes on Metamodernism* (2010b). 28 March 2013. http://www.metamodernism.com/2010/10/14/what-meta-means-and-does-not-mean/.

Aquinas, St Thomas. *Summa Theologiae: A Concise Translation*. London: Eyre and Spottiswoode, 1989. Print.

Armitstead, Claire. 'The Smile off Your Face: Review'. *The Guardian* (2013). 19 October 2013. http://www.theguardian.com/culture/2013/mar/04/smile-off-your-face-ontroerend-goed-review.

Armstrong, Isobel. *The Radical Aesthetic*. Oxford: Blackwell, 2000. Print.

Artaud, Atonin. *The Theatre and Its Double*. Trans. Richards, Mary Caroline. New York: Grove Press, 1958. Print.

Assmann, Aleida. 'Authenticity – The Signature of Western Exceptionalism?' *Paradoxes of Authenticity: Studie Son a Critical Concept*. Ed. Straub, Julia. Bielfeld: Transcript, 2012. 33–50. Print.

Aurelius, Augustinus. *On Lying*, 2nd edition, Vol. 14. 18 vols. Trans. Sister Mary Muldowney (RSM) et al. Fathers of the Church. Ed. Deferrari, Roy Joseph. Washington, DC: The Catholic University of America Press, 1965a. Print.

Aurelius, Augustinus. *Against Lying*, 2nd edition, Vol. 14. 18 vols. Trans. Jaffee, Harold B. Fathers of the Church. Ed. Deferrari, Roy Joseph. Washington, DC: The Catholic University of America Press, 1965b. Print.

Auslander, Philip. *From Acting to Performance*. London and New York: Routledge, 1997. Print.

Auslander, Philip. *Liveness: Performance in a Mediatized Culture*. 1999. London and New York: Routledge, 2008. Print.

BAC. 'Battersea Arts Centre Homepage'. London, 2013. 5 February 2015. https://www.bac.org.uk/content/29454/about_us/past_shows/london_stories.

Bailes, Sara Jane. *Performance Theatre and the Poetics of Failure: Forced Entertainment, Goat Island, Elevator Repair Service*. London and New York: Routledge, 2011. Print.

Bainbridge, William. *The Virtual Future*. London: Springer, 2011. Print.

Banham, Gary. 'Kant and the Ends of Criticism'. *The New Aestheticism*. Eds Joughin, John J. and Simon Malpas. Manchester and New York: Manchester University Press, 2003. 193–207. Print.

Barboza, David. 'Iphone Maker in China Is under Fire after Suicide'. *The New York Times Online*. 26 July 2009. Print.

Barker, Martin. *Live to Your Local Cinema: The Remarkable Rise of Livecasting*. Basingstoke: Palgrave Macmillan, 2013. Print.

Barthes, Roland. *Image-Music-Text*. Trans. Heath, S. London: Fontana, 1977. Print.

Baudrillard, Jean. *Simulacra and Simulation*. 1981. Trans. Glaser, Sheila Faria. Ann Arbor: University of Michigan Press, 2010. Print.

Behler, Ernst. 'On Truth and Lie in an Aesthetic Sense'. *Revenge of the Aesthetic: The Place of Literature in Theory Today*. Ed. Clark, Michael P. Berkley: University of California Press, 2000. 76–92. Print.

Bell, Elizabeth. *Theories of Performance*. Los Angeles, CA: Sage, 2008. Print.

Benjamin, Walter. *Illuminations: Essays and Reflections, Edited and with an Introduction by Hannah Arendt*. New York: Schocken Books, 1969. Print.

Benjamin, Walter. *The Work of Art in the Age of Mechanical Reproduction*. 1936. Trans. Underwood, J. A. Penguin Great Ideas. London: Penguin, 2008. Print.

Bennett, Susan. *Theatre Audiences: A Theory of Production and Reception*. London: Routledge, 1990. Print.

Beumers, Birgit. 'The Performance of Life: Documentary Theater and Film'. *Russian Review Special Issue: The Desire for the Real: Documentary Trends in Contemporary Russian Culture* 69.4 (2010): 615– 637. Print.

Biesenbach, Klaus. *Marina Abramovic: The Artist Is Present*. New York: Museum of Modern Art, 2010. Print.

Billington, Michael. 'Stuff Happens'. *The Guardian* (2004). 25 February 2014. http://www.theguardian.com/stage/2004/sep/11/theatre.politicaltheatre.

Billington, Michael. 'Talking to Terrorists'. *The Guardian* (2005). 25 February 2014. http://www.theguardian.com/stage/2005/apr/28/theatre.politicaltheatre.

Billington, Michael. 'Enron'. *The Guardian* (2009). 21 March 2014. http://www.theguardian.com/stage/2009/sep/23/enron-review.

Blast Theory Homepage. 24 February 2016. http://www.blasttheory.co.uk/
projects/rider-spoke/.

Blau, Herbert. *The Audience*. Parallax Series: Revisions of Culture and Society.
Baltimore: Johns Hopkins University Press, 1990. Print.

Bleeker, Maaike. 'Theatre of/or Truth'. *Performance Paradigm* 3 (2007): 14. Print.

Boal, Augusto. *Theatre of the Oppressed*. 1979. New York: Theatre
Communications Group, 2011. Print.

Bok, Sissela. *Lying: Moral Choice in Public and Private Life*. Sussex: The
Harvester Press, 1978. Print.

Botham, Paola. 'From Deconstruction to Reconstruction: A Habermasian
Framework for Contemporary Political Theatre'. *Contemporary Theatre
Review* 18.3 (2008): 307– 317. Print.

Bottoms, Stephen. 'Putting the Document into Documentary'. *The Drama
Review: A Journal of Performance Studies* 50.3 (2006): 56–68. Print.

Bourriaud, Nicolas. *Relational Aesthetics*. Trans. Pleasance, Simon and Fronza
Woods. Paris: Les Presses Du Réel, 2002. Print.

Bowie, Andrew. 'What Comes after Art?' *The New Aestheticism*. Eds Joughin,
John J. and Simon Malpas. Manchester, New York: Manchester University
Press, 2003. 69–82. Print.

Brantley, Ben. 'A Story to Question, Word for Word'. *The New York Times*
(2013). 25 February 2014. http://www.nytimes.com/2013/11/20/
theater/reviews/taking-care-of-baby-from-manhattan-theater-club
.html?adxnnl=1&adxnnlx=1393322870-1a2g4sU1AGWxJOPpHlsIuQ.

Brittain, Victoria et al., eds. *The Tricycle: Collected Tribunal Plays 1994–2012*.
London: Oberon Books, 2014. Print.

Broadhurst, Susan. *Liminal Acts: A Critical Overview of Contemporary
Performance and Theory*. London and New York: Cassell, 1999. Print.

Brockett, Oscar G. *History of the Theatre*. Boston: Allyn & Bacon, 1995.
Print.

Brown, Alison Leigh. *Subjects of Deceit: A Phenomenology of Lying*. Albany:
State University of New York Press, 1998. Print.

Bruzzi, Stella. *New Documentary: A Critical Introduction*. London: Routledge,
2000. Print.

Burke, Gregory. *Black Watch*. 2007. London: Faber and Faber, 2010. Print.

Butler, Judith. *Undoing Gender*. London and New York: Routledge, 2008. Print.

Campbell, Jeremy. *The Liar's Tale: A History of Falsehood*. New York and
London: W. W. Norton & Company, 2001. Print.

Canton, Ursula. 'We May Not Know Reality, but It Still Matters – A Functional Analysis of "Factual Elements" in the Theatre'. *Contemporary Theatre Review* 18.3 (2008): 318–327. Print.

Carr, David. 'Theater, Disguised as Real Journalism'. *The New York Times* (2012). 23 March 2012. http://www.nytimes.com/2012/03/19/business/media/theater-disguised-up-as-real-journalism.html?pagewanted=all.

Cavendish, Dominic. 'Punchdrunk: Plunge into a World of Extraordinary Theatre'. *The Telegraph Online* (2013). 31 October 2013. http://www.telegraph.co.uk/culture/theatre/theatre-features/10127892/Punchdrunk-plunge-into-a-world-of-extraordinary-theatre.html.

Chakrabortty, Aditya. 'The Woman Who Nearly Died Making Your Ipad'. *The Guardian Online* (2013). 5 August 2013. http://www.theguardian.com/commentisfree/2013/aug/05/woman-nearly-died-making-ipad.

Chatzichristodoulou, Maria. 'Blast Theory'. *British Theatre Companies 1995–2014*. Ed. Tomlin, Liz. London: Bloomsbury, 2015. Print.

Costa, Maddy. 'Ontroerend Goed: Are You Sitting Uncomfortably?' *The Guardian Online* (2011). 28 March 2013. http://www.guardian.co.uk/stage/2011/nov/07/ontroerend-goed-theatre-audience.

Courtney, Richard. 'Drama and Aesthetics'. *British Journal of Aesthetics* 8.4 (1968): 373–386. Print.

Culler, Jonathan. *Framing the Sign: Criticism and Its Institutions*. Oxford: Basil Blackwell, 1988. Print.

Damian, Diana. 'Tim Etchells on the Coming Storm'. *Exeunt Magazine* (2012). 26 November 2012. http://exeuntmagazine.com/features/tim-etchells-on-the-coming-storm/.

Derrida, Jacques. *Die Schrift Und Die Differenz*. Trans. Gasché, Rudolph. Frankfurt: Suhrkamp, 1976. Print.

Derrida, Jacques. *Specters of Marx*. London: Routledge, 1994. Print.

Derrida, Jacques and R. Klein. 'Economimesis'. *Diacritics* 11.2 (1981): 2–25. Print.

Dickson, Andrew. 'Internal: The Ultimate Test for Edinburgh Audiences?' *Guardian Theatre Blog* (2009). 1 August 2012. http://www.guardian.co.uk/stage/theatreblog/2009/aug/17/internal-edinburgh-audiences.

Dietschi, Daniel. *Hinführungen Zur Authentizität: Die Ideen- Und Begriffsgeschichtliche Aufbereitung Eines Modernen Persönlichkeitsideals*. Würzburg: Königshausen & Neumann, 2012. Print.

Docherty, Thomas. 'Aesthetic Education and the Demise of Experience'. *The New Aestheticism*. Eds Joughin, John J. and Simon Malpas. Manchester and New York: Manchester University Press, 2003. 23–35. Print.

Domsch, Sebastian, ed. *Amerikanisches Erzählen Nach 2000: Eine Bestandsaufnahme*. Munich: Edition Text & Kritik, 2008. Print.

Dutton, Dennis. 'Bookmarks'. *Philosophy and Literature* 14.1 (1990): 232–238. Print.

Eagleton, Terry. *The Ideology of Aesthetic*. Oxford: Blackwell, 1990. Print.

Easo Smith, Molly. 'The Theatre and the Scaffold: Death as Spectacle in *The Spanish Tragedy*'. *Revenge Tragedy*. Ed. Simkin, Stevie. London: Palgrave, 2001. 71–87. Print.

Eco, Umberto. *Faith in Fakes: Travels in Hyperreality*. 1973. London: Vintage, 1998. Print.

Edgar, David. 'A Hard Time for British Plays: David Edgar Defends the Vibrancy of British Playwriting'. *Hard Times* 91 (2012): 7–12. Print.

Eshelman, Raoul. 'Performatism, or the End of Postmodernism'. *Anthropoetics: The Electronic Journal of Generative Anthropology* 6.2 (2001). 26 September 2012. http://www.anthropoetics.ucla.edu/ap0602/perform.htm.

Etchells, Tim. *Quizoola!: Performance Text*. Sheffield: Forced Entertainment, 1997. Print.

Etchells, Tim. *Certain Fragments: Contemporary Performance and Forced Entertainment*. London: Routledge, 1999. Print.

Etchells, Tim. 'A Text on 20 Years with 66 Footnotes'. *Not Even a Game Anymore: The Theatre of Forced Entertainment*. Eds Helmer, Judith and Florian Malzacher. Berlin: Alexander Verlag, 2004. Print.

Etchells, Tim. 'Incomplete Alphabet: Some Notes after Twenty Years of Forced Entertainment'. *A Performance Cosmology: Testimony from the Future, Evidence from the Past*. Eds Christie, Judie, Richard Gough and Daniel Watt. London and New York: Routledge, 2006. 140–144. Print.

Etchells, Tim. 'An Island, a Prison Cell, a Hotel Bed, a No Man's Land: Some Thoughts about Quizoola! 24 from Tim Etchells' (2013). 17 September 2013. http://notebook.forcedentertainment.com/?p=797.

Faulkner, Paul. 'What Is Wrong with Lying?' *Philosophy and Phenomenological Research* 75.3 (2007): 535–557. Print.

Favorini, Attilio. 'History, Memory and Trauma in the Documentary Plays of Emily Mann'. *Get Real: Documentary Theatre Past and Present*. Eds Forsyth, Alison and Chris Megson. Performance Interventions. Basingstoke: Palgrave, 2009. 151–166. Print.

Féral, Josette. 'Theatricality: The Specificity of Theatrical Language'. *SubStance* 31.98/99 (2002): 94–108. Print.

Fiebach, Joachim. 'Theatricality: From Oral Traditions to Televised Realities'.
SubStance 31.98/99 (2002): 17–41. Print.

Fischer, Jessica. 'British Art Now'. *Hard Times: Theatre in Britain* 91 (2012):
58–60. Print.

Fischer-Lichte, Erika. 'Theatralität Und Inszenierung'. *Inszenierung Von
Authentizität.* Eds Fischer-Lichte, Erika and Isabel Pflug. Tübingen and
Basel: Francke, 2000. 11–27. Print.

Fischer-Lichte, Erika. *Performativität: Eine Einführung.* Bielefeld: Transcript,
2012. Print.

Fischer-Lichte, Erika. 'Classical Theatre'. *The Cambridge Companion to
Theatre History.* Eds Wiles, David and Christine Dymkowski. Cambridge:
Cambridge University Press, 2013. Print.

Fischer-Lichte, Erika. 'The Art of Spectatorship'. *Journal of Contemporary
Drama in English* 4.1 (2016): 164–179. Print.

Forced Entertainment. *Quizoola!.* Dir. Tim Etchells, The Junction, Cambridge.
17 February 2008. Performance.

Forced Entertainment. 'Forced Entertainment Homepage'. Sheffield, 2012.
Forced Entertainment. 1 August 2012. http://www.forcedentertainment
.com/page/1/Home.

Forced Entertainment. '#Quizoola! 24'. n.d. 17 September 2013. http://
notebook.forcedentertainment.com/?p=772.

Forsyth, Alison and Chris Megson. 'Introduction'. *Get Real: Documentary
Theatre Past and Present.* Eds Forsyth, Alison and Chris Megson.
Performance Interventions. Basingstoke: Palgrave, 2009. 1–5. Print.

Fortier, Mark. *Theory Theatre: An Introduction.* London: Routledge, 2002. Print.

Foster, Hal. *The Return of the Real: The Avant-Garde at the End of the Century.*
Cambridge, MA and London: MIT Press, 1996. Print.

Foucault, Michel. 'Of Other Spaces'. *Diacritics* 16.1 (1986): 22–27. Print.

Fox, Loren. *Enron: The Rise and Fall.* New York: Wiley-Blackwell, 2003. Print.

Freud, Sigmund. 'Introductory Lectures on Psychoanalysis'. *The Standard
Edition of the Complete Psychological Works of Sigmund Freud.* 1916. Ed.
Strachey, James. Vol. 16. London: Hogarth Press, 1963. Print.

Funk, Wolfgang. *The Literature of Reconstruction: Authentic Fiction in the New
Millennium.* London: Bloomsbury, 2015. Print.

Funk, Wolfgang, Florian Gross and Irmtraud Huber, eds. *The Aesthetics of
Authenticity: Medial Constructions of the Real.* Bielefeld: Transcript, 2012.
Print.

Gardner, Lyn. 'I Didn't Know Where to Look'. *The Guardian* (2005).
15 October 2013. http://www.theguardian.com/stage/2005/mar/03/theatre2.

Gardner, Lyn. 'We Make Our Own Ghosts Here'. *The Guardian* (2007).
1 August 2012. http://www.guardian.co.uk/stage/2007/sep/12/theatre
.edgarallanpoe.

Gardner, Lyn. 'How Intimate Theatre Won Our Hearts'. *The Guardian* (2009).
1 August 2012. http://www.guardian.co.uk/culture/2009/aug/11/intimate
-theatre-edinburgh.

Gardner, Lyn. 'London Stories – Review'. *The Guardian* (2013). 15 October 2013.
http://www.theguardian.com/culture/2013/sep/18/london-stories-review.

Geertz, Clifford. 'Deep Play: Notes on the Balinese Cockfight'. *Daedalus* 101.1
(1972): 1–37. Print.

Geertz, Clifford. 'Thick Description: Toward an Interpretive Theory of
Culture'. *The Interpretation of Cultures: Selected Essays*. New York: Basic
Books, 1973. 3–30. Print.

Glenn, Joshua. 'Fake Authenticity'. *Hilobrow* (2010). http://hilobrow
.com/2010/06/01/fake-authenticity/.

Goffman, Erving. *The Presentation of the Self in Everyday Life*. New York:
Double Day, 1959. Print.

Gomme, Rachel. 'Not-so-Close-Encounters: Searching for Intimacy in One-
to-One Performance'. *Participations: Journal of Audience and Reception
Studies* 12.1 (2015): 281– 299. Print.

Gordon, Mel. *Lazzi: The Comic Routines of Comedia Dell'arte*. New York:
Performing Arts Journal Publications, 1983. Print.

Goulish, Matthew. 'Peculiar Detonation: The Incomplete History and
Impermanent Manifesto of the Institute of Failure'. *Not Even a Game
Anymore: The Theatre of Forced Entertainment*. Eds Helmer, Judith and
Florian Malzacher. Berlin: Alexander Verlag, 2004. Print.

Gran, Anne-Britt. 'The Fall of Theatricality in the Age of Modernity'.
SubStance 31.98/99 (2002): 251– 264. Print.

Gratza, Agniszka. 'Quizoola!'. *FriezeBlog* (2013). 31 January 2015. http://blog
.frieze.com/quizoola/.

Grau, Oliver. *Virtual Art: From Illusion to Immersion*. Cambridge, MA:
Cambridge University Press, 2003. Print.

Green, Chris. 'Forced Entertainment'. *Performa Magazine* (2013).
28 March 2013. http://performamagazine.tumblr.com/post/42953624125/
forced-entertainment.

Gross, Florian. "'Brooklyn Zack Is Real'": Irony and Sincere Authenticity in 30 Rock'. *The Aesthetics of Authenticity: Medial Constructions of the Real.* Eds Funk, Wolfgang, Florian Gross and Irmtraud Huber. Bielefeld: Transcript, 2012. 237–260. Print.

Groves, Nancy. 'London Stories'. *What's on Stage* (2013). 15 October 2013. http://www.whatsonstage.com/london-theatre/reviews/09-2013/london -stories_31982.html.

Guignon, Charles. *On Being Authentic.* Thinking in Action. London: Routledge, 2004. Print.

Hall, Edith. *Greek Tragedy.* Oxford: Oxford University Press, 2010. Print.

Hamilton, James R. "'Illusion' and the Distrust of Theater'. *The Journal of Aesthetics and Art Criticism* 41.1 (1982): 39–50. Print.

Hare, David. *Stuff Happens.* London: Faber & Faber 2006. Print.

Harper, Steve. 'Everytime You Go Away... You Take a Piece of Me with You'. *Contemporary Theatre Review* 10.3 (2000): 87–95. Print.

Haselstein, Ulla, Andrew S. Gross and Mary Ann Snyder-Körber. 'Introduction: Returns of the Real'. *The Pathos of Authenticity: American Passions of the Real.* Eds Haselstein, Ulla, Andrew S. Gross and Mary Ann Snyder-Körber. Heidlberg: Universitätverlag Winter, 2010. Print.

Hassan, Ihab. 'Beyond Postmodernism: Toward an Aesthetic of Trust'. *Beyond Postmodernism: Reassessments in Literature, Theory, and Culture.* Ed. Stierstorfer, Klaus. Berlin and New York: Walter de Gruyter, 2003. Print.

Hassan, Ihab. 'A Plague of Mendacity: A Plea for Truth, Trust and Altruism' (2004). 16 May 2012. www.ihabhassan.com/plague_of_mendacity.htm.

Hayden, Andrew. 'Subversion on Stage: Can Theatre Change the World?' *Theatre Blog with Lyn Gardner* (2011). 28 August 2014. http://www.theguardian.com/ stage/theatreblog/2011/jan/06/theatre-change-world-belarus.

Heathfield, Adrian. 'As If Things Got More Real: A Conversation with Tim Etchells'. *Not Even a Game Anymore: The Theatre of Forced Entertainment.* Eds Helmer, Judith and Florian Malzacher. Berlin: Alexander Verlag, 2004. 77–99. Print.

Hebbel am Ufer. 'I Feel a Great Desire to Meet the Masses Once Again'. Berlin, 2006. Hebbel am Ufer. 22 March 2014. http://www.archiv.hebbel-am-ufer .de/archiv_de/kuenstler/kuenstler_7664.html.

Hegel, Georg Wilhelm Friedrich. 'Lectures on Fine Art'. *The Norton Anthology of Theory and Criticism.* Ed. Vincent B. Leitch et al. London and New York: W. W. Norton, 2010. Print.

Heidegger, Martin. 'On the Essence of Truth'. Trans. Krell, David Farrell. *Basic Writings: From Being and Time (1927) to the Task of Thinking (1964)*. Ed. Krell, David Farrell. San Francisco: Harper Collins, 1993. Print.

Highberg, Nels P. 'When Heroes Fall: Doug Wright's *I Am My Own Wife* and the Challenge to Truth'. *Get Real: Documentary Theatre Past and Present*. Eds Forsyth, Alison and Chris Megson. Performance Interventions. Basingstoke: Palgrave, 2009. 167–178. Print.

Hoffmann, Beth. 'Radicalism and the Theatre in Genealogies of Live Art'. *Performance Research* 14.1 (2010): 95–105. Print.

Hoggins, Tom. 'Punchdrunk to Perform "Immersive" Theatrical Prequel to the Video Game Resistance 3'. *The Telegraph* (2011). 21 August 2011. http://www.telegraph.co.uk/technology/video-games/8714455/ Punchdrunk-to-perform-immersive-theatrical-prequel-to-the-video -game-Resistance-3.html.

Horowitz, Anthony. *The House of Silk*. London: Orion Books, 2012. Print.

Hughes, Jenny. *Performance in a Time of Terror: Critical Mimesis and the Age of Uncertainty*. Manchester: Manchester University Press, 2011. Print.

Hulse, Seth. 'Monolithic Authenticity and Fake News: Stephen Colbert's Megalomania'. *The Aesthetics of Authenticity: Media Constructions of the Real*. Eds Funk, Wolfgang, Florian Gross and Irmtraud Huber. Bielefeld: Transcript, 2012. 63–90. Print.

Iezzi, Teressa. 'Punchdrunk's Felix Barrett Drops You in His Theater with No Directions Home'. 2012. 29 November 2012. http://www.fastcocreate.com/1679201/punchdrunks-felix-barrett-brings-theater-to-life-literally.

Irmer, Thomas. 'A Search for New Realities: Documentary Theatre in Germany'. *The Drama Review: A Journal of Performance Studies* 50.3 (2006): 16–28. Print.

Ishwerwood, Charles. 'Speaking Less Than Truth to Power'. *The New York Times* (2012). 23 March 2012. http://www.nytimes.com/2012/03/19/theater/defending-this-american-life-and-its-mike-daisey-retraction.html.

Jacobi, Philip. *Postmillenial Speculative Fiction and the Culture of Longing*. Trier: WVT, 2016. Print.

Jameson, Fredric. Postmodernism, or the Cultural Logic of Late Capitalism. *Post-Contemporary Interventions*. Eds Fish, Stanley and Fredric Jameson. Durham: Duke University Press, 1991. Print.

Jay, Martin. *The Virtues of Mendacity: On Lying in Politics*. Charlestonville and London: University of Virginia Press, 2010. Print.

Jones, Alice. 'Is Theatre Becoming Too Immersive?' *The Independent Online* (2013). 31 October 2013. http://www.independent.co.uk/ arts-entertainment/theatre-dance/features/is-theatre-becoming-too -immersive-8521511.html.

Kalisch, Eleonore. 'Aspekte Einer Begriffs- Und Problemgeschichte Von Authentizität Und Darstellung'. *Inszenierung Von Authentizität*. Eds Fischer-Lichte, Erika and Isabel Pflug. Tübingen and Basel: Francke, 2000. 31–44. Print.

Kan, Anneka Esch-Van. 'The Documentary Turn in Contemporary British Drama and the Return of the Political: David Hare's *Stuff Happens* and Richard Norton-Taylor's *Called to Account*'. *A History of British Drama: Genres – Development – Model Interpretation*. Eds Baumbach, Sibylle et al. Trier: Wissenschaftlicher Verlag, 2011. 413–428. Print.

Kant, Immanuel. *Lectures on Ethics*. Cambridge: Cambridge University Press, 1997. Print.

Kant, Immanuel. *Groundwork of the Metaphysics of Morals*. Trans. Abbott, Thomas Kingsmill. BN Publishing, 2010. Print.

Kant, Immanuel. *The Critique of Judgment*. Ed. Meredith, James Creed. 2013. http://web.ebscohost.com/ehost/ebookviewer/ebook/ nlebk_1085930_AN?sid=67fbc47c-844e-498d-8945-dbbec5408353@ sessionmgr11&vid=1&lpid=lp_1. EPUB file.

Kelly, Dennis. *Taking Care of Baby*. 2007. London: Oberon Books, 2013. Print.

Kent, Nicolas. 'Srebrenica'. *The Tricycle: Collected Tribunal Plays 1994–2012*. Eds Brittain, Victoria et al. London: Oberon Books, 2014. 201–290. Print.

Kershaw, Baz. *The Radical in Performance: Between Brecht and Baudrillard*. London: Routledge, 1999. Print.

Keyes, Ralph. *The Post-Truth Era: Dishonesty and Deception in Contemporary Life*. New York: St Martin's Press, 2004. Print.

Kirby, Alan. 'The Death of Postmodernism and Beyond'. *Philosophy Now* 58 (2006): 2 February 2016. https://philosophynow.org/issues/58/The _Death_of_Postmodernism_And_Beyond.

Kirby, Alan. *Digimodernism: How New Technologies Dismantle the Postmodern and Reconfigure Our Culture*. New York and London: Continuum, 2009. Print.

Knaller, Susanne. 'The Ambigousness of the Authentic: Authenticity between Reference, Fictionality and Fake in Modern and Contemporary Art'. *Paradoxes of Authenticity: Studie Son a Critical Concept*. Ed. Straub, Julia. Bielefeld: Transcript, 2012a. Print.

Knaller, Susanne. 'Authenticity as an Aesthetic Notion: Normative and Non-
Normative Concepts in Modern and Contemporary Poetics'. *The Aesthetics
of Authenticity: Medial Constructions of the Real*. Eds Funk, Wolfgang,
Florian Groß and Irmtraud Huber. Bielefeld: Transcript, 2012b. 25–40. Print.

Knudsen, Stephen. 'Beyond Postmodernism: Putting a Face on
Metamodernism without the Easy Clichés'. *ARTPulse* (2013). http://
artpulsemagazine.com/beyond-postmodernism-putting-a-face-on
-metamodernism-without-the-easy-cliches.

Kristeva, Julia. *The Powers of Horror: An Essay on Abjection*. New York:
Columbia University Press, 1984. Print.

Lacan, Jacques. *The Four Fundamental Concepts of Psychoanalysis*. Trans.
Sheridan, Alan. Ed. Miller, Jacques-Alain. New York: W. W. Norton, 1998.
Print.

Lachman, Michal. 'History or Journalism: Two Narrative Paradigms in Bloody
Sunday. Scenes from the Hutton Inquiry by Richard Norton-Taylor'. *Studia
Anglica Posnaniensa* 43 (2007): 305–314. Print.

Lane, David. *Contemporary British Drama*. Edinburgh: Edinburgh University
Press, 2010. Print.

Lehmann, Hans-Thies. *Postdramatisches Theater*. Frankfurt: Verlag der
Autoren, 2008. Print.

Lepage, Robert. 'Polygraph'. *The Routledge Drama Anthology and Sourcebook*.
Eds Gale, Maggie B. and John F. Deeney. London: Routledge, 2010. Print.

Lepecki, André. '"After All, This Terror Was Not without Reason": Unfiled
Notes on the Atlas Group'. *The Drama Review: A Journal of Performance
Studies* 50.3 (2006): 88–99. Print.

Lepecki, André. 'In the Mist of the Event: Performance and the Activation
of Memory in the Atlas Group Archive'. *The Atlas Group (1989–2004): A
Project by Walid Raad*. Cologne: Verlag der Buchhandlung Walter König,
2007. Print.

Logan, Brian. 'For Your Eyes Only: The Latest Theatrical Craze Features a
Single Performer with a Single Audience Member'. *The Independent* (2010)
. 15 October 2013. http://www.independent.co.uk/arts-entertainment/theatre
-dance/features/for-your-eyes-only-the-latest-theatrical-craze-features-a
-single-performer-with-a-single-audience-member-1995795.html.

Love, Catherine. 'London Stories: A 1-on-1-on-1 Festival'. *Exeunt Magazine*
(2013). http://exeuntmagazine.com/features/london-stories/.

Lukowski, Andrzej. 'London Stories'. *Time out London* (2013).
15 October 2013. http://www.timeout.com/london/theatre/london-stories.

Lyotard, Jean-Francois. *The Postmodern Condition: A Report on Knowledge.* Manchester: Manchester University Press, 1984. Print.

Machiavelli, Nicolo. *The Prince.* 1532. Trans. Marriott, W. K. Everyman's Library. London: J. M. Dent & Sons, 1945. Print.

Machon, Josephine. *(Syn)Aesthetics: Redefining Visceral Performance.* Basingstoke: Palgrave, 2009. Print.

Machon, Josephine. *Immersive Theatres: Intimacy and Immediacy in Contemporary Performance.* London: Palgrave, 2013. Print.

Mair, Judith and Silke Becker. *Fake for Real: Über Die Private Und Politische Taktik Des So-Tun-Als-Ob.* Frankfurt (Main): Campus Verlag, 2005. Print.

Majetschak, Stefan. *Ästhetik Zur Einführung. Zur Einführung.* Hamburg: Junius-Verl, 2007. Print.

Malzacher, Florian. 'There Is a Word for People Like You: Audience – The Spectator as Bad Witness and Bad Voyeur'. *Not Even a Game Anymore: The Theatre of Forced Entertainment.* Eds Helmer, Judith and Florian Malzacher. Berlin: Alexander Verlag, 2004. Print.

Marks, Peter. '"Black Watch" Review: Scottish Battalion's Iraq Story Is Authentic, Astonishing'. *The Washington Post* (2011). 25 February 2014. http://www.washingtonpost.com/wp-dyn/content/article/2011/01/30/AR2011013004534.html.

Marshall, Cynthia. *The Shattering of the Self: Violence, Subjectivity, and Early Modern Texts.* Baltimore: Johns Hopkins University Press, 2002. Print.

Martin, Carol. 'Bodies of Evidence'. *The Drama Review: A Journal of Performance Studies* 50.3 (2006): 8–15. Print.

Martin, Carol. 'Living Simulations: The Use of Media in Documentary in the UK, Lebanon and Israel'. *Get Real: Documentary Theatre Past and Present.* Eds Forsyth, Alison and Chris Megson. Performance Interventions. Basingstoke: Palgrave, 2009. 74–89. Print.

McKenzie, Jon. *Perform or Else: From Discipline to Performance.* London: Routledge, 2001. Print.

McMillan, Joyce. 'Internal'. *The Scotsman* (2009). 10 October 2010. http://www.edinburgh-festivals.com/viewshow.aspx?id=1587074.

Mechelen, Marga van. 'The Representation of the True Artificial Body'. *Semiotic Bodies, Aesthetic Embodiments, and Cyberbodies.* Ed. Nöth, Winfried. Kassel: Kassel University Press, 2006. Print.

Megson, Chris. '*Half the Picture*: "A Certain Frisson" at the Tricycle Theatre'. *Get Real: Documentary Theatre Past and Present.* Eds Forsyth, Alison and Chris Megson. Basingstoke: Palgrave, 2009. 195–208. Print.

Mele, Alfred R. *Self-Deception Unmasked*. Princeton NJ: Princeton University Press, 2001. Print.

Mitchell, David. *Cloud Atlas*. London: Hodder Headline, 2004. Print.

Moore, Allan. 'Authenticity as Authentication'. *Popular Music* 21.2 (2002): 209–233. Print.

Murray, Craig. 'Her Majesty's Man in Tashkent'. *The Washington Post* (2006). 21 March 2014. http://www.washingtonpost.com/wp-dyn/content/article/2006/09/01/AR2006090101418_pf.html.

Nakas, Kassandra. 'Double Miss. On the Use of Photography in the Atlas Group Archive'. Eds Raad, Walid, Kassandra Nakas and Britta Schmitz. Cologne: Verlag der buchhandlung Walter König, 2007. Print.

Nakas, Kassandra and Britta Schmitz. 'Preface'. *The Atlas Group (1989–2004): A Project by Walid Raad*. Eds Raad, Walid, Kassandra Nakas and Britta Schmitz. Cologne: Walter König, 2007. Print.

Nietzsche, Friedrich. *Philosophy and Truth: Selections from Nietzsche's Notebooks of the Early 1870's [sic]*. Atlantic Highlands, NJ: Humanities Press, 1979. Print.

Norris, Christopher. *What's Wrong with Postmodernism*. London: Harvester Wheatsheaf, 1990. Print.

Norris, Christopher. *Truth Matters: Realism, Anti-Realism and Response-Dependence*. Edinburgh: Edinburgh University Press, 2002. Print.

Norton-Taylor, Richard. 'Justifying War: Scenes from the Hutton Inquiry'. *The Tricycle: Collected Tribunal Plays 1994–2012*. Eds Brittain, Victoria et al. London: Oberon Books, 2014a. 417–510. Print.

Norton-Taylor, Richard. 'Nuremberg'. *The Tricycle: Collected Tribunal Plays*. Eds Brittain, Victoria et al. London: Oberon Books, 2014b. 113–194. Print.

Norton-Taylor, Richard. 'The Colour of Justice'. *The Tricycle: Collected Tribunal Plays 1994–2012*. Eds Brittain, Victoria et al. London: Oberon Books, 2014c. 291–416. Print.

Nünning. *Unreliable Narration: Studien Zur Theorie Und Praxis Unglaubwürdigen Erzählens in Der Englischsprachigen Erzählliteratur*. Trier: WVT, 1998. Print.

Oddey, Alison and Christine White, eds *Modes of Spectating*. Bristol: Intellect, 2009. Print.

Osipovich, David. 'What Is a Theatrical Performance?' *The Journal of Aesthetics and Art Criticism* 64.4 (2006): 461–470. Print.

Otto-Bernstein, Katharina. *Absolute Wilson: The Biography*. Munich: Prestel, 2006. Print.

Paget, Derek. *True Stories? Documentary Drama on Radio, Screen and Stage.* Cultural Politics. Manchester: Manchester University Press, 1990. Print.

Paget, Derek. 'The "Broken Tradition" of Documentary Theatre and Its Continued Powers of Endurance'. *Get Real: Documentary Theatre Past and Present.* Eds Forsyth, Alison and Chris Megson. Performance Interventions. Basingstoke: Palgrave, 2009. 224–238. Print.

Patel, Roma. 'Touched by Human Hands: City and Performance'. *Modes of Spectating.* Eds Oddey, Alison and Christina White. Bristol: Intellect, 2009. Print.

Phelan, Peggy. *Unmarked: The Politics of Performance.* Repr. ed. London: Routledge, 1996. Print.

Plato. *The Republic.* Trans. Griffith, Tom. Cambridge: Cambridge University Press, 2000. Print.

Poster, Mark, ed. *Jean Baudrillard: Selected Writings.* London: Blackwell, 2001. Print.

Potolsky, Matthew. *Mimesis.* New Critical Idiom. London: Routledge, 2006. Print.

Prebble, Lucy. *Enron.* London: Methuen, 2009. Print.

Pringle, Stewart. 'The Drowned Man'. *Exeunt Magazine* (2013). 31 October 2013. http://exeuntmagazine.com/reviews/the-drowned-man/.

Punchdrunk. *The Masque of Red Death.* Dir. Felix Barrett, Maxine Doyle, in Association with the Royal National Theatre, Battersea Arts Centre, London. 20 September 2007. Performance.

Punchdrunk. *The Drowned Man: Program Book.* London. 2013. Print.

Punchdrunk. *The Drowned Man.* Dir. Felix Barrett, Maxine Doyle, in Association with the Royal National Theatre, London St. 31, London. 25 November 2013. Performance.

Quizoola24 Twitter Feed. '#quizoola24'. 2014. 26 November 2014. http://www.mjharvey.org.uk/things/quizoola24/.

Raad, Walid. 'The Atlas Group'. n.d. 22 March 2014. http://www.theatlasgroup.org.

Raad, Walid. *I Feel a Great Desire to Meet the Masses Once Again.* 2007. Festival D'Automne. Centre Pompidou, Paris. 13 October 2007. Performance.

Raad, Walid and The Atlas Group. *My Neck Is Thinner Than a Hair: Documents from the Atlas Group Archive.* Vol. 2. 2 vols. Cologne: Verlag der Buchhandlung Walther König et al., 2005. Print.

Raad, Walid, Kassandra Naka and Britta Schmitz, eds. *The Atlas Group (1989–2004): A Project by Walid Raad.* Cologne: Walther König, 2006. Print.

Rancière, Jacques. *The Emancipated Spectator*. London: Verso, 2009. Print.

Rancière, Jacques. *The Politics of Aesthetics: The Distribution of the Sensible*. London: Continuum, 2011. Print.

Read, Alan. *Theatre and Everyday Life: An Ethics of Performance*. London and New York: Routledge, 1995. Print.

Read, Alan. *Theatre, Intimacy & Engagement: The Last Human Venue*. Studies in International Performance. Eds Reinelt, Janelle and Brian Singleton. 1. Publ. ed. Basingstoke: Palgrave Macmillan, 2008. Print.

Read, Alan. 'From *Theatre & Everyday Life* to *Theatre in the Expanded Field*: Performance between Community and Immunity'. *Journal of Contemporary Drama in English* 2.1 (2014): 8–25. Print.

Rebhandl, Bert. 'I Feel a Great Desire to Meet the Masses Once Again'. *Frieze Magazine* (2007). 22 March 2014. http://www.frieze.com/issue/review/i_feel_a_great_desire_to_meet_the_masses_once_again/.

Reinelt, Janelle. 'Toward a Poetics of Theatre and Public Events'. *The Drama Review: A Journal of Performance Studies* 50.3 (2006): 69–87. Print.

Reinelt, Janelle. 'The Promise of Documentary'. *Get Real: Documentary Theatre Past and Present*. Eds Forsyth, Alison and Chris Megson. Performance Interventions. Basingstoke: Palgrave, 2009. 6–23. Print.

Remshardt, Ralf. 'Die Dreigroschenoper (The Threepenny Opera)/The Masque of the Red Death'. *Theatre Journal* 60.4 (2008): 639–643. Print.

Röttgers, Kurt. 'Lügen(-)Texte – Oder Nur Menschen?' *Dichter Lügen*. Eds Röttgers, Kurt and Monika Schmitz-Emans. Essen: Die Blaue Eule, 2001. Print.

The Royal National Theatre. 'In the Beginning Was the End: Dreamthinkspeak at Somerset House' (2013a). 25 November 2013. http://www.nationaltheatre.org.uk/shows/in-the-beginning-was-the-end-dreamthinkspeak-at-somerset-house.

The Royal National Theatre. 'The Drowned Man: A Hollywood Fable' (2013b). 25 November 2013. http://www.nationaltheatre.org.uk/shows/the-drowned-man-a-hollywood-fable.

Ruthrof, Horst. *The Body in Language*. London and New York: Cassell, 2000. Print.

Saussure, Ferdinand de. *Course in General Linguistics*. LaSalle, IL: Open Court, 1988. Print.

Scarry, Elaine. *The Body in Pain: The Making and Unmaking of the World*. New York and Oxford: Oxford University Press, 1985. Print.

Schaper, Rüdiger. *Spektakel: Eine Geschichte Des Theaters Von Schlingensief Bis Aischylos*. München: Siedler, 2014. Print.

Schechner, Richard. *Public Domain: Essays on the Theatre*. New York: Avon Books, 1970. Print.

Schechner, Richard. *Performance Studies: An Introduction*. London: Routledge, 2006. Print.

Schmitz, Britta. 'Not a Search for Truth'. *The Atlas Group (1989–2004)*. Eds Raad, Walid, Kassandra Nakas and Britta Schmitz. Cologne: Verlag der Buchhandlung Walter König, 2007. Print.

Schmitz-Emans, Monika. 'Diskursive Mimikry: Zur Gattung Und Poetik Des Fiktiven Forschungsberichts'. *Mimikry: Gefährlicher Luxus Zwischen Natur Und Kultur*. Ed. Andreas Becker et al. Zeiterfahrung Und Ästhetische Wahrnehmung. Schliengen: Edition Argus, 2008. 270–287. Print.

Schnabel, Ulrich. 'Mein Wahres Gesicht: Heute Ist Das Echte, Authentische Gefragt. Doch Was Ist Das? Und Wie Findet Man Es?' *Die Zeit*. 14 August 2014: 27–30. Print.

Schuhbeck, Birgit. 'Less Art, More Substance: New Tendencies in Contemporary Theatre'. *Notes on Metamodernism* (2012). 30 July 2012. http://www.metamodernism.com/2012/02/22/less-art-more-substance -new-tendencies-in-contemporary-theatre/.

Schulze, Daniel. 'Fake Acting – Real Experience: Theatre as a Form of New Authenticity'. *Critical Contemporary Culture* 2 (2012). http://www .criticalcontemporaryculture.org/article-daniel-schulze-fake-acting -real-experience-theatre-as-a-form-of-new-authenticity-daniel-schulze -university/.

Schulze, Daniel. 'Blood, Guts and Suffering: The Body as Communicative Agent in Wrestling and Performance Art'. *Journal of Contemporary Drama in English* 1.1 (2013): 113–125. Print.

Schulze, Daniel. 'The Passive Gaze and Hyper-Immunised Spectators: The Politics of Theatrical Live-Broadcasting'. *Journal of Contemporary Drama in English* 3.2 (2015). Print.

Sedlmayr, Gerold. *Wir Sind Hier Nur Zu Gast: Gedichte*. Poesie 21. Ed. Leitner, Anton G. Deiningen: Verlag Steinmeier, 2014. Print.

Shakespeare, William. 'Hamlet'. *The Arden Shakespeare*. Eds Proudfoot, Richard, Ann Thompson and David Scott Kastan. London: Thomson, 1997a. Print.

Shakespeare, William. 'Macbeth'. *The Arden Shakespeare*. Eds Proudfoot, Richard, Ann Thompson and David Scott Kastan. London: Thomson, 1997b. Print.

Sheperd, Simon and Mick Wallis. *Drama/Theatre/Performance*. 2004. The New Critical Idiom. Ed. Drakakis, John. London: Routledge, 2010. Print.

Shields, David. *Reality Hunger*. New York: Alfred A. Knopf, 2010. Print.

Sierz, Aleks. 'Beyond Timidity: The State of British New Writing'. *PAJ: A Journal of Performance and Art* 27.3 (2005): 55–61. Print.

Sierz, Aleks. 'Reality Sucks: The Slump in British New Writing'. *PAJ: A Journal of Performance and Art* 30.2 (2008): 102–107. Print.

Sierz, Aleks. *Rewriting the Nation: British Theatre Today*. London: Methuen, 2011. Print.

Sierz, Aleks. 'British Theatre Today: A Report on Its Health'. *Hard Times* 91 (2012): 2–6. Print.

Slovo, Gilian. 'The Riots'. *The Tricycle: Collected Tribunal Plays 1994–2012*. Eds Brittain, Victoria et al. London: Oberon Books, 2014. 855–911. Print.

Smith, David. 'In Bed with the Boys from Fife'. *The Observer* (2008). 25 February 2014. http://www.theguardian.com/stage/2008/jun/29/theatre .reviews1.

Soans, Robin. *Talking to Terrorists*. London: Oberon Books, 2005. Print.

Sommerstein, Alan H. *Greek Drama and Dramatists*. London and New York: Routledge, 2000. Print.

Spencer, Charles. 'Fine Journalism and Wonderful Drama'. *The Telegraph* (2004). 22 March 2014. http://www.telegraph.co.uk/culture/theatre/ drama/3623902/Fine-journalism-and-wonderful-drama.html.

Steck, Melanie. 'Was Ist Noch Echt Im Deutschen TV?' *BILD*. 25 August 2014: 1, 4. Print.

Straub, Julia. 'Introduction: The Paradoxes of Authenticity'. *Paradoxes of Authenticity: Studies on a Critical Concept*. Ed. Straub, Julia. Bielefeld: Transcript, 2012. 9–29. Print.

Suk, Jan. 'Bodies? On? Stage? Human Play of Forced Entertainment'. Paper given at the annual conference of the Society for Contemporary Drama in English (CDE), Mühlheim, Germany, 9 June 2012.

Suk, Jan. 'Stepping Off the Stage: Live Art Aspects in *Bloody Mess*'. *Hradec Králové: Journal of Anglophone Studies* 1.1 (2014): 55–62. Print.

Taylor, Charles. *The Ethics of Authenticity*. Cambridge, MA and London: Harvard University Press, 1991. Print.

The Coca Cola Company, Conversations Staff. 'A History of Coca Cola Advertising Slogans'. 2012. 21 October 2014. http://www.coca -colacompany.com/stories/coke-lore-slogans.

Tomlin, Liz. *Acts and Apparitions: Discourses on the Real in Performance Practice and Theory, 1990–2010*. Manchester: Manchester University Press, 2013. Print.

Trilling, Lionel. *Sincerity and Authenticity*. Cambridge, MA: Harvard University Press, 1972. Print.

Trivers, Robert. *Deceit and Self-Deception: Fooling Yourself the Better to Fool Others*. London: Allen Lane/Penguin, 2011. Print.

Turkle, Sherry. *Alonetogether: Why We Expect More from Technology and Less from Each Other*. New York: Basic Books, 2011. Print.

Upton, Carole-Anne. 'The Performance of Truth and Justice in Northern Ireland: The Case of Bloody Sunday'. *Get Real: Documentary Theatre Past and Present*. Eds Forsyth, Alison and Chris Megson. Performance Interventions. Basingstoke: Palgrave, 2009. 179–194. Print.

Vermeulen, Timotheus and Robin van den Akker. 'Notes on Metamodernism'. *Journal of Aesthetics & Culture* 2 (2010): 30 July 2012.

Vrij, Aldert. *Detecting Lies and Deceit: Pitfalls and Opportunities*. Wiley Series in Psychology of Crime, Policing and Law. Eds Davies, Graham and Ray Bull. Chichester: John Wiley & Sons, 2008. Print.

Weidle, Roland. 'Mimetic Narration: Documentary Theatre and the Staging of Truth'. *Narrative in Drama*. Eds Tönnies, Merle and Christina Flotman. Contemporary Drama in English. Trier: Wissenschaftlicher Verlag, 2011. Print.

Weinrich, Harald. *The Linguistics of Lying*. Seattle and London: University of Washington Press, 2005. Print.

White, Gareth. 'Odd Anonymous Needs: Punchdrunk's Masked Spectator'. *Modes of Spectating*. Eds Oddey, Alison and Christina White. Bristol: Intellect, 2009. Print.

White, Gareth. 'On Immersive Theatre'. *Theatre Research International* 37.3 (2012): 221–235. Print.

Wilde, Oscar. *The Complete Works of Oscar Wilde*. New York: Harper Perennial, 2008. Print.

Williams, Bernard A. O. *Truth & Truthfulness: An Essay in Genealogy*. Princeton and Oxford: Princeton University Press, 2002. Print.

Williams, David. 'Writing (after) the Event: Notes on Appearance, Passage and Hope'. *A Performance Cosmology: Testimony Form the Future, Evidence from the Past*. Eds Christie, Judie, Richard Gough and Daniel Watt. London and New York: Routledge, 2006. Print.

Williams, Raymond. *The Long Revolution*. Harmondsworth: Penguin, 1961. Print.

Wilson, Laetitia. 'The Ups & Downs of One-on-One'. *RealTimeArts Magazine* (2012). 15 October 2013. http://www.realtimearts.net/article.php?id=10597.

Wittgenstein, Ludwig. *Philosophical Investigations: The German Text with a Revised English Translation*, 3rd edition. Trans. Anscombe, G.E.M. London: Blackwell, 2001. Print.

Yablonsky, Linda. 'The Epic Performance'. *The Art Newspaper* 225 (2011): 48–49. Print.

Yates, Daniel B. 'Submit Your Questions for Quizoola!' *Exeunt Magazine* (2013). 28 March 2013. http://exeuntmagazine.com/features/your-questions-for-quizoola/.

Young, Stuart. 'Playing with Documentary Theatre: *Aalst* and *Taking Care of Baby*'. *New Theatre Quarterly* 25.1 (2009): 72–87. Print.

Zarrilli, Philip B. et al. *Theatre Histories: An Introduction*. London: Routledge, 2009. Print.

Zerihan, Rachel. 'Live Art Development Agency Study Room Guide on One to One Performance'. *n.a.* (2009). 24 April 2013. http://www.thisisliveart.co.uk/resources/Study_Room/guides/Rachel_Zerihan.html.

Concept Index

Performances, Companies, Practitioners Index

Person Index

CPSIA information can be obtained
at www.ICGtesting.com
Printed in the USA
LVOW13*1529161117
556554LV00010B/195/P